Speaking My Mind

*

The author with Prime Minister Menachim Begin, Israel 1983

To my friend
Kalu + family

Speaking My Mind

Rhodes Boysa

The Autobiography of

RHODES BOYSON

PETER OWEN

London & Chester Springs

PETER OWEN PUBLISHERS
73 Kenway Road London SW5 0RE
Peter Owen books are distributed in the USA by
Dufour Editions Inc. Chester Springs PA 19425–0007

First published in Great Britain 1995
© Sir Rhodes Boyson 1995

ISBN 0–7206–0901–1

A catalogue record for this book is available from
the British Library

Printed and made in Great Britain by Biddles of Guildford

Preface

*

This book arose from a Foyles Literary Luncheon, at which Peter Owen and I were among the guests of honour. We had arrived early and talked together, and Peter mentioned that it was time I wrote another book. He suggested an autobiography, but I, cheerful and optimistic as always, said it was still far too early in my life for me to do so!

I then proposed that I should write a book covering my contemporary reactions to the political, economic and educational changes of the last sixty years which I have lived through and in which I have participated. The copious daily notes I kept over the years have greatly helped me in this endeavour.

What therefore I have attempted is a careful recollection of the moods, oral and written battles and changes of my time and why they came about, rather than a straightforward autobiography. I enjoy the noise and bustle of daily life, but here I am a camera looking at the changes and assessing my part in them. I had originally thought of calling the book 'A Changed World', but the present title, *Speaking My Mind*, is more apt, since this is precisely what I have always done while taking part in the debates of each decade.

Rhodes Boyson

To the Lancashire that made me
and the London that adopted me.

Contents

*

Contents

1

Secure in My Village

*

I was privileged to be born and live my first ten years in an
almost self-contained Lancashire village where everyone knew my
father, my mother and my forebears. There were two cotton mills,
in one of which my father first worked, numerous small streams
and the rough cow-grazing farms came down to the edge of the
steep, terraced streets, and the road from Haslingden to Accrington
out of the Rossendale Valley cut the village in two.

The year was 1925 and the village was called Rising Bridge,
while its small railway and goods stations was called Baxenden.
It had a small council house estate built of brick and two recrea-
tion grounds, one even rougher than the other. The rest of the
houses were built of local stone. There was a co-operative store,
along with a few shops, a public house and a working men's
club surrounded by hen pens, allotments and smallholdings. The
total population was under a thousand.

We lived next door to one of the cotton mills and my earliest
memories are of waiting for the mill engine to start up at 7.30 in
the morning, when I was allowed to get up, the sound of cotton
wagons being shunted during the night in the sidings of the local
railway station, and later being allowed by my mother to accom-
pany her to take my father his mid-morning drink and cake in
the mill. The warmth of the fellowship at the Wesleyan Methodist
church in the village, whose events I must have attended from
the time of birth, cocooned me from any fear of the world outside.

My father's family of Huguenot stock had come north from

Cambridgeshire to work in the mill towns at the time of the Industrial Revolution and originally settled in the village of Rhodes, near Middleton, in south-east Lancashire. From there they moved to the Rossendale Valley, having already acquired the name Rhodes as a family name of territorial origin. My paternal grandfather, York Rhodes Boyson, was a free-thinker and socialist and was blacklisted by all the east Lancashire cotton employers as a dangerous trade unionist and thence had made his living from a smallholding and a fish-cart. Never a teetotaller, but a huge, powerful, jolly man, he had a liking when he was in money for visits to local hostelries. He insisted, however, on his children attending the village Methodist chapel and he himself regularly attended the Sunday afternoon men's classes.

My father was conceived in 1885 at a time of relative trade depression, when money was short and one child had already died and Grandmother told me that she cried every day wondering how she could feed another mouth. This is a reminder of Samuel Laycock's poem:

> *Welcome Bonny Brid*
> 'Th'art welcome, little bonny brid,
> But shouldn't ha' come just when tha did;
> Toimes are bad.
> We're short o' pobbies for eawr Joe,
> But that, of course, tha didn't know,
> Did ta, lad?'

I am sure that my father's melancholy must have been caused by his experiences in the womb.

My father's wide-ranging intellect and his many interests had been a continued source of wonder in Rising Bridge and at times he alarmed the villagers with his left-wing radicalism. His decision to register as a socialist conscientious objector during the 1914–18 war, believing that it was a capitalist plot to wipe out millions of the working class on both sides, shocked the village.

My father started life as a half-timer in the mill at the age of ten. To begin with he was a little piecer and by the time of the First World War became a cotton spinner – one of the aristocrats of the factory – as well as a part-time trade-union officer of the Haslingden Operative Spinners Association. Father never really regained full health from the days of his imprisonment in the

First World War, although he was physically always a very powerful man. He also never fully recovered from the fact that in that period of the First World War and the immediate post-war years it was his working-class friends who turned on him because of his views, and it was the factory owner and the overseer and the village attenders of the Anglican church who did most to try and help him. Indeed, his Conservative employer, who served on the committee which 'tried' conscientious objectors, visited him and begged him to apply for conscientious objection on religious and not socialist grounds. When Father returned at the end of the war, it was again the factory owner and overlookers who ensured that he had his spinning-mules back, against the wishes of his brother spinners. His employer declared: 'If Bill Boyson does not get his mules back I will shut the mill.' A Conservative, working-class, activist family who owned 18 Hoyle Street, where we lived, kept the house empty for his return when Mother drew out her savings to go to London to hire a room to be near my father's prison.

Father was, however, soon restored to be the village adviser again on all issues and within two years he was again a part-time officer of his union, becoming a full-time official some years later. He continued to amaze the village, but they became very proud of him. Though his ideas and reading were wide, his habits remained those of the Lancashire working class with his cloth cap, his scarf, his pipe, his twist tobacco and his love of soccer and cricket. I grew up in awe of him.

By 1930 he was president of both the Haslingden Labour Party and the Rossendale Divisional Labour Party, and in 1933 he was elected as Labour councillor for the ward, which included the village and which never before or since elected a Labour man or woman. Within a short time he became the chairman of both the finance committee and the housing committee of a council made up originally of thirteen Conservatives, eight Liberals, two Independents and himself as the only Labour member. One of his proud boasts was that he had chaired every Labour leader from Hardy to Clement Attlee.

My mother came from a very different background. A simple soul in the best sense, her first ambition was to be a teacher and her second to keep a lodging-house in Blackpool. She achieved neither, but she still prayed to her Maker every day. Her family farmed Higher Barn Farm on the bleak Haslingden moors near

Rising Bridge for generations. She was the youngest of fourteen children on the farm and she taught in the Sunday school all her life. When she was ninety-one she laid the foundation stone for the new Methodist chapel in the village. She then died cheerfully, her life complete.

Mother, born in 1886, had originally been led to believe that as the youngest in her family she would go to grammar school. At the last moment her father decided otherwise and she was sent to the mill as a half-timer at the age of ten and hated every day of it. Her only chance of escape was marriage. Father, not surprisingly, was one of the last unmarried men left in the village. He was also secretary of the Methodist Young Men's class and, unlike his own father, teetotal. These two last points must have outweighed for the Barnes family his strange views and almost total lack of social graces. He was thirty-one and she was thirty when they married.

Mother knew my father's views when she married him in 1916, but she stood by him and withstood the anger of the town and the taunts of the cheap 'union jack' lobby. She came from a Liberal family with a brother killed in the Boer War, while others of her family served in the trenches of Flanders. The windows of all the other Boysons in the town were smashed regularly, since they were all religious conscientious objectors, but the windows of 18 Hoyle Street were never touched and the neighbours helped to clean up the house when Father and Mother returned from London.

My mother, who believed totally in the power of prayer, asked God daily in the village chapel for a child. She loved children and she also knew that no respectable Methodist's wife with a baby went to work, and thus childbirth provided an escape from the dreaded factory whistle. My mother's happiest day was when she knew she was with child and she could forget the cotton worker's adage: 'Prepare to meet thy loom.' A child, even I, would also be companion for her, since Father was always out at meetings or busy reading mighty tomes on economics and politics. Though never violent, he had black moods which went on for days and he then never spoke. At such times I played cricket and football on the hard stone sets in the road outside and the neighbours welcomed me at all times.

The Methodist church was a great pillar in our lives. Sunday morning service was followed by Sunday school in the afternoon. Then on Sunday evening from the age of five or six I had to stand on the table and repeat the morning sermon to my maternal grandmother, my auntie and stray relatives and neighbours while my parents were at church. It was good training for a preacher, a teacher and a politician. After I had repeated the sermon – sometimes to applause, sometimes to argument – we did the Sunday night chores: we cut up the salt from large blocks for the week, newspapers were cut up for toilet paper and other newspapers were transformed into tapers which my father used to light his pipe, pushing them into the coal fire. The loo, a wastewater 'tippler' at the end of the short yard, had an awesome 15–20 foot drop which caused me to shudder on dark winter evenings and to pee against the wall so that I could quickly return to the light and safety of the house.

Despite my father's moods there was much visiting among relatives at weekends and bank holidays and Father held court wherever he went. We looked forward to such visiting, since they improved his moods. We walked over the moors to neighbouring towns where we had relatives and came back by train or tram. There was difficulty, however, with visiting one of my mother's brothers, since he was such a strong Conservative. Father ceased to take part in this visit and I had to sit on a horsehair chair, which pricked my bare legs every time I moved. I decided I did not like Conservatives. The visit was only made tolerable by my auntie plying me with chocolate biscuits. This uncle died after the Second World War and my return from the Royal Navy, and as a young married schoolteacher I helped to carry his coffin. When the will was read I learnt that he had left me his Sunday boots. I walked home half amused and half annoyed.

The Methodist minister called regularly at our home. One year a new superintendent minister was appointed and upon his first preaching in our village he asked to have a tea (4.30 p.m.) meal with us. He requested Mother to make no special preparations. This instruction was ignored and we borrowed cloths, plates, knives and forks from at least a dozen houses. 'I am glad you made no special preparation for my visit,' said the superintendent as he was leaving – a remark which convinced me that there was more than one England! At that time a Methodist minister could run a car, buy books and have a middle-class standard of living.

I went to the Anglican village school clad in short trousers, shirt, jersey and clogs soled with irons. I ran the half-mile to and from school striking sparks from the gritstone pavements. I always pretended I was driving a train. The Labour MP for Rossendale in 1924 and in 1929 was an engine-driver. I decided I would like to be an MP and an engine-driver.

Discipline in the school was sensibly tough. I could read before I went to school, but I could not number. My teacher was so amazed that I could read fluently but could not number that she thumped me on the back on the first day until I cried, and I decided I had better number. I needed no second lesson and I remembered this when I became a schoolmaster. Classes were reasonably large, but socially homogeneous. We had the three Rs, history, geography, Bible stories, music, art and craft, sport on the Church of England field and even a little country dancing, at which I certainly did not excel. I also learnt the Anglican creed and I was surprised to find that it did me no harm.

Two events in my church primary school career are as clear as the day they happened: a fight and a July Friday. There is an old Lancashire sport called 'purring', in which both combatants wear iron-tipped clogs and kick each other until one gives in because of lack of moral fibre. I fought one such match in a meadow near the school when I was about six or seven years old, with the older boys making a ring around us. My opponent was from my class and we battled for the favours of a young damsel. We kicked and kicked with tears pouring down our cheeks until the big boys separated us, honour having been satisfied on both sides. We remained good friends and I do not remember ever fighting again. The damsel in question is, I believe, now dead and I am not sure if she even knew that she had inspired our bloody encounter.

My mother was horror-struck when some of the bigger boys took me home and banged on the door and ran away. Her anger at my fighting was at first weakened by her concern at the state of my legs. She summoned a neighbour, a local untrained midwife and medical adviser, who decided no bones were broken. I was then put to bed and Father was told, but once assured I had not lost a leg, he returned to his books and papers and his ever-smouldering pipe.

In the morning my mother decided to summon the doctor. This decision appalled me. My opponent would be at school and I would be missing. I would never live this down. When Mother set out after breakfast I dressed quickly, left home and got to school in time to shake hands with my opponent. They were gentlemanly days! Meanwhile, Mother and the doctor were gazing at an empty bed and I soon had to pay for my actions. There were no school meals and Mother met me at the school gates at noon. She clouted me all the way home, watched by passing children. I was no longer a hero! I was then promised worse to come – my father was to be told that evening.

At the end of afternoon school I tried to walk home very slowly. My father was a big man and I had grown smaller by the afternoon. I was then locked in the house and my playmates were given short shrift when they knocked on the door. They were informed: 'He is waiting for his dad.'

The mill engine stopped at 5.30 p.m. and soon I heard mill clogs coming up the street. Mother pulled me outside and there was Father as usual reading a book as he climbed the steep street. She told him what I had done and Father seemed half amused and half shocked. She then made a mistake she never repeated. She said, 'He is goin' to grow up like thy father.' Father withdrew a hand which was rising to hit me, opened the house door and pushed me into the living-room. He then took Mother into the holy of holies – the front parlour, used only on Sundays – and shut the door. I heard his voice rise in ice-cold anger I had never heard before. Grandfather was dead and Father loved and worshipped him. Grandfather had all the happiness and joy – even in liquor – that my father envied. Mother was left sobbing in the parlour. Father was in the living-room. I went to my bedroom. There was no meal and soon no sound. Then I remember Father coming upstairs and saying, 'Get over to thy grandmother's and auntie's.' I passed Mother and fled. Grandmother and Auntie knew what had happened. Grandmother then talked to me as if I was an adult and told me that she had cried every day when she carried my father. I was ten years older when I went to bed that night.

I remember Dr Evans, the doctor. I was told that when he first set up in the town he had no patients, just a rented house and he could be seen scrubbing the front steps and cleaning the windows. He became adviser to thousands in the neighbourhood – there were no joint practices then and he was on call day and night.

I also remember as yesterday one late July day. I was eight or nine and it was the Friday before the Haslingden Wakes Week, when the whole town stopped and the great majority went on holiday to Blackpool. The sun was shining and tomorrow we would be going to that great Mecca of the north. For the last school lesson we were taken out to the nearby hayfield to see a shire-horse pulling a mowing machine, while one could smell the hay ripening in neighbouring fields. The birds were singing and I wished the clock and calendar could stop. I knew that I would never forget that moment as one of the happiest, if not the happiest, in my life.

Many years later – in 1988 – when I had ceased to be a minister, the whole village petitioned me to help to save the village school from closure. Again it was a July day just before the Wakes Week and most of the village – mothers, grandparents, aunties, those I had grown up with – turned up to meet me at the school. The schoolchildren sang and recited poems and gave me a beautiful sketch of the school done by an eleven-year-old. This also was a blessed moment. The school was saved!

Blackpool to a 1920/30s Lancastrian was something unique. Almost the whole village went to Blackpool by special train from Baxenden station. After we left Preston Station we stood by the train window to catch the first sight of what to us was the most amazing structure in the universe – Blackpool Tower. There were then three railway stations like the three piers – North, Central and South. The nonconformists and some Anglicans stayed in the north – very sedate; some Anglicans stayed by the central pier; and the Roman Catholics stayed in the south.

Most of our village children met every day on the sands, according to the tides and the weather. We made sand-castles, watched Punch and Judy shows and played cricket and soccer. When the tide was in we visited the Tower, the zoo, the aquarium. On Friday afternoon we spent all the money we had left at the pleasure beach. We had no sense of danger, the village was here – it was Rising Bridge by the sea.

We had family battles, however, as to whether we spent the day with our mates or the family. If it was the latter we had to wear our best clothes and walk with Mother and Father along the promenade and the piers. I most enjoyed being with my mates, but when I was with Mother and Father and assorted family I was proud that every few yards someone would call out and come over to talk to Father. He introduced me to them as his 'lad' and I felt very important. By the tenth such occasion in an hour, however this excitement palled and I decided the following day to return to the sands.

Though Blackpool had a few big hotels, the vast majority of us stayed in small boarding-houses and lodging-houses. It was a working-class resort. One person once said to me that it had the worst hotels in the country but the best boarding- and lodging-houses because working-class Lancastrians demanded value for money.

We never went into a big hotel or indeed any hotel. We stayed in the same lodging-house every year and booked for the following year before we left for the train back to Baxenden. We did not even stay in a boarding-house where the landlady bought and cooked the food. Such boarding-houses were increasing in number in the 1930s. We stayed in a clean, wholesome lodging-house where Mother provided the food to be cooked. We took the non-perishable foods with us on the train and Mother shopped every day for the perishables.

Thus on our outgoing journey to Blackpool we were loaded up with parcels, bags and cases. We walked from the North Station the half-mile to the lodging-house like a refugee caravan. Once, I carried the bowl with our breakfast eggs in it, which had been carefully garnered over weeks and kept in lime. I dreaded dropping any and facing a breakfastless week.

The landlady was a Methodist who came from our village, and every year Mother explained to me how she had 'got on in life', at which Father snorted fiercely and I tried to shut Mother up in case Father developed a black mood. The thought of my father managing a lodging-house made me laugh even at the age of six!

The lodging-house had no lounge. We simply hired a bed and a cook and we were turned out after meals, whatever the weather. There was just a form outside to sit on if one was early for the meal or if Mother had forgotten something. Mealtimes were rigid. A cooked breakfast was followed by a cooked dinner (lunch), and then we had a cold tea and finally a hot drink and biscuits when we came in at 8 or 9 p.m. We were always in bed by 10 p.m. The same people came to the same lodging-house each year, and Father talked politics when he got the chance – much to Mother's fury.

On Sunday we had to go to the nearest Methodist church and Sunday school to have my Sunday school card marked so that I had a 100 per cent attendance over the year and received a book prize. Public morality was enforced in the lodging-house by the unmarried males and females being on separate floors.

I heard tales of boarding-houses where people did not bring

their own food and I thought they must be very grand. We children also heard rumours of houses far from the front where up to seven people slept in one bed and they were allowed to stay out late. We laughed about this and wondered whether they had a rota system for the bed. It all seemed very sociable. We were hurried by Yate's Wine Lodge as the site of the Devil and we could smell his alcoholic black breath. For years the smell of alcohol turned my stomach over and made me sick.

One great joy I had at Blackpool was that I was given money to have a comic every day – an amazing luxury. Normally I had *The Wizard* once a week, but at Blackpool I had *The Hotspur*, *The Skipper* and others. I thus found Blackpool a literary paradise!

The Lancashire working-class holidays were made possible by the widespread number of savings clubs: Christmas, holiday and so many other kinds. Father put in so much a week in a holiday club and received it all back on the Friday before we went. He was a very important man that day. Such clubs were an extension of building and co-operative societies and other local saving accounts. One year we even had a second holiday in Blackpool at Haslingden's September holidays, where we had a Friday and a Monday off. I then saw the Illuminations for the first time and walked the length of them on two evenings. Those nights I slept with stars in my eyes.

Ironically, since the Second World War Blackpool has changed again. It has moved to self-catering flats and small, full-board hotels. But it will always be the Mecca of my childhood. I am always excited to revisit it, and when I wake up in another world and see a green tram clanging past and the Illuminations above I shall know that I am in paradise.

2

The 'Hungry' Thirties in Lancashire

*

Despite the security of my village life I had two nagging worries. Both centred on my father. The first was minor: he never played with me or even watched me play, except on the sands at Blackpool when he might put his paper down to note but not comment on what I was doing. My second concern was the threat of unemployment. It was all round me, and my father, as a trade-union official, was on only a three-month contract, to be voted back at a general or committee meeting each quarter day. His reappointment in the middle and late 1930s was opposed by a Communist/Popular Front cell, since he had no time for the hard left and suspected the dictatorship in Russia. His mood became blacker as each three-month end approached.

I also had an older cousin who went to bed early each night and got up in the early hours for fear of oversleeping. Every morning spinning mills and weaving sheds had queues outside of men and women needing work, and if anyone was a minute late then their mules or looms would be passed to the head of the queue and the laggard might not get another job for years. My cousin never had a full night's sleep for the rest of his life.

Immediately after the First World War the cotton trade boomed and many new mills were built. It was, however, a false dawn and the number employed in cotton and Britain's share of world trade steadily declined. Haslingden was a cotton town and I grew up in a cotton village and, what was worse, Haslingden's trade was in shoddy and waste cotton, the lower end of the market where Lancashire met most competition. Britain had weakened herself and lost markets in the First World War and cotton manufacture had increased greatly in India, Japan, the United States and China to challenge our erstwhile supremacy. In 1912 eight thousand million yards of cloth were made in Britain, 85 per cent in Lancashire. By 1924 the amount was reduced to five thousand six hundred million yards and was still falling.

In 1929, 555,000 people were employed in cotton and this figure fell to 518,000 in 1932, 409,000 in 1937 and 393,000 in 1938. The number of spindles fell from 58 million in 1931 to 41.8 million in 1938, and the number of looms declined from 658,000 to 461,000. I grew up in a town under sentence. In 1939, despite the Spindles Board 'buying out' spindles to close mills down, only 75 per cent of remaining cotton spindles and 68 per cent of looms were in use. Cotton had the highest unemployment of any industry. In 1931, 44.7 per cent of insured cotton workers were unemployed. In addition, there were many cotton workers on short time. After 1931 and the National Government and the flight from an overvalued gold standard, a period of low interest rates reduced unemployment, but this did little to help industrial Lancashire, Scotland, West Cumberland, Tyneside and Northern Ireland. Neville Chamberlain, then Chancellor of the Exchequer, could say in 1935 that the country had left 'Bleak House' and might now move to 'Great Expectations', but Lancashire still had 'Hard Times'.

It was the south of England that saw the industrial revival. Between 1929 and 1936 output per person in manufacturing industry increased by 20 per cent in Britain as against 13 per cent in Germany and an actual fall in the United States. This increased productivity in the 1930s under the National Government enabled us to stand up to Germany in 1939. But it was really 1939 and the outbreak of war before there was real revival in Lancashire. The housing boom in the south did not touch Haslingden, where very few houses, apart from council houses, were built in the 1930s. Hundreds of thousands in Lancashire and thousands in Haslingden continued to live in fear of the dole, especially after the family means test was introduced in the early 1930s, whereby help was given only if the income of all others living in the house – grandparents to grandchildren – was taken into account. Even the produce of allotments was measured!

I also saw as a small boy the clash of capital and labour. Wages were reduced further in one Haslingden mill and Father and his union called a strike. For months, and it seemed years, pickets met the 'blackleg' strike-breakers who came in by coach daily from other towns. Father would take me occasionally on his shoulders and walk the three and a half miles in the morning to the mill from home and put me on a wall to watch as he argued with the strike-breakers and organized his pickets. When they had entered the mill, he talked to his own men and he carried me back for another three and a half miles home, or we called at the Trades Club in the town. Sometimes, however, his men played football with the police after the mill had started and Father watched them. I also remember that when there was a works soccer knock-out competition at the time of the strike, Father would take me suddenly on his shoulders to watch the matches after the pickets had dispersed in the evening and the blacklegs had all disappeared. I sat on his shoulders for the one-hour games and then he walked me home again or carried me. I was very small and Father rarely spoke to me, but I liked those occasions and felt proud of him because again everybody knew him and I was sorry when the strike ended, particularly as Father lost. It was the only strike he did lose. He preferred negotiation and, particularly after he became a councillor and town leader, was widely respected and consulted by the employers.

3

The Politics of the 1930s

*

How did Lancashire's economic depression in the 1930s affect the political attitude of my family, my neigbours and even myself? It was depressive. People had difficulty in thinking long-term and conversation often concentrated on who was at work and who was on the dole. The village was basically Conservative, as was Haslingden, and the fall of the Labour Party in 1931 reinforced the view of the village 'angels in marble' – the working-class Conservatives – that Labour did not understand economics and economic decisions should be left to the monied class. I remember my father being angered by one workman saying to him that those who had money obviously understood it and should make decisions for the rest of us. Father's time, in any case, was largely taken up in fighting appeals regarding unemployment pay for individual members of his union.

I can still remember clearly Father's horror at the National Government triumph of 1931 when only forty-six Labour Members were returned to Parliament. Rossendale was lost, with Labour coming third behind both a National Government Conservative candidate and a National Government Liberal candidate. Father was very bitter about what he considered the betrayal of Ramsay MacDonald, Philip Snowden and J.H. Thomas. The difference in electoral commitment then to now can be seen by the large attendance at all the public meetings in Rossendale for all parties and the fact that one-ninth of the 46,000 electors signed the nomination papers of a candidate.

There was a close tie in the village and the town between reli-gion and politics. The Anglicans were largely Conservative. The nonconformists were largely Liberal, with some having turned to Labour. The Roman Catholics, overwhelmingly of Irish descent, were Labour. It was very similar in the early 1960s when I left Haslingden but it has greatly changed now.

My father's union members were overwhelmingly of Irish descent and they protected him from the Communist left. Father, despite his total acceptance of Lancashire working-class habits and life, was in politics and religion a genuine dissenter and he thus needed the protection of friends because of his firm opinions on so many subjects on which he totally refused to compromise. He was lucky that there was a clear Methodist/Roman Catholic dislike of Russia and of the local Communists on one side, while there was a sus-picion of Anglican political dominance on the other side. The Roman Catholics were the praetorian guard of my father and he was good with them and they greatly admired him. Our house rever-berated regularly to two accents – Lancashire and Irish. I sat in the corner and listened to all the political discussions on week-end evenings.

By 1930 the threat of Germany and Italy was increasing. Mussolini boasted in that year that 'right unaccompanied by might is an empty word'. The 1930 German elections raised the number of National Socialists in the Reichstag from 12 to 107. The following year Japan began her conquest of Manchuria. Dark clouds warned of the future.

Labour was largely pacifist in the inter-war years. When it at-tained office in 1924, it slowed down work on the Singapore naval base and stopped work on two cruisers and two submarines. Father believed in the League of Nations and later supported the Peace Pledge ballot, but he was never a pacifist.

The Conservative Government was slow to react to the new threats. The huge number of deaths and horrific injuries in the trenches of the 1914–18 war haunted the memories of those who survived and they wanted no more war. Every street in Haslingden had widows of the carnage of the trenches, and women who would never marry their boy-friends because they had been killed in Flanders and no surplus men were left as bachelors. The clouds of the First World War hung over Haslingden until 1939.

The whole country was not only tired of war but it was also tired. American suggestions of collective action against Japan were rejected and Japan moved to attack China. By 1932 Germany was plainly rearming.

The Government's attitude was affected by the Oxford Union debate of 1933, when by 275 to 103 votes the members affirmed that 'this House will in no circumstances fight for its King and Country' and the peace ballot of the following year was participated in by 11½ million adults who voted three to one against military action in all circumstances.

Even more important was the East Fulham by-election of October 1933. The Conservative candidate, advocating rearmament, was soundly defeated by a Labour candidate, who accused the Conservatives of preparing for war. A Conservative majority of 14,521 was replaced by a Labour majority of 4,841. My father still wore a white poppy on Remembrance Day to indicate his feelings and, at his request, my mother also wore a white poppy, but she was never happy with it and took it off at the first opportunity.

The Clay Cross and Kilmarnock by-elections also showed large swings to Labour and George Lansbury, as Labour's leader, advocated total disarmament.

The threat to freedom and civilized values was shown at home as well as abroad. The British Union of Fascists, set up in 1931, arose partly out of Oswald Mosley's failed New Party. At its peak it had 20,000 members, largely drawn from low-paid office workers and the growing middle class. Haslingden, made up of mill-owners, a small professional class largely of teachers and a large working class, had to my knowledge and the knowledge of my father no Fascist members.

The biggest Fascist meeting was at Olympia, London, in 1934, with 15,000 inside and 5,000 outside. The true colours of this movement were seen in the brutal beating up of hecklers and opponents. My father was horrified and he talked about it for days. Always an internationalist, he was also receiving information from Germany as to what was happening to trade-union leaders there.

Rearmament was certainly slow in coming in Britain. The budget for the armed services was £116 million in 1926/7. It was reduced to £110 million by the Labour Government in 1930/1 and to £102 million by the National Government in 1932/3, and it would be 1935 before there was a significant increase in expenditure. None of the political parties comes well out of their defence and foreign policies in the 1930s. Labour favoured collective responsibility and the League of Nations yet, like the Liberal Party, refused to vote the armaments to make collective responsibility a reality. The Conservatives feared to come out clearly for rearmament in case this caused them to lose the general election. My father was indecisive. He hated the Fascists yet feared the slaughter in another major war and the limitations on democracy that could follow military leadership.

Late 1935 was the turning-point. At the Labour Party Conference on 1 October Ernest Bevin destroyed the left-wing pacifism of Lansbury and Stafford Cripps's opposition to effective international sanctions. Bevin accused his opponents of taking 'your conscience round from body to body asking to be told what to do with it'. Father was there and agreed with Bevin. Six weeks later came the general election and Labour increased its MPs to 154, but more importantly the Government with five years of rule ahead could decide its own policies without looking over its shoulder all the time. The scene would change.

4

Personal Isolation

*

The year 1935 was also traumatic in my life. No one asked a happily secure boy of ten whether he wished to change his house, his locality and his school. I was simply informed that, with my paternal auntie, my father was to build two semi-detached houses near the centre of Haslingden. I just could not understand why we were to leave the village which more than fulfilled all our wants. I was aware that Mother – a farmer's daughter – tried in our backyard to grow pansies in boxes, but they got little light and when she put glass over them children's balls came over and smashed it. I had always known that she wanted a garden. It was only later that I came to realize that she also wanted a modern house. If she could not have a lodging-house at Blackpool, she could surely have an inside toilet and hot water and a modern fireplace and a lawn and flower-beds instead of the two up and two down end-of-row terraced house with its coal-fire heating the boiler and the oven alongside.

Ironically, my father never used the bath in the new house; I think he still believed the widely held miners' legend that full immersion weakened the back and he washed himself every Friday bit by bit while standing up.

Father was already widely respected on the council and it was a new and fulfilling life for him. Parliament was too far from his native Lancashire and Haslingden town hall was to become the centre of his life. The house was thus to be built within easy walking distance of the town hall and also of the Trades Club.

How could a working man who never earned a big wage afford to build a three-bedroom, semi-detached house – one of the last stone houses built in Haslingden from the local quarries? I still have Father's account book. He checked all expenditure – even for books – and kept Mother on a very tight budget. He had £199 at the end of 1920 and every year until his death this sum was added to. We must also remember that the 1930s were years of a falling cost of living. By 1925 he had £601, by 1930 £1,151 and by 1934 £1,501 when he inherited £250 from his mother. The following year he had the semi-detached house built for £605 and for the rest of his life this was the figure that stood in his accounts. On Mother's death in 1979 I sold it for £9,750. A high payment insurance policy matured in 1935 and this helped to build the house.

Self-help and thrift were taught in the church and Sunday schools and Father and Mother lived it. Father walked whenever he could and, apart from newspapers, books and his beloved pipe, he craved little from life. Mother was a very careful housekeeper, able to cut bread and meat in the slimmest slices. She headed the self-caterers in all Sunday school and Labour Party teas. Auntie, my father's only sister and a widow, could afford her house because she had put a large insurance policy on her husband's life and he was killed being thrown from a horse. He had been in partnership with my paternal grandfather.

Every time I visited the building site of our new houses – and we went every weekend – I became more depressed. The more excited Mother became and the more satisfied Father, the greater became my despair that I was to be transplanted into alien soil. I ceased to talk to them and retreated into my own loneliness.

The arrival in Colldale Terrace was even worse than I expected. There was no one of my own age in the avenue of semi and detached houses: it was not even a terrace. How different were its fenced gardens with houses isolated from each other from the steep village street with people going in and out of each other's houses all day. The clogs I had always proudly worn except when going to Sunday school were not worn by many at the town's county primary school, and to join a new school in the last year before transfer to grammar or secondary elementary school was the worst time possible. I fitted in neither at the school nor in the terrace, nor did I try to fit in. I completed nightly without enthusiasm the homework set for the scholarship class but evinced little interest in my day's schooling. I was bullied at school but did not respond. I lived the worst year of my life. I became a loner and my childhood ended on the first night I went to bed in 11 Colldale Terrace after spending a day at my new school.

Meanwhile, Father enjoyed his increasing visits to the town hall and the Trades Club and his wide reading. Mother became active in one of the Methodist churches, where she already had friends, and she also soon became a member and officer of the Town Women's Co-operative Guild. Occasionally I returned to Rising Bridge to see my best friend in the village who had lived next door at number 16 Hoyle Street, but he was already making new friends and I found that I could no longer bowl or bat well at cricket or play football proficiently. When my village friends asked me what was wrong with me, I did not go again. That first summer Blackpool was not even fun and I just walked with Mother and Father on the promenade like a well-trained dog, and the comics were now an escape and not an adventure.

Worse was to come. On the day of the 11-plus examination Blackburn Rovers were playing at home. Father had occasionally taken me to a match, but this Saturday a friend's father invited a few of us in the new class to go with him to watch the game. It was important that we got there on time and in a rare effort of will I encouraged the others to also leave the examination early and set off for the game. I had not completed the examination. I did not care!

I thought no more about this until the results came out. I had failed. My father could not believe it. For the first time in my life he really hit me, sending me sprawling across the room. He was a big man who had boxed when he was young. He had also spent a lifetime in self-education, his wife had wanted to go to the grammar school and be a teacher, and now their son had failed his 11 plus! Mother cried and was silent, Father remained very angry. Out of both belief and pride there was no way I was not to go to a grammar school.

A family meeting was held. The fee payers, as against the free places, were charged £9 a year – £180 in present currency. It seemed a lot to my parents, who weighed up every penny. My auntie offered to pay a third, Father would pay the rest and I was sent off for a second examination. I tried hard – I did not want a second 'beating' and the even more painful tears of my mother. I also disliked my present school, which was a further incentive to effort. I passed.

Father and Mother were now satisfied and reverted to their varied interests. They were careful of what they spent on clothes and for the first term at the grammar school I was the only pupil not in uniform, a point brought home to me weekly by my form teacher, as if I had not myself noticed. I again felt further out of it. At the end of the first term I was the only one in my class not to attend the junior school party. An attractive girl asked me to 'take her' but I did not reply. I had learnt by then that conversations ended quicker if I did not answer. With the new demands of the grammar school fees, I did not even have a Sunday suit.

I no longer enjoyed soccer. I no longer had any friends and I became more morose. I took little interest in school work but I began to read widely every evening in my bedroom, both library books – particularly books about the sea – and the mighty political and economic tomes of my father's. I also read both the books of the Left Book Club and the Right Book Club bought by my father who, with his usual intellectual fairness, liked to study both sides of the question. I became an expert on all kinds of knowledge apart from school work and occasionally astonished my class and my teachers by my depth of information on odd subjects. This must have made me appear even more odd.

My first school report put me twentieth out of twenty-nine in the B form of a two-form grammar school. Only my mathematics and science were good. In the second year, however, I discovered history and an exciting history master who was the most prominent Lancashire historian of his age, and I immediately became top in his subject. I found history took me out of myself and I read all the history books in the local library. History also interested me because it was linked with politics and the numerous books in my father's library.

Only one other subject really brought me to life: woodwork, which I hated. I have no finger dexterity and, however I tried, my efforts in the weekly double lesson came to nought. It was only a matter of time before the woodwork master and I came to blows. Fortunately my father was the chairman of governors at the school and the headmaster, in an amazing act of prescience, removed me from the subject and put me in charge of advertisements for the school magazine, which allowed me every week to absent myself from woodwork classes and collect advertisements from all tradesmen in the town. I remembered this wise decision of the head when I became a headmaster.

Three years later two events and one interest began to bring me back into society. I had always wanted a sister and in September 1939 one arrived in the shape of a girl evacuee from Salford. I adored her and looked forward to coming home from school and playing with her. I was desperately sorry when the bombing of Salford ceased and she went home, but I am still in touch with her. My mother was also very sorry when she went home, since she always wanted a daughter as well as a son.

The second event was the taking out of my tonsils, which were found to be diseased, and I felt much fitter afterwards and took a greater interest in life, although this was still largely shown in wide reading especially in economics and politics. In the fourth and fifth years of my grammar school I slowly came alive again and began mixing socially with my classmates and competing vigorously in sport. I also began to look forward to joining the Royal Navy and sailing the seven seas.

5

The Outbreak of the Second World War

*

My personal problems in the late 1930s mirrored in a tiny way the country's problems from 1935 to 1940. The choice for our country from 1935 onwards was to rearm or to surrender to events. There was a Conservative Government with a big majority, the Peace Pledge Union membership would fall from 1936 and Italy's invasion of Abyssinia and Hitler's reoccupation of the Rhineland in the same year totally challenged the existing order.

It is arguable that if the League of Nations had acted effectively against Italy in 1936 and if Britain and France had been prepared to use force against the reoccupation of the Rhineland, the six-year war of 1939–45 could have been prevented, with its loss of life and changed map of the world. We now know that Hitler's generals opposed the occupation of the Rhineland, fearing Allied intervention, and if such intervention had occurred they would have withdrawn. The fact that Britain and France did nothing increased Hitler's control of Germany and the army and encouraged his own aggressive instincts.

Labour did little beyond making verbal protests, and it voted against the 1936–7 rearmament budget when Germany was already spending £1 billion a year on rearmament.

Hitler's brutalities brought Labour and trade-union leaders, like my father, to total condemnation and increased opposition to Hitler and Mussolini. But some Labour leaders, including my father, also suspected that the Conservative Government wanted to fight an imperialist war and would not make the necessary alliance with Russia to build up, along with France, an alliance that could both outman and outgun Germany and Italy.

Spain became a major divide between the Labour and Conservative Parties and made the Labour Party more suspicious of the ultimate aims of the Conservative Government. The Popular Front Government, elected in 1936 in Spain, was opposed by the army generals and the Roman Catholic Church in Spain and a bitter civil war was fought. People like my father considered that the British Government policy of non-intervention favoured General Franco, particularly as Italy and to a lesser extent Germany gave open support to the Spanish Nationalists.

Some 110,000 regular servicemen from Italy and a smaller number of German servicemen fought in Franco's armies, and armaments were poured in and assessed for their use in later conflicts. Russia helped the Republicans, although her distance from Spain proved a considerable handicap. Two thousand Britons fought with the International Brigade on the side of the Republicans and I remember my sorrow that I was too young to volunteer to fight with the Brigade.

There was at this time a great flowering of left-wing literature which alarmed not only the Conservative Party but the Labour Party which, while supporting the Spanish Republicans, did not want a Popular Front in Britain. There is no doubt that the influence of this literature on the younger generation planted the seeds for the Labour general election victory of 1945.

Marxist ideas were then permeating the British left. John Strachey and H.N. Brailsford were writing. Russia was seen in a very favourable light and the Webbs had reissued their *Soviet Communism: A New Civilisation* without the previous final question mark. Penguin Books arrived in 1935 and Pelican tracts in 1937. I immediately began to save up to buy and collect them. The Left Book Club was founded in May 1936 with a monthly book for 2/6 (12½ pence now but then equal to our £2.50 spending power). Within a year there were 50,000 members and we awaited the arrival of these books like the early Christians awaited the epistles of St Paul. Four hundred local discussion groups were set up and Father and I occasionally attended the Blackburn group.

The Spanish Civil War also tended to turn British politics on its head. The left was for intervention on behalf of the Republicans to counter Nazi and Fascist help to the Nationalists, while the Conservatives advocated non-intervention.

32

Feelings about Russia also varied. The left wished her to be an ally of Britain and France against Germany and Italy, while the Conservatives were suspicious of her policies and reliability and the purges of 1937 indicated that Russia was, like Germany and Italy, a totalitarian state with no love of liberty and justice.

Thus we had a phoney peace from 1936 to 1939. Neville Chamberlain, the Prime Minister, felt that Germany and Italy could be contained or bribed for peace, Labour wanted peace without paying the insurance policy of rearmament and collective security, and Liberal support was declining and the party did not even speak with one voice. Labour ceased to vote against rearmament expenditure from July 1937 and then abstained on such votes, although the party voted against conscription in March 1939, six months before the outbreak of war. A Popular Front of the left had no attractions to the Labour leadership at home or abroad.

In 1937 Japan made further inroads into China. In 1938 Hitler entered Vienna and incorporated Austria in the greater Reich and then turned his ambitions to Czechoslovakia, absorbing much of this country in two gulps in September 1938 and March 1939.

Labour was confused in its attitude. It came out for resistance to Germany in September 1938, then supported the four-power talks which gave the Sudetenland to Germany and then voted against the Munich agreement when Mr Chamberlain advocated peace rather than conflict 'because of a quarrel in a far-away country between people of whom we know nothing'.

War or surrender became inevitable when the German/Russian pact was signed on 23 August 1939, and eight days later Hitler invaded Poland, to which country France and Britain had given a defence guarantee. Chamberlain still hesitated before declaring war and was only forced into it by the pressure of the Labour Party and his Cabinet colleagues.

I well remember the declaration of war on Sunday, 3 September 1939. That Sunday morning I did not go to church but was allowed to stay at home. We had no wireless – Father considered wireless sets not only expensive but also rivals to the written word – so at 10 a.m. my father and I walked up to Meadows Farm, which was then farmed by my Uncle Herbert for the Haslingden Industrial Co-operative Society. There we heard the declaration of war by the Prime Minister, his ultimatum to Hitler having expired at 11 a.m.

I then walked home with Father and, passing the drill hall, we saw the Haslingden detachment of the Territorials marching away to the railway station. I saw my father's friend Ervin Russell, then a sergeant but who came back six years later as a major, and many others whom I knew. A man beside me in the crowd said to my father, 'Thars lucky. T'War'll be o'er afoor he's owd enough to feight.' Father smoked his pipe and said nothing.

So ended four years of hesitation. A tired and visionless Neville Chamberlain had hoped that Hitler and Mussolini could be bought off; a Liberal Party, which shamed its past, was revived to its greatness only by the odd speech of Lloyd George; and a Labour Party, at last weaned from its pacifism, was bewildered by events. Delay had meant, however, that Britain was united in and out of Parliament. Almost all Britain now saw war as inevitable and accepted that no one could deal sensibly with Hitler. Only the Independent Labour Party opposed the declaration of war and it was a spent force. The Communists made fools of themselves by first coming out in favour of war and then, at the command of Moscow, opposing it.

There were fewer pacifists than in the First World War and they made clear that it was *all* war and not this particular war they opposed. In the Second World War conscientious objections were allowed on political as well as religious grounds, but few took advantage of this concession. The First World War was largely for King and Country, but the Second World War was to ensure that the lights of freedom and decency and the rule of law were not snuffed out everywhere. I was fourteen when war was declared and I had no intention of following my father as a conscientious objector. The matter was never discussed by the two of us. This was a different war!

When I looked at an atlas it did, however, strike me as odd that we had not gone to war for Czechoslovakia, which was probably easier to defend than Poland, but I decided that the adult world was always strange.

For almost a year a phoney war followed a phoney peace. The Cabinet was simply strengthened by Winston Churchill and Anthony Eden. It was 13 December before the first British soldier was killed, although the Royal Navy was regularly in action and the Merchant Fleet had begun to make its sacrifices of men and ships. A crisis was needed to bring the matter to a head and this occurred in May 1940 in the débâcle on the Narvik (Norway) expedition. History has many ironies and this is one of them, since it was Churchill who wanted and planned the failed expedition. Yet its failure broke Chamberlain and brought Churchill to the premiership.

At the end of the Commons debate on 7 and 8 May 1940, 41 Conservatives voted with Labour and 60 abstained and a 240 Conservative majority was reduced to 81. Churchill became Prime Minister. The previous Sunday I had, as usual, walked up to King Street Methodist Church with my father and mother for the evening service. Everyone stopped Father and asked him about the war. He replied that all would be well, but I knew from the tone of his voice that he did not believe it. A week later we walked to the church again and everyone again spoke to Father, but this week when he replied his tone of voice was different. He believed that Churchill as Prime Minister would enable us to win the war.

Father had always been suspicious of Churchill because of Tonypandy, when he had sent troops to South Wales during a mining dispute, and because of his being responsible for the return of Britain to the gold standard in 1925 at too high a parity. Conservatives were suspicious of Churchill because of his opposition to the India Bill and his support of Edward VIII, and many of the general public remembered the failures of his Antwerp and Dardanelles expeditions. But war brings strange bedfellows and my father gave Churchill his total support, and indeed admiration, for five years until the war was won. Then he and millions more thanked him for his efforts and voted for his removal from government!

6

Sixth Form Life

*

I had a happy two years in the sixth form of Haslingden Grammar School. I became more outgoing again and was accepted as such by my friends in the school, the King Street Methodist Church and in the town generally. I played sport for the school and began to have a full political life outside it. School thus fell into perspective and was just part of my life – an enjoyable part, but one that was balanced by many other interests.

I had already begun to show my independence in the fifth form. I had told my art teacher that there was no way I could pass art and that I should study the history of art instead on my own: I did and passed. I also decided to study biology by myself and again I passed at school certificate standard.

In the sixth form for Higher School Certificate I studied five subjects: English, history, French, mathematics and economics. I studied economics by myself, and because of timetable difficulties I attended only a few of the mathematics lessons. It was a mistake to carry on with French. I had worked hard and had private tuition to achieve a credit at School Certificate level so I could reach the matriculation standard required for entry to university. I was, however, totally uninterested in the subject and I had wanted to drop French when France capitulated in 1940. I am also slightly tone deaf, especially in French. My headteacher, however, considered my interest in literature would, via the sixth form French set books, pull me through. I failed and did not even get the equivalent of an ordinary School Certificate pass!

I did very well, however, in history, English and economics. I studied economics by myself, read one textbook and wrote one essay. Ever since, I have considered economics to be an easy or even a non-subject. There are the laws of supply and demand and the need for a look at the history of various economies with their booms and slumps. Everything else is largely mumbo-jumbo and the work of economic witch-doctors. I came to the conclusion that economists muddy the waters so that the rest of society cannot see how shallow they are. Having stated that, I must to be fair add that I had read widely in politics and history and even Marxist economics and this must have shown in my examination papers.

I was very busy in my church and Sunday school, and in addition to being a Sunday school teacher I was put on 'trial' as a local preacher. I began to read theology and thought for a time I should become a minister and preach a social gospel! We had a very happy group of young people at King Street Methodist Church, which was alas broken up by the call of the armed forces. I played table tennis regularly there and we had jolly parties and I stayed out late with no evil intent.

I also took on two allotments to help the war effort and grew potatoes and sold them to neighbours. I introduced the use of treated human sewage to this allotment area, and there was great amazement when my first cartload arrived. Growing flowers, especially pansies and carnations, was another hobby. I won trophies in all the local shows and have kept the prize cards I received. I then thought that I would become a carnation specialist after the war and I still have a strong desire to own a carnation nursery where other people do the work and I walk round once or twice a day.

The Sixth Form Debating Society, which met every Monday afternoon, was a delight. We discussed the post-war world and I was then a full socialist in every way. My socialism was, however, more religious than Marxist. I had not yet discovered the religious 'Fall of Man'. I was all for a redemptive environment and believed that if people were well treated they would be filled with brotherly and sisterly love. Competition between people and shops just seemed wasteful. Capitalism certainly brought the moral fall of economic man. Many of the sixth form agreed with my views and the others tolerated me as a strange ornament or even 'seer' who was quite pleasant, provided I was taken in small doses.

I also became very active in the Haslingden Labour Party, taking office and advocating a post-war full socialist peaceful revolution in Britain. The Left Book Club was still pouring out left-wing literature and influencing the Labour Party's thinking on future policies. In many ways my views were the views of those years. There was a sea change in political opinion in the war years. Modern wars are won only by the total conscription of capital and labour. Wars are thus collectivist and people then hold that, since a country has won a war by conscripting capital and labour, capital and labour should similarly be conscripted to win the peace. This was a major factor in the Labour victory of 1945. Father and the Labour movement were also deeply concerned that there should be no post-war return to massive unemployment and the means tests of the 1930s.

In 1942 William Beveridge's celebrated Report was published, building on the work of the Fabians and the Webbs. When I read it again – as I did when I became Social Security Minister – it was obvious that it was concerned with past problems, but it was then held by many of us in the Labour movement as a beacon of light for the post-war world. We were all excited by its possibilities and I can remember the almost wild enthusiasm and hopes of those early years.

The Conservatives in Parliament received the Beveridge Report more coolly. The Labour MPs not in government divided the House and voted for an amendment, giving it warmer approval. This was the only time in the coalition government that the Labour Party divided the Commons. Yet Beveridge presumed the continuance of a capitalist society and rejected the view that an insurance scheme could be replaced by a government-funded social security system.

To guarantee post-war peace I joined the Federal Union movement, which was dedicated to world federal union so that wars between states would be impossible. While in the lower sixth I then called a public meeting, which was well attended, and a Rossendale branch was set up, of which I became secretary. Filled with enthusiasm I built this branch up to be one of the most successful Federal Union branches. One cousin of mine was chairman, another cousin was treasurer and my father was president – a little nepotism goes a long way! I also addressed Federal Union meetings all over the North Country and North Wales, and the audiences must have been slightly surprised when they found their speaker for the evening was a callow sixteen-year-old with a great zeal for figures and instant solutions. These were my first journeys away from home by myself. Alas, the Rossendale branch collapsed when the approach of my Higher School Certificate examinations called me back to study. I was at that time and remained for some years a Christian socialist. I was also influenced by the Marxist view of the inevitability of socialism.

My final sixth form activity was linked with my volunteering to join the Royal Navy. I had read so many sea books in my years of isolation that it had to be the Royal Navy. Haslingden, however, had not a Sea Cadet Corps but an Air Training Corps, and this I joined. I then told my mother that I wished to join the Royal Navy. She said I should discuss this with my father and my headmaster. The headmaster was surprised, but agreed after commenting that he thought I might find problems with my left-wing views in that particular service. I had then to wait to have a proper conversation with my father, who was always busy. An interview was arranged after two weeks in our small three-bedroomed semi. I stated my case and Father took his pipe out of his mouth, spat into the fire and said, 'Since thi cannot play cricket, thi'd better join Navy.' I never really knew what this meant, except that Father had approved. Father's great sporting love was cricket, especially Haslingden in the Lancashire League; and he was most disappointed that while I could play other sports I was no good at cricket. Presumably if I had been good at cricket I should have been put in a reserved occupation! I can imagine my father asking my mother some weeks after I joined the Navy, 'Where's Rhodes? I haven't seen 'im recently!'

I was interviewed in Manchester by two imposing naval figures. The conversation went well but I was tested not on ship but on aircraft recognition. I knew none, so they quickly brought the interview to a close before I made further gaffes, and I was accepted. I became an expert at Morse code in the Haslingden Air Training Corps, but I never improved in aircraft recognition.

In the long summer break between completing my Higher School Certificate papers and receiving the results in late August I climbed the Haslingden and Helmshore hills every day and read on my back and heard and saw the skylarks high above me. It was a timeless summer punctuated by a week of pea picking and a week at ATC camp. Part of me wished this interregnum would go on for ever.

Strangely enough my years of service in the Royal Navy were also an interregnum. My political views were exactly the same when I came ashore in 1947 as when I enlisted. I did six months with the Cardiff University Naval Division, training for naval service while taking part in all the university activities and passing a part one BA examination in Anglo-Saxon, philosophy and English. I then did the course at the notorious HMS *Ganges* with its famous mast, and I knew when I left that training ship I was fitter than I would ever be again in my life.

I was fortunate to be sent out to the East Indies Fleet and to take leaves in Ceylon and India. I was twice promoted. The Indian experience – I was based for several months in Bombay – has been very helpful in my constituency, which has large numbers of constituents who originate from Gujarat and other places in north-west India.

I never disguised, for good or ill, my views while I was in the Royal Navy. I was a socialist. I became sympathetic towards Russia, I favoured Indian home rule. I certainly understood why Churchill lost the 1945 election. The country had moved to the left and 90 per cent of non-commissioned servicemen had only one wish in 1945 – to get back home quickly – and while they appreciated Churchill's war leadership, they feared he would delay demobilization by more military adventures.

The Royal Navy further reinforced my already systematic methods of work. A nonconformist home, a strict school and the tight discipline of the Royal Navy gave me a privileged start in life, for which I am always grateful.

7

Switch to Education

*

As soon as I returned from the Royal Navy I married Vicky, my first wife, and began my studies at Manchester University, reading politics and modern history. Marilyn, my elder daughter, was born in 1949 while I was still completing my first degree. For the first fifteen months we lived with my father and mother and then we bought a terraced two-bedroomed 'overlookers' house a mile and a half away. I was more mature now and Father was beginning to mellow. He was, however, still the proverbial intellect of the town with cutting phrase, and the town saw me as his son. Father and I met regularly at meetings, I called on my parents most days, and we always had the Sunday high tea at 11 Colldale Terrace. It was a pleasant and secure routine. Yet at Labour Party meetings I had become much more radical than my father and we were often involved in major arguments, to the concern of the rest of the party. In 1947 I must have been a real thorn in the flesh for him although, with his usual toughness, he took it all in his stride.

In the 1945 general election Rossendale returned Mr G.H. Walker, a linotype operator, as its new MP, with a majority of 5,588 on a minority vote. This was a Labour gain from the Conservatives. My father rejoiced in this victory and I from afar shared his enthusiasm.

In the November council elections of 1945 – the first such elections since 1938 – Labour gained two seats from the Tories and one from the Liberals in Haslingden. The make-up of the council was then Conservatives ten, Liberals eight, Labour five, with one independent. Father, who had been made a magistrate in 1941, was re-elected in Acre Ward, topping the poll with 723 votes. At the first meeting of the new council he was elected Haslingden's first Labour alderman and stayed on the aldermanic bench the rest of his life, to become the father of the town council.

Father also stood for the Haslingden seat on the Lancashire County Council on 4 March 1946, against Captain Baxter, MC, a prominent local Conservative, and was defeated. The fact that Father had been a conscientious objector in the 1914–18 war did not help, and my serving in the forces in the Far East was no substitute. The Conservative advertisement for the election began: 'An appeal to ex-servicemen and women to support an Ex-service Candidate who is in favour of Pensions to Parents of families of servicemen. . . .' The Haslingden British Legion also sent out a letter: 'We recommend for your support in the County Council election Captain W.H. Baxter, MC. . . .' Father lost by 595 votes in a 6,000 poll. In the same year, 1946, only one ward returned a Labour member in Haslingden.

Meanwhile I had been editing pamphlets which drew blood from the local Tories and when, in April 1947, there was a by-election in Syke Ward, I was asked to stand. This was a ward we had won by 613 votes in 1945 and by 595 votes in 1946. We worked the ward very hard, doing a 100 per cent canvass, but the Labour Party was becoming more unpopular. This was at the height of a coal shortage, which was causing short time in all the mills and making life hard in the town. I lost by 480 votes in a high poll.

I was shattered and it was ten years before I stood for the council again. I often wonder how different my life would have been if I had won. Would I have gone on to stand for Parliament in the Labour interest and been elected and eventually been trapped in the Labour Party of the late 1970s, moving to the left and being unelectable? At what stage would I have changed my views and what would I have done about them? Would I have joined the Social Democratic Party at that time? Who knows? One cannot replay history. Instead, I threw myself into other activities. I became spokesman for the Haslingden ex-Servicemen's Housing Association. I became a Methodist lay preacher and Sunday school teacher, and I started work on local history. I also completed my degree. I attended occasional Labour meetings, but really began to move to their reserve list.

At Manchester University I took no part in politics at all. I felt as an ex-serviceman a generation away from the young undergraduates and I returned to wide reading. I was, however, elected a member of the Board of Management of the Haslingden Industrial Co-operative Society, one of the oldest in the country and whose history I wrote for its centenary in 1951. These six years as an elected director gave me my first business experience.

I also became a WEA youth lecturer and an assistant warden of Haslingden's Civic Youth Club. My father encouraged my educational interests – education was his great love and he was chairman of the Rossendale Education Executive for very many years. My mother, who had always wanted me to be a teacher, also encouraged my educational interests and Vicky, my wife, was a teacher. I suspect my parents thought that education would be more likely to keep me at home in Lancashire rather than politics, which could take me to London and elsewhere.

After a very successful teacher training year at Manchester University, specializing in junior education, I applied to local Rossendale schools for a junior school post but was unsuccessful. Teaching and medicine are classic examples of the inability of government to get the numbers right. There was then a surplus of junior school teachers in East Lancashire.

When I came away from the third unsuccessful interview my local divisional education officer took me on one side and suggested that I might like to start in a secondary modern school the following day in charge of a department. I immediately accepted, so I arrived in secondary schools as a primary school reject! I also failed to ask what the subject was and had to ring up to find out. I was to be in charge of English. I knew nothing about secondary modern schooling, but spent the evening with a very successful secondary modern school headmaster. I thus arrived at Ramsbottom County Secondary School the following morning with a new and detailed English syllabus, much to the amazement and possible alarm of the headmaster.

Ramsbottom Secondary Modern School had no visible honours board on which Albert, who was eaten by the lion, or anybody else could be listed. The school was run-of-the-mill, healthy and cheerful, with no airs and graces and little idea of what it was supposed to achieve. The headmaster held it together loosely and some of the boys from isolated villages were very tough and could have been characters in nineteenth-century fiction.

The year 1951 saw the raising of the school-leaving age to fifteen, a reform that certainly did not commend itself to the fourteen-year-olds in the school who the previous year could have gone to work. The staff agreed entirely with the children. I was to have 4C for double periods several times a week in a dilapidated technical school building some two and half miles away from the main school. It contained more illiterates, semi-illiterates and lesson resisters than would normally have been found in a whole township. I had been warned of the illiteracy. Never daunted, I read on the bus journey from Haslingden to Ramsbottom Neville Cardus writing on cricket in the *Manchester Guardian*. I proposed to read this to 4C when we first met and then ask them if they would like to be able to read it themselves.

This first lesson with 4C – which would have been more aptly called 4Z – was held in a laboratory of the technical school. It took some fifteen minutes to get the class inside and then I began to read Cardus. Within seconds, water and gas taps were turned on and all kinds of Olympic wrestling began to take place on the floor. It was obvious that my pupils were not enthusiastic either for cricket or Neville Cardus or the *Manchester Guardian*.

Then began a battle for control in this detached building, which lasted two months and almost drove me out of teaching. There seemed original sin here, if not the presence of the original serpent itself. Bit by bit I gained control and I never reported my problems to the headmaster. The final victory was in part of the curriculum not mentioned in any teaching practice – climbing and kicking!

That November we had a very heavy snowfall and when I went out to the small playground to call in 4C they pointed to the roof, on which sat the demon boy of the class. I tried to recall the lectures of Professor Oliver at Manchester University on the philosophy of education, but this kind of situation had scarcely been covered by them. Thank goodness for the more practical experience of the Royal Navy. Drainpipes and rigging were and are for climbing and I recalled the famous mast at HMS *Ganges*, where I had served time as a boy seaman. I climbed the drainpipe to the roof and collected the boy and we came down the drainpipe together. I held him by various parts of his anatomy, thumping and kicking him all the way down whenever I got the opportunity. As I approached the ground a great cheer went up, followed by cries of 'Good old sir', and the class rushed inside for the first time probably since it was constituted.

After victory, peace was made. I was now given all kinds of information by the class. The demon boy had a dishevelled stray dog he worshipped. I gave him permission to bring it once a week to a double lesson, provided it behaved. The mongrel was brought in on an old piece of string and sat beside the boy. The class approved both of the dog and of me.

My faith in my class control greatly increased when I saw the boy in question continue to cheek in public one of the strongest members of staff. A few days later another member of staff took me to the staff-room door following afternoon school and he opened it six inches to show me the boy and the same member of staff fighting underneath the staff-room table. We locked the door and went home!

The class developed its own play, which was never written down but recalled as in ancient oral traditions and involved all the boys in it. Every double lesson ended with the performance of the play, which resulted in the death of all participants. Similarly, if we had any visitors – which was rare, because most people fled at the sight of the class – the play was performed. In one year the number of its performances rivalled those of *The Mousetrap*.

Never again, when I became a headmaster in London, did I meet boys who could be as difficult as those in Lancashire. Class rebellions are easier to deal with than the lonely revolts of the long-distance runners of the north.

To balance this very difficult class there was the pleasure of 2A, which was my form class. Young, keen and cheerful they were, with many other classes a delight, but I suspect there must still be 4Cs in a number of schools. Corporal punishment cannot stop the occasional 4Z arising, but I suspect that its presence could deter many incipient 4Cs. Those Members of Parliament who voted to end corporal punishment in state schools should have been locked in the laboratory with 4C on one of its more lively days. Anyone who met 4C would have been surprised that it was the lion that ate Albert and not Albert who ate the lion!

That first year I produced a Christmas play and I started a school magazine. The previous summer I had led a party from Haslingden Youth Club hostelling in Germany, and I then organized from the school a youth hostel holiday in Germany every year.

After being appointed head youth warden in Clayton-le-Moors, I was asked by Lancashire County Council to form a civic youth club in Ramsbottom which would meet in the school where I taught. I did so and the club became famous throughout the county. I remained its head warden until my appointment to my first headship.

The success of my youth hostel parties in school encouraged me to set up a travel firm taking Lancashire tourists to Germany, France and Switzerland. This firm continued for three years, but I had to bring it to a close because of its time demands and I decided that teaching was now my real career. This was my second taste of the commercial world.

After four years of enjoyable teaching I began to think more deeply about the ethos of British secondary education, especially with regard to the secondary modern schools. The elementary schools that preceded them knew exactly what their aims were: the three Rs, general knowledge, good habits of work and pupils left to apprenticeships and general work. Similarly the grammar schools knew what their task was: to give the taste of high culture and training for university and the professions.

The secondary modern schools were a government confidence trick which led inevitably to the campaign for comprehensive schools. They were so general that no one knew what their purpose was. I remember attending a conference addressed by a senior Lancashire education officer early on in my time at Ramsbottom, at which he said secondary modern schools were the schools of the future and that their exciting and yet non-examinable curriculum would become so popular that in five years no one would wish to go to grammar schools. I thought he must have been thinking of drainpipe climbing in the snow and I wondered which grammar school his children were attending! I began to be cynical about the attitude both of politicians and education officers to the reality of the classroom and the individual school.

Ramsbottom Secondary Modern School was basically kept going by a number of ex-servicemen trained after war service on emergency teacher training courses. These were one-year courses taught in residential camps by heads and deputy heads on secondment. They might be short of lectures on the philosophy of education, but they were superb at class control and in real-life situations. On teaching practice for my Teacher's Certificate I had been put with one such person who passed on to me the 'craft' of teaching. I thus came early to the view that departments of education and teacher training colleges were generally a waste of time, but what mattered was seeing a master teacher with his or her class. I still hold that view.

I raised money towards the cost of school journeys by running a canteen each morning break. We sold biscuits, crisps and Oxo on cold winter days at a penny a cup, or one penny for the hot water if 4C brought their own cubes. For some months we also had meat pies from a friendly father van-driver who obtained them from a famous factory at very low cost. One day, however, several staff and many pupils fell ill and we then discovered that the pies were rejects. All staff and pupils recovered and were probably tougher for the experience but we cancelled the order. One day the county raised with the school the low take-up of milk by the children. Not surprisingly, most pupils preferred hot Oxo to frozen milk on a February day.

I continually invited the captain of the merchant ship we had 'adopted' to visit us. One December as a skylark with one other ex-service member of staff I decided to inform the school that the captain was to come on the last day of term and my colleague, who was a well-known local amateur actor, prepared to hire Merchant Navy uniform – beards and other theatrical requirements. Alas, at the last moment we had to cry off since we found the headmaster was minded to invite the chairman of the council, the governors and local councillors. Discretion was the better part of valour if Ramsbottom was not to be my last as well as my first school. A telegram was sent from Manchester and the school had to overcome its disappointment.

In my fifth year I became most concerned about the waste of talent in secondary modern schools and the low expectations. At the age of thirteen many of our brightest boys passed an examination to go to two local technical schools – Bury and Radcliffe. This depressed the morale of the boys who failed and the girls who were not allowed to sit. One boy did stay on for a fifth year at the school, but this was to play soccer for Lancashire schoolboys and not to attempt examinations.

I decided that I would stay on at the school more than five years only if the school was prepared to introduce extended courses for School Certificate, City and Guilds and Lancashire and Cheshire Institute examinations. The headmaster declined and I began to read the teacher vacancy columns in *The Times Educational Supplement*.

I applied for a post in nearby Bolton and was interviewed and appointed. Then Lancashire moved into action. I was by then well known through German youth hostelling and language teaching, the running of a very successful town youth club and a good school magazine and many other out-of-school activities. I was informed that a secondary school headship in my Rossendale Valley was vacant and that I might like to apply. I did.

The interview was at Rawtenstall Town Hall. There was the local divisional officer, a senior county official and some four to five local councillors from the Divisional Executive and from the governing body of the school. The officials asked numerous questions on youth hostelling, youth work and so forth. I also made my views clear that I considered that secondary modern schools were going nowhere and they needed a tighter ideology and extended meaningful courses leading to examinations. I was appointed. I ran all the way to Rawtenstall town centre to telephone my wife and my father and mother and I felt that I could have run for ever. I was just thirty years old and I had been given my own command. Life was very good.

I heard years later that, without my knowledge, one of Haslingden's Labour councillors had walked a round trip of eight miles to see a Conservative councillor who sat on the appointment panel to ensure that he would be present at the interview for this headship. He apparently agreed and said, 'He may be Labour but he is a good schoolmaster and his father will like him staying at home.'

I remembered that day the advice of my grammar school headmaster when I first told him that I was becoming a schoolmaster. He said that I must teach confidently, but if I introduced two new activities into the school when I first joined and made them over a few years the gold stars of the school, I would certainly be appointed to a headship. Unthinkingly I had done this in my youth hostelling and with the youth club and consequently I had become a headmaster. The grammar school headmaster also gave me a testimonial when I applied for this first headship. It ended: 'He is indeed a man of action and ideas rather than an aesthetic spectator. He will get things done.'

Yet it was with some sadness that I left Ramsbottom Secondary Modern School. I had been close to the children. It was fun there, but I wanted the final responsibility of running a school.

The building in which I worked at Ramsbottom has now been demolished and a new primary school built on the site. I opened the new building when I was a Minister of State and I have a picture of it in my room at the Commons.

Soon after I was elected for Parliament I was invited to return to Ramsbottom Youth Club, now in its own building. I did and, without my knowledge, my favourite 2A had organized a 'This Is Your Life'. Some thirty-seven of the forty-one in that class came in one by one and all had done well. I wish I had a video of that evening.

Some years later a boy who was in one of the lower forms at Ramsbottom, but was by then an army NCO, asked to see me at the Commons. He had just married and brought his bride to meet me. He told her and reminded me that he was illiterate when he was first taught by me, but that by means of a mixture of the stick, willpower and compassion he was reading after six weeks. He pointed to his sergeant's stripes and said, 'These are really yours, sir.' On such days to have been a schoolteacher is to have been a member of a great and honourable profession.

8

My First Headship

*

The day after I was appointed a headmaster I visited my new school. All I knew was that it was an ex-central school – originally a selective school up to the age of fifteen – which was now a mixed secondary modern school. When I arrived in mid-afternoon the school had closed for its annual cross-country. I was amazed by the building and its setting. It was a converted nineteenth-century stone country mansion with lodge-houses at each end of a fine winding drive set in spacious, beautiful grounds on the fringe of the semi-wild Lancashire countryside. The grounds had tennis-courts, lawns, magnificent rhododendrons, a stream and a pond. My headmaster's room was large with huge windows. I was spellbound. My life certainly was to be 'in pastures green'.

I intended to make Lea Bank a purposeful school with useful courses, tough discipline, high morale and activities for everyone. If Lea Bank could not be made into a Guards battalion, it could certainly have the morale of a good county regiment. I could see immediately that my predecessor had been a fine disciplinarian and that the school was in excellent shape. There were no signs of 4C and the school was very civilized, with an adult relationship between pupils and staff. I was determined to develop extended courses, as I had promised at my interview, and I took a copy of the school timetable and individual teachers' timetables home with me.

In the summer holidays I drew up a full timetable, including a fifth-year class for extended courses. I made contact with parents to ensure they knew that such courses would now be available. I also informed them that there would be a full uniform based on the crest of Lea Bank, which was a red fox on green, since the nineteenth-century Ashworths, the owners of the house at that time, had been masters of the Rossendale foxhounds. I also announced that there would be a German youth hostelling holiday in my first year. I was a young man in a hurry.

I have always considered that schools must have a close partnership with parents. After announcing my plans I stated that if in any year there were fewer applicants for places than there were vacancies in the school, the governors would have my resignation. I also made clear, through the local press, that I considered myself responsible to parents in the last resort and not to the education authority.

As soon as the school year opened, I knew that I would have opposition from most of the school teaching staff. Some were aware of my family's politics and they feared the politicization of education – something of which I would never be guilty. Others just wanted the school to free-wheel, and I had to put them on tandem bicycles with a parent sitting in front of each of them. Perhaps I did too much myself – visits, timetables, events, school journeys, instead of encouraging others, but a young man has to learn.

Two of the teaching staff had been at the school when it had been a central school and they welcomed my changes. I reminded them of the great days of the school. Both lived locally and the standing of the school mattered to them. One was fortunately the senior mistress: a lady of great wisdom, full of common sense and local knowledge. The children saw her as powerful as Gagool in *King Solomon's Mines*.

The first year had very difficult staff-headship relationships without there ever being a total breakdown. By the end of the year, however, two things happened. First, I made sure that the school would always be in the news and it became very popular with parents, potential parents and the junior schools that fed into us. Second, the other valley secondary modern schools, and particularly the grammar school, did not like what we were doing and tried to prevent my changes. This provided the dynamic tension whereby all staff had to decide on whose side they were. There were no resignations.

I also began to lecture on education and write letters to the press on educational issues. I remember well two letters. One was on sport and the other was on the future of secondary education. The one on sport was to a national paper commenting with tongue in cheek how remarkable it was that the 11-plus examination not only divided the intellectually able from the less able but the most vigorous pupils from the least vigorous, since the allowance per pupil for games in grammar schools was twice as much as in secondary modern schools. Within three months sports allowances in Lancashire were changed to give the same allowance to pupils of the same age, irrespective of the type of school. I began to admire and use the power of the press.

The second letter, to *The Sunday Times*, was published on 2 February 1958. It made clear my views that the bipartite system was untenable unless secondary modern schools were allowed or preferably encouraged to develop meaningful and examination-tested extended courses. The letter ended: 'The knowledge that others in such a [secondary] modern school are succeeding and going to college or a student apprenticeship is the greatest educational tranquilliser for parents and is worth 1,000 pamphlets describing the methods of selection! What parents fear in the 11+ is not technical error, but an alternative choice which will cut their children off from later educational opportunities.'

I also became suspicious of education officials and their theories. As soon as I announced that Lea Bank would have extended courses, I was visited by a county official who pointed out to me how almost infallible was the 11-plus examination so that there were very few, if any, in my school who could sit the School Certificate with any chance of passing or even benefiting from extended courses. I nodded sagely but said nothing and he went away convinced he had changed my mind. When a fortnight later he heard that the extended courses had started, he returned and repeated the previous argument. Again I nodded but said nothing. It is a model I have used regularly since. Be nice to officials, listen to them and nod wisely but ignore their advice and do what you believe is right. Officials then decide there is something strange about such a person and leave him or her alone. This they did with me.

Ironically, four years later the Lancashire Education Committee policy was reversed and external examinations were encouraged in secondary modern schools and I was visited by the same senior official to ask me to lecture at a county conference on the advantages of extended courses in secondary modern schools. I then decided that if one says what one believes, one is eventually in fashion!

I have always been a believer in prizes for all and varied examinations for all. Everyone must be able to achieve something. On our prize nights we had General Certificate of Education certificates in various subjects, Union of Lancashire and Cheshire Institute certificates, Rossendale leaving certificates set and marked in the school after an examination covering basic literacy, numeracy and general knowledge, 100 per cent (a year) attendance certificates and public service certificates. We also had form prizes, subject prizes, school sports colours and inter-house trophies. All the sixteen-year-olds were prefects and we had form captains.

The prize day was held in the largest dance hall in the area, which was very prestigious, and the sight of the whole school in uniform with a silence in which you could have heard the proverbial pin drop and the attendance of hundreds of parents and local notabilities made clear to all that this was a successful school proud of its achievements. Staff relationships were no longer any problem.

What effect did extended courses have? In the first place they lifted the morale of the whole school. Those who stayed on and passed examinations were delighted. The others who left at fifteen still had the reflected glory of having been to a school which was something special and the pollen of the examination successes rubbed off on them.

In my last year at Lea Bank nine pupils – 15 per cent of our intake of that year – sat the General Certificate of Education, achieving on average 5.3 subject passes each. They were taught alongside the fourth-year pupils who were staying on in a teaching group of just over twenty, which was economic in staffing. The school did so well in external examinations that the Lancashire County Council had to change its scheme for special allowances in secondary modern schools, or all my teaching staff would have been on one.

Discipline was never a problem at Lea Bank but, as at Ramsbottom, I met the bloody-minded solitary individual who demonstrated what must be a northern, or at least a Lancashire trait. In this case it was a powerful boy who showed the loneliness of the long-distance runner. He did his work, did not cheek staff but he ceased to speak to them even when spoken to and continually stared at them with piercing eyes. He began to stand outside the house of a member of staff for hours in the evenings and the member of staff began to crumble. I had to take action. I decided to run with him at lunch-times for two or three miles. We changed, set out, returned and showered with hardly a word passing between us. I pulled him out of lessons where problems might arise and he sat and read or just sat in my room. Finally he got a job as a miner; I did not enforce school attendance and we let him leave early. Yet he continued to return very occasionally at lunch-times and knocked on my door and we ran together. In my last week he knocked one day, we ran together and returned and he just said 'Thank you' and gave me a present. I think it was a tin of my favourite tobacco which I smoked at that time – Balkan Sobranie. Not a further word passed between us. We shook hands and I saw him no more.

My father was now the town's elder statesman. He had already received the MBE and in 1957 he was given the Freedom of the Borough. With my wife and two daughters we attended this ceremony and it tempted me to consider standing again for the local council. I had not been active in politics for some years, but had kept up nominal membership of the Labour Party, largely out of respect for my father. The local Liberal Party had indicated that they hoped for my allegiance at some stage and I had also spoken to a Conservative friend about a likely vacancy for a Conservative councillor in my father's old ward which could interest me. Father somehow heard of this conversation through the Haslingden bush telegraph and, despite his rigid 10 p.m. bedtime, arrived at my home one evening at 10.30 p.m. and awaited my return from a theatre trip to Manchester to speak to me. He informed me that there would be a vacancy in Syke Ward, which I had fought in 1947, and that he would like me to stand as a Labour candidate. Since I did not feel deeply committed to any party at that time but just wished to serve the town, I thought about the matter, attended the next meeting of the Haslingden Labour Party and agreed to stand in their interest in Syke Ward.

There were two vacancies in this ward and I was elected as the second councillor with a majority of 317 over the third candidate. The following year I came up for re-election and was returned unopposed, something I continue to try to persuade my Labour and Liberal opponents in Brent North to repeat. I had left the valley when I came up for re-election again in 1961 and the seat was won by the Conservatives.

As I wrote earlier, one cannot replay history, changing events and the cast, but looking back I occasionally wonder what would have happened if I had been officially asked to stand as a Tory in 1957 and had accepted before my father's visitation? Would I have agreed and would I have become so fully involved that I stayed in the valley, became known throughout Lancashire and was asked to stand for a Conservative parliamentary seat in 1959 or 1964?

Haslingden Council then ran virtually without party whips, and chairmen and vice-chairmen were shared out among the three parties. Haslingden, with a population of 14,000, made sure that the allegiance of its councillors was first to the town and only secondarily to the party. This was real local government: something that was lost in the reorganization into the large boroughs by, of all parties, the Conservative Party!

My first speech in the council was not as it would have been if I had been elected in 1947. Then it would have been on a deeply felt socialist theme, now it was on a common-sense understanding of the needs of my council house electors. Haslingden was building semi-detached council houses, all with the same size of garden whether people wanted one or not. I suggested that people should be given a choice between having semi-detached houses with gardens, with no gardens or land at all, or with solid concrete bases on which people could repair their cars or motor bikes and be handymen. To treat all the same seemed senseless to me.

On one important issue I disagreed with and voted against my party. This was the automatic subsidizing of council house rents by all ratepayers. This meant that old age pensioners in my ward on low incomes owning their houses or paying rent to private landlords subsidized council house tenants often with two, three or more wages in one house. This seemed to me against social justice.

I chaired a public meeting for Tony Greenwood, the Labour MP for Rossendale, in the 1959 general election, but I took no part in Labour activities outside the town. My other semi-political activity was that I was elected to the committee of the Rossendale branch of the National Union of Teachers, but this was non-party political. I had not then concluded that unions were no longer a force for good, even for their members.

There might also have been a more Machiavellian aspect to my election to the NUT Committee for Rossendale. My radical educational policies could bring me opposition from teachers –

especially other headteachers – in the valley, and even in the beginning from my own staff, and to be on the local committee of the NUT could be helpful to me. It is never wise to fight on too many fronts at the same time.

Since my school-days I have always been interested in the history of Rossendale. I chose to do the long essay in my degree course on local history and I now decided to do an MA degree by thesis on the history of the Poor Law in north-east Lancashire from 1834 to 1871. I visited the Lancashire Record Office in Preston and local libraries on evenings, Saturdays and holidays and completed my thesis. I obtained my degree in 1960. My father was very proud of this achievement. Part of the thesis was published in the *Transactions of the Lancashire and Cheshire Antiquarian Society* in 1960, and when I read the paper my old history master – Dr G.H. Tupling – who had given me my love of history when I was at Haslingden Grammar School, was present.

I seem to have been in education a quinquennium man. I taught at Ramsbottom for five years. I was head of Lea Bank for five years and two terms. After five years I had itchy feet. The itch was, however, not to leave education for politics but to take a bigger challenge in the educational scene. I saw my future entirely in education and scholarship at that time. I was beginning to think more deeply about educational organization. As a practising teacher I wanted evolutionary and not revolutionary change and the careful monitoring of all changes. I had not made my mind up as to my attitude to the movement to comprehensive secondary school education. I wrote a letter in *Education* at the time of the Notting Hill riots which illustrated my then attitude. In this letter I expressed 'a certain sympathy with advocacy of the common school', but I considered the case was 'over-stated'. I was interested in its educational side, not in the claims for greater cohesion. I ended: 'Many modern schools are producing excellent results intellectually and in their social products. If "parity" was real and not a politician's catchpenny and we had equality with the grammar schools in staffing ratios . . . we could do more.'

In real life and even, to a large extent, in religion I have always advocated salvation by works and not salvation by faith alone. In my view, comprehensive schools should have been tried in set areas and their results monitored carefully and compared with the results in bipartite areas. I had by now passed beyond simple beliefs in politics and education and I wanted carefully evaluated experiments before we turned the whole educational organization of our country upside-down.

However, I was keen to take part in such experiments. I thus looked round for an opportunity. I read *The Times Educational Supplement* and applied for six headships of large schools. The first to call me for interview was the London County Council, which had long had a high educational reputation and where there was a policy of moving towards comprehensive education through the erection of well-built and well-funded comprehensive schools. I was interviewed twice and offered the headship of the Robert Montefiore Secondary School, an ex-central school where the London County Council wished for extended courses, including sixth form studies, to be expanded. The area of the school also attracted me. My Huguenot forebears had lived in East London when they first came to England.

I was sorry to leave my native valley. Like my father, my instincts and judgements are those of Lancashire nonconformity. I knew, however, that if I was to move to the big league, now was the time and London the place. I thus felt like my forebears who travelled from Cambridgeshire to the Lancashire cotton valleys in the early nineteenth century. I wished to be where the action was. I also was aware that in some way I had to move from the proximity of my father. I respected him greatly and he rarely tried to intervene in my life, but he was a very powerful man with a formidable presence and I had to work out for myself where I was going. One part of me hated leaving the valley and my parents, the other part wished to be in the big league. The big league won.

I remember much from Lea Bank, my first headship. In my first year we had a competition for a Christmas poem for the Christmas card. One boy from a very large family, which was still increasing, wrote:

> Joseph was walking here and there,
> He really looked quite mad,
> But all that was wrong with him
> Was he was going to be a dad.

Much human poignancy there.

On my last day at Lea Bank a scribbled note arrived on the main notice-board: 'Jumble Sale in Mr. Boyson's Room, 6.30–9.00 p.m. All his old canes will be sold.'

On my departure, the following poem was written by the senior mistress:

Lea Bank bids farewell with nostalgic tears,
To the stormy petrel ranging for five years
Through assemblies and holidays, GCEs and renown
A whirlwind, a kaleidoscope, a fluttering gown. . . .

So now farewell and Godspeed
To Montefiore in its greater need.

I regularly receive letters from ex-Lea Bankers and see them when I revisit the valley. In 1991 I also returned for a pupil and staff reunion and hundreds turned up, including the two head-masters, Mr Pearson and Mr Wood, who followed me. Alas, the school was closed in 1970. This made me very sad. Granted the buildings were not ideal, but they still had a unique atmosphere and presence and beauty. The place was loved by pupils and parents and the people of the area.

In that year, 1970, I was the guest of honour at the last prize day of Lea Bank before it closed and its pupils were sent to larger schools some distance away. That year twenty-one pupils received GCE (O) certificates. The average pass was between four and five subjects, ignoring single-subject entries. All passes were in main-line subjects like English, mathematics and history. Seventeen other pupils passed in groups of CSE subjects. My belief in the poten-tial of average ability pupils when well taught and motivated was certainly vindicated.

I wrote to the Department of Education and Science, objecting to the closure of Lea Bank. It was a casualty of our sad age, with its transient fashions and soulless building regulations. The edu-cational establishment had decreed large comprehensive schools were the way for the future and all children had to be squeezed into this mould. The reply from the Department ignored all the success and popularity of the school. It read: 'Of the classrooms at present in use only three conform to the required size and another five classrooms are exceptionally small.' Yet no one had died for lack of air – the rooms were of a height mountainous compared with present-day schools, and the narrow corridors stopped the jostling of pupils as occurs in many schools. Assem-blies could be held daily for all children to be together on stairs, corridors, hall and rooms, which is now impossible in many modern schools. Ironically, the very success of Lea Bank in giving pupils success in extended courses, which helped to inspire a movement for comprehensive schools, was what eventually closed it. Revolutions almost always devour their children.

For the 1991 reunion everyone gathered to sing the school song and I stood where I had always taken assembly, at the bottom of the beautiful staircase by my room. It was a very emotional moment. My mind went back not only to staff and pupils I had known, but to my father and mother, both now dead. My parents always attended the prize days and, as chairman of the local Education Executive, Father sat on the platform. He was proud of me and I was pleased he was. He had hoped that Lea Bank would keep me in the valley, but it proved to be the springboard that took me out of it.

9

My East End Headship

*

The Robert Montefiore School in Vallance Road in east London was also an ex-central school. It was a typical three-decker Nelson 'frigate' board school with a two-decker Nelson 'frigate' alongside, with various outbuildings nearby. London was and is still dotted with such buildings. It had some 700 pupils and 40 staff. It took pupils up to School Certificate level and had a very strong commercial section for girls and the occasional boy, teaching shorthand and typing and other office skills. The Spitalfields area of east London had long been largely Jewish and the school was renamed in the First World War the Robert Montefiore School after the first elected member of the London County Council killed on active service. When I arrived, the school was still more than half Jewish, with the rest from varied backgrounds. The movement of Jewry from the East End of London, however, to northwest London had already begun. By 1994 there are as many Jews in north-west London as there were in the East End in 1914.

The school was cheerful, noisy and healthy but, apart from certain departments, lacked tightness and discipline. By taking over the school at the beginning of the summer term I was given the opportunity to organize a sixth form for the next academic year and to prepare a timetable directed towards where I saw the future of the school. I was astonished to find that there were no assemblies. There were four halls but none that would hold all the children. A further obstacle was that when a Jewish assembly was called, almost all children decided they were Christian; and if a Christian assembly was called, most changed their faith, at least temporarily, to Jewish or Muslim. I think assemblies are essential for giving a school unity, and to show staff and pupils that 100 per cent discipline is possible. Full assembly control is essential for a headteacher. I decided that on four days a week there would be senior and junior assemblies in separate halls, with the deputy head and myself taking a week in each in turn. On the fifth day we would have house assemblies once we had built in a house system, since we had four small assembly areas.

On the first day at my new school I contacted the local leaders of the major religions represented there and we agreed twelve hymns which were basically all in praise of the one God. I then approached educational warehouses and bought four huge sets of ten of their hymns which we could hang high in the halls to be seen by all. After school closed for that first day, these were hoisted to the ceiling in the four halls with the help of the schoolkeepers and the woodwork and metalwork masters. Then in the two larger halls, which were to be used for senior and junior assemblies the following day, the floors were marked out like a parade-ground so that each class and form teacher knew where they stood. We went home that evening weary but content.

In the morning the school was shell-shocked. Teachers and pupils were kept in their classrooms until they were sent for, and then they were shown where they stood for assemblies. I then took the senior assembly standing on a gymnasium buck, and my deputy took the junior assembly. Two teachers played the piano and we sang number one hymn. We worshipped the one God and I explained when we prayed that pupils could open or close their eyes according to the habits of their faith. I had not allowed at this stage for a small minority who prostrated themselves and knocked their neighbours over. I then decided that the one God would not like anyone injured in prayer and all were to remain standing.

As soon as the first assembly was over, some wished to rush home to inform their relatives of the new regime. They found the gates locked with the schoolkeeper on guard along with his Alsatian dog. Pupils were let in but none were let out.

Meanwhile on that second day my deputy had joined me where I was still standing on the buck. A fifteen-year-old boy came to talk to me. He surprised me by fingering my waistcoat and asking me how much I had paid for my suit. Before I could reply, he said he guaranteed that his father could give me a better deal! Seeing my astonishment, my deputy took me on one side and assured me with obvious delight that I had been accepted as an East-Ender and they obviously liked me!

It took me some time to appreciate and fully understand the East End accent. One morning I stopped the hymn singing on the line 'Holy, Holy, Holy, all the saints adore thee' because it sounded as if they were singing 'early, early, early', but I was assured by a senior member of staff that this was simply the local accent. I did not ask them how they managed with my Lancashire accent.

I had been brought up as a northern nonconformist, with relatives called Jacob and Ezekiel and other biblical names. My mother had taught me from birth the history and the suffering of the Hebrew people and my father had told me in the thirties that the treatment of the Jews in Germany had even exceeded the suffering of trade-union leaders whom he knew there. I had, however, met only two Jews before I came to London. One came to live in Haslingden from Manchester at the height of the Manchester blitz. He joined the Labour Party and, as a sixth former, I often visited him for a political chat. The second, who was very clever and artistic, served with me in the Royal Navy and we shared a cabin for some weeks. What I had not expected was the cheerfulness, hospitality, warmth, loyalty, colourfulness, noise and generosity of the East End. It was an amazing and different culture from what I had been accustomed to. There was at first no school uniform and the yard was a blaze of colour. The children were for you or against you; there was no neutral ground! I was also very surprised on the first morning break to observe a number of tables and blackboards appear in the yard giving the odds on the day's horse races. Betting was brisk. The teachers disappeared to the staff-room and for all I knew they then placed their own bets by runners while they had their tea and coffee.

For the first few weeks I did permanent yard duty at breaks and lunch-times. The tick-tack men disappeared, the boys' lavatories were patrolled and smoking there ended. Nevertheless smoking continued in the girls' lavatories. These were roofless and a minute after the start of morning break smoke billowed up as from a coal-fired ocean liner. The women staff, though now also patrolling the yard, drew the line at visiting the girls' lavatories. It was time for a second unexpected stroke – the first being the assemblies.

Harry Greenway, MP, who had taught at the Robert Montefiore

School, has described on the floor of the House of Commons what this strike was. I instructed my caretaking staff to obtain lengths of fire hose and connect these to the water hydrants. When at morning break smoke began billowing out of the girls' roofless lavatories, the caretakers and duty staff opened the hydrants and the hoses were put over the girls' lavatory doors, which were immediately locked from the outside. Great screams were then heard and the whole yard stopped and called out that there were girls inside and I replied, 'Of course there are, but the lavatories were on fire and we are saving them.' The yard soon picked up and enjoyed the joke and all gathered round the girls' lavatories and shouted back at the screaming girls inside.

After five minutes we turned off the hydrants, released the girls, who were totally drenched and needed new hair-styles, and the yard laughed as the 'lavatory girls' were taken inside. No one smoked there again.

Before long almost everyone was wearing school uniform; there was a most effective house system, a school magazine, frequent home and overseas holidays and expeditions and much tighter discipline. The academic work improved without killing the fine, open spirit of the school which I had inherited. I took two large parties a year to Lancashire and Scotland.

The first sixth form began after the summer break. We chose the subjects offered according to the competence of staff and the wishes of the pupils. When the pupils applied for university entry the following year, they had only their School Certificate passes to show and these were often in odd subjects. I thus wrote to a number of universities on their behalf, receiving no help from the trendy sort, but I was encouraged by the future Lord James, then the new vice-chancellor of York University and the former high master of Manchester Grammar School, who in the first year of intake there took a couple of our boys. Both did well, one going on to research.

For the first two years in London I kept a house in Haslingden until I was certain I would remain in the south and until my second daughter, Diana, was ready for transfer to secondary school. We then moved to Chingford, which was convenient for my school. This was a real separation for my parents and I remember the sadness of their voices when we rang them on the first Sunday afternoon – a time of day that for years we had spent with them as a family.

The biggest problem at 'Robert Monte', as everyone affection-
ately called it, was to obtain continuity of staffing. Few wanted
to teach in the East End and the school had a chequered history.
I not only made a yearly timetable and a terminal timetable, but
I had to adjust the timetable every Monday morning if not every
day when I knew which teachers were available. We had a permanent staff of about forty, with another ten transient supply
teachers or anybody who walked in on the day. 'Robert Monte'
was like a Merchant Navy command with casual labour coming
on and off at every port. I was at the school for five years and a
term and I always found first the London County Council and
then the Inner London Education Authority most helpful. In my
last year at the school 80 per cent stayed on beyond the school-
leaving age, with forty-nine pupils obtaining one or more ordinary level passes in their School Certificate. Another thirty-five
sat the CSE examination.

I remained a nominal member of the Labour Party and voted
Labour at the 1964 general election. I also served for two years
as an elected member of the East London National Union of Teachers Committee before I switched my free time to a major research
topic, which was ultimately to change the pattern of my life. I
was still a supporter of comprehensive school experiments, but
wished them carefully monitored. Indeed, I chaired the first meeting
of the Comprehensive Schools Committee in London, but I ceased
to attend when I realized the rest of the committee were total
believers if not zealots in their support of such schools.

When in Lancashire I had been researching the Poor Law in
Bolton as part of my MA thesis I had noted that decisions were
often very different when a Liberal-elected guardian named Henry
Ashworth was present. He was obviously a man of immense
personality and influence. I set out to know more about this man.
Ashworth lived from 1794 to 1880 at The Oaks, in Turton near
Bolton, as his residence. With his brother Edmond, he was a major
cotton manufacturer employing several hundred men and women.
He was a Quaker, a leading Liberal and an ex-chairman of the
Manchester Chamber of Commerce. He was a close friend and a
relative of John Bright, and one of the closest confidants of Richard
Cobden, who often stayed with him and with whom he corre-
sponded regularly. I also discovered that A.P. Wadsworth, then

editor of the *Manchester Guardian* was collecting material on Henry Ashworth, as was yet another historian who was connected with the Bury Yeomanry. In addition, I met the late Robert Walsh of Bromley Cross, Bolton, a well-read and reliable local historian who had some Ashworth material. I began to visit Walsh and the Turton district regularly with Christopher Aspin, of Helmshore, Rossendale, another fine local historian who has published a number of books and who wrote for many years on business and music for the *Manchester Evening News*.

Bob Walsh told me that at Henry Ashworth's death in 1880 the counting-house at the New Eagley mill, where all his papers were kept, was locked and for more than seventy years everything was left untouched. Then the mill stopped and was sold and the locals broke in. The scene must have been like the room in *Great Expectations*. The building was then pillaged by people seeking penny blacks, foreign stamps and anything else they fancied. Some intruders took barrow-loads home nightly. Bob Walsh gathered as much of this material as he could and he pointed me to others who had acquired material from the mill.

Christopher Aspin drove me over to Turton on several occasions and we contacted a man who was believed to have sold foreign stamps to overseas collectors. I bought from him a sack of all the material that he had left, minus the stamps, and returned to Haslingden with my treasure trove. Much of it proved to be dross. Meanwhile, Wadsworth had died and I bought from a bookseller some of his material, while the rest was placed in the John Rylands Library in Manchester.

I then decided that the way was clear for me to write a biography of Henry Ashworth. After I came to London I spoke of this to Dr Michael Edwards, who knew me as an historian, when we were dining one evening, and he suggested I should do this research for a doctorate under the auspices of the London School of Economics. The LSE agreed and for the next four years I spent every spare moment of my time – evenings, weekends and holidays – at the British Museum, the Colindale Newspaper Library, at county record offices and the Bolton and Manchester Libraries. My supervisors were Dr D.C. Coleman and Professor Theo Barker.

As well as being the history of one of the most important cotton firms of the nineteenth century, the thesis traced the ideology of the manufacturers in the Anti-Corn Law League, which was probably the most effective lobbying body in British history.

It also covered their attitude to factory legislation, education, working-class movements and all the political and commercial issues of the 1830–80 period. It was a privilege to study the private and public thoughts of a body of men – the Classical Liberals – who with a coherent philosophy changed the face of British politics, at least temporarily.

For four years I communed almost daily with these free-market radicals and I came to know and generally accept their views on almost every issue apart from patriotism, the nation state and law and order. They saw the free market breaking down national differences; I saw the free market strengthening each nation state. There are even undertones here of the Maastricht debate. On law and order I was always a hard-liner.

This research helped me redefine my own political beliefs. I had lost faith in socialism on religious grounds when I truly discovered the third chapter of Genesis and the Fall of Man. I then accepted that man was not perfectible in this life, and I needed a philosophy of damage limitation. I was once described as the last man personally converted to the free market and the free society by Richard Cobden. Theses, like ideas and books, have consequences.

In 1964 ILEA allowed me to take a term's sabbatical leave at Corpus Christi College, Cambridge, as a schoolmaster fellow commoner. I spent the whole term working on my Henry Ashworth thesis. I was thus there at the time of the October 1964 general election victory of Harold Wilson. Up to the date of the election, in which I voted Labour, I somewhat reluctantly defended the Labour Party in the senior common room. Immediately after the election, when the Wilson government gave blanket subsidies to the shipbuilding industry without firm reciprocal commitments from the trade unions to end restrictive practices and overmanning, I tore up my Labour membership card. That, I thought, would be the end of my involvement in politics.

I finished my Ph.D. thesis within the four years usually given to full-time students. I did this while I was running a large school, and while doing classroom teaching and making daily timetables. Thus when I became Minister for Higher Education in 1979 I had little sympathy for Ph.D. students who in four years full-time could not finish their theses.

In 1970 my thesis, suitably rewritten as a book, was published by the Oxford University Press under the title *The Ashworth Cotton Enterprise: The Rise and Fall of a Family Firm 1818–1880*. All his life Henry Ashworth was a Manchester man, but he finished up in Oxford!

By 1966 I was ready for new challenges. The first came in education. I enjoyed 'Robert Monte', but the horizons were limited. The school was in old buildings and it did not have a full comprehensive intake and the location created staffing problems. I was switching back to school education again and I needed a big comprehensive school in which I could try out my ideas. I applied for the first headship of Highbury Grove School and the vacant headship of Woodberry Down School in Hackney. The Highbury Grove interviews came first and I was appointed to the most exciting challenge of my career. I was to combine in brand-new buildings a reputable grammar school, a good secondary modern school and a residual school with the problem boys of the area into one united comprehensive school.

I was sad to leave 'Robert Monte', but it had increasing problems of area, staffing and building. My headship there brought me in close touch with the vibrant and exciting Jewish community of that area. I still keep contact with many old Robert Montefiorians and they and I look back on our time at the school with pleasure. Where else would you have a head boy who was a recognized tick-tack man who was released for this special occupation at the main races?

Alas, the Robert Montefiore School, which was always a very difficult school to discipline, ran into difficulties after I left it. By 1975 'A' level courses had ceased and only eight of the 150 fifth-year pupils were entered for 'O' level examinations, and none passed in any subject. The changing population of the East End was a factor in this great decrease. Never was there a school more loyal to you if they liked you than 'Robert Monte', never a school more bloody-minded if they did not. Never was there a school where one had so many laughs and headaches. It really was a Merchant Navy command.

10

The Launch of Highbury Grove

*

I knew by instinct that Highbury Grove would be my last head-ship and I was determined to put into practice there all that I had learnt from my previous schools. For the first year, 1966–7, the three schools still ran separately. I was technically the head of the grammar school while Barnsbury School had for the first term its existing head and Laycock School retained its existing head for the whole year. I spent one day a week at Barnsbury learning about their staff and boys, but the Laycock headmaster remained for the year in total control of his school. This was a residual school for difficult boys for the whole area and he was a fine headmaster whose powers of discipline could put even me to shame. He allowed me to visit his school once only and have a quarter of an hour's talk with each member of staff who was applying to come into the new school. I, of course, then arranged to see such applicants after school at Highbury when we were not subject to such time restraints.

It was advantageous that I was based at the Highbury Grammar School until it was demolished in the summer of 1967. Parents and boys at Highbury had opposed the amalgamation and my presence there with a credible academic record put their minds at rest. I also taught all sixth formers at least once weekly. Being on the site of the new buildings was also advantageous because I had considerable say in how they were finished and even had some walls moved.

I drew up with the local London inspector a staffing plan for the school. There were to be two deputy heads, six housemasters and numerous heads of departments of various grades. We first appointed the two deputies, the deputy head of the Grammar School becoming technically the senior over the deputy head of Barnsbury School. The first deputy was a wise man and a fine academic, and the second deputy an excellent disciplinarian. The two men, after certain misunderstandings, got on very well and the three of us ran the school in what became a very pleasant and easy relationship.

At the beginning, however, the second deputy was rather aggrieved and felt he was going to be a flogging machine while the first deputy would have the intellectual responsibilities. In the second week of the new school I asked the second deputy to go down to a nearby mixed comprehensive school at lunch-time where one of our boys was apparently attacking their pupils. He hesitated and I said briskly, 'I must not spoil your lunch break, I'll go', and before he could say anything I went. At the nearby school a large boy in Highbury Grove uniform was being held down by staff and pupils. I collected him like a heavy parcel and frog-marched him to the gate, meeting relatively little resistance, and brought him back to Highbury. Amazingly, no housemaster claimed the boy – nobody knew him. Then the boy confessed: he had been expelled from another school and had wandered about the area for the last term. He had then read about Highbury Grove School, and from his illicit market gains he had bought our uniform and decided to be our free-ranging agent, attacking boys from other schools.

I called a meeting with my deputies, had the boy caned as an initiation ceremony and informed him to his great amazement and even greater pleasure that he was now a Highbury Grovian, and woe betide him unless he mended his ways. I passed him over to one of my stricter housemasters and he never offended again. Nor did my second deputy! Alas, both deputies are dead and I greatly regret that we cannot meet for the occasional drink at the House of Commons to talk about Highbury Grove's great days.

We then advertised for and appointed a sixth form master. This was the fourth post in seniority and it was vital that we appointed the right man. We did so in one of the few outside appointments. He was excellent and went on to a distinguished educational career.

When this sixth form post to supervise 200 sixth formers was advertised I had a temporary secretary whose mind was elsewhere. This was the advertisement she typed, a copy of which I kept:

Highbury Grove, Highbury Grove, N.5.

(New Comprehensive School for 1,300 boys opening in September 1967 in completely new buildings with a suite of Sisal Farm accommodation).

Master as Head of Sisal Farm Studies. Grade E (£660) allowance available. Duties to include responsibility for course and subject choices and general progress of some 200 Sisal farms on academic, technical and non academic courses, to cover entries for university, college and industry, and general studies.

If I had not checked this advertisement it certainly would have made the 'No Comment' feature of the national newspapers.

Then the six housemasters were appointed. All of them came from the feed schools – three from Barnsbury, two from Laycock and one from Highbury. The heads of department were then appointed.

By now I had instituted a weekly meeting after school, which staff from all three schools who wished to come into the new school could attend, and we had drinks and occasionally food and a free agenda where we could discuss anything about the new school. This gave the more junior members of staff the chance to participate and kept the senior staff on their toes. It was a totally unwhipped meeting.

It was a meeting of this informal group that insisted, against my wishes, on keeping the Highbury Grammar School colours of black, purple and silver, and I had a battle to get even the badge changed. It was staff largely from Barnsbury and Laycock who made this decision and the Highbury staff abstained. Here was a classic example that certain decisions should be taken collectively and freely, since if I had suggested this it would have been resented by the Barnsbury and Laycock staff. As it turned out, the retention of the school colours meant that local parents automatically retained their respect for the school.

We developed a new badge with the help of the art and technical departments. This badge represented the high-rise flats and offices of the area and the reaching out for the conquest of space. I then explained the significance of the colours: purple represented red for courage and blue for spirituality; silver was the moon colour, clean and virtuous; while black represented the underlying dark mystery of life. These definitions were never challenged, at least in my presence!

By the end of the Christmas term all appointments were made and we were fully staffed for the following September. A weekly meeting of the heads of houses, a weekly meeting of heads of departments and occasional meetings of joint heads of houses and heads of departments, as well as the informal meetings, continued throughout the following two terms. My deputies, the sixth form master and I attended them all. I also encouraged and arranged for staff to visit other comprehensive schools to see what staff there of equivalent rank did and I asked them all to report to me in writing afterwards what they had learnt.

The housemasters were to be the key to discipline. The houses were named after one earl and five dukes, the first letter of the name of these aristocrats being the same as the first letter of the colour of the house: Bedford, blue: Gloucester, green: Marlborough, mauve; Oxford, orange; Richmond, red; York, yellow. Each of the housemasters had a large room for assemblies and the serving of lunch to boys, and all had their own private office alongside.

I introduced similar clean lines in the teaching departments. I divided the rest of the school building into departments with the head of department in each case responsible for his or her area in and out of lesson time, and again I arranged that each head of department had a private room even if we had to take over a broom cupboard to accommodate it.

The heads of houses grasped their responsibilities and asked for more. Some of the heads of departments, however, preferred the extra money to their extra responsibilities, but a firm line was taken and collective pressure brought them to heel.

Once the school came together in 1967 I continued the weekly heads of houses meeting, and we also had a weekly joint meeting of the heads of departments and heads of houses. All had open agendas. The meetings for all members of staff continued for some time after the school opened, and then attendance declined and they came to a natural end.

Another major decision was how we organized the teaching groups. I have never been an egalitarian. I am a believer in an open society where people move if they have the ability and the desire to do so. I also believe that children differ as much in their intellectual ability as they do in their physical make-up. We are all made gloriously different, and these differences are, both in sport and in the classroom, an organizational and not a moral matter. To educate very bright children and less able children together is the height of cruelty. The least able will never excel and will become bloody-minded, while the most able will become big-headed and arrogant.

There were roughly eight classes in each year once the school had been run in. We decided to divide them for teaching purposes into three A classes, four B classes and one remedial class in each year. Each of the A classes was of equal spread of ability, the same with the four B classes, while the organization of the C group was left to the head of remedial, who proved to be one of the finest of teachers. His classes started at 8 a.m. and went on to 5 p.m. or even 6 p.m.

I then promised to make a timetable whereby the three A-band classes in each year were taught the same academic subjects at the same time, while the four B bands in each year were also taught the same academic subjects at the same time. This allowed each head of department to decide whether they wished to stream tightly the A and B bands or arrange the A and B bands as equal ability classes. Mathematics and languages streamed both the A and B bands, while general art subjects continued to teach children within their broad bands.

After three years we decided to unstream totally the first year, apart from the remedial pupils, and teach them in house groups for the first term and then have an examination at the end of November upon which we would do the banding. The reason for this was the huge difference between the standards of teaching in the junior schools. Certain junior schools never sent us a non-reader, while others sent us one-third non-readers every year. Usually the best-taught pupils were from church schools in old buildings that the local authority was trying to close.

In the fifth year of the school we decided to teach all the first year, again apart from the remedials, in house groups. The house-masters particularly were pleased with this decision, since it gave them easier lesson contact with their boys in the first year, although it added to their already heavy responsibilities.

All I was interested in was the efficiency of the teaching. Each head of department had to write down for me at the beginning of each year what he and his staff intended to achieve with each year group over the coming year. This list was then put in the school safe and at the end of the year it was taken out to check with the head of department and his staff how accurate the forecasts had been.

My governors were very helpful and I had only one battle with them, which I had to win. Some governors wished to call the new school the North Islington School. I fought against this tooth and nail. Names matter and Highbury was remembered in the area as a place of carriage property – horses and carriages up to 1914 – and parents always want their children to go up- and not down-market in their schooling. Highbury was also an area of fine houses on Highbury Fields and elsewhere and it had been the name of the grammar school. Since this was to be also a major soccer school, the retention of the name of Highbury, linked with nearby Arsenal, was very important. After a one-month battle, I won. Names and emblems matter to boys, who are team animals, and although I did not threaten to do so, I even considered resigning if I lost that battle.

Our relationship with parents was also important and I linked them from the beginning with the housemasters. All the boys in the existing three schools had been broken up into houses, with the same proportion from each school in each house. Invitations were then sent out in the winter of 1966–7 for parents to attend an evening meeting according to the year group their sons were in. These invitations were sent out by the housemasters, but the meetings were addressed by me.

More than 80 per cent of parents attended these meetings. They were held in the hall of the grammar school, with suppliers of the new uniform in attendance. Parents who did not attend their first meeting were then 'summoned' to one of two other meetings, again by a letter from the housemasters. This time the letter regretted that the parents had not been able to attend the previous meetings because they were probably abroad, while some were handicapped, and a promise was made that if they were unable to attend one of the last two meetings, they would be visited unannounced at home one evening by a number of staff. The threat worked and each house was left with a hard core of say a dozen parents who were then visited unannounced! Even these parents generally turned up at future meetings. I made clear at all these meetings that we took on families not boys; responsibility for their behaviour in school was to be shared between the parents and staff.

The new entry for 1967 were put into houses before the first-year parents' meeting, boys from the same primary school going as far as possible into the same house so that we had built-in friendship patterns. Again as far as numbers allowed, future boys from junior schools would always go into the same houses so that junior school heads and staff would have permanent contact with the same housemasters.

At the end of the 1966–7 year we organized a number of get-togethers of staff and wives and even their children at sherry parties. No man will work harder than his wife lets him and it was vital that wives also felt that they belonged to Highbury Grove and that their husbands were important people because they taught there.

In September 1967 we staggered the entry to the new school with first years and sixth formers on the first day, the second and fifth formers on the second and the more difficult third and fourth years on the third day. Timetables were ready and within an hour every boy was in a lesson. Any boy without uniform was immediately sent home and the housemaster had to sort out a full solution for the following morning. The grand hall was not yet completed so I took the daily assembly in the gymnasium, standing on a buck once again! This time we had 1,350 boys and 70 staff.

By 1.30 p.m. on the second day I knew that we had won. The fifth-year pupils at Highbury Grammar School for some strange reason always carried umbrellas to show their seniority. It was after lunch on that second day that I saw five fifth form boys – four ex-Barnsbury and one ex-Laycock – all in impeccable uniform pass by my window carrying rolled umbrellas. It was plain that the umbrellas had not been pillaged from ex-Highbury boys but bought with honest coinage of the realm as a mark of belonging. I shall never forget that sight. Boys and men – unlike women – are almost totally tribal creatures and a new Highbury Grove tribe had been created.

The housemasters were put in charge of pupil attendance. They also took the weekly house assemblies. Registers were marked in mixed first- to fifth-year house groups twice a day, with the sixth form in each house having their own house tutor group. All inside house arrangements and appointments were entirely at the discretion of the housemasters. Sixth form attendance was, however, reported to the sixth form master by each of the sixth form house tutor group staff. It was important that the sixth formers, who had their own common room, were treated in a relaxed yet responsible fashion.

In a large school with a number of gates morning registers can mean simply that pupils are there for some part of the day, maybe only for registration. Thus, once a week in the first months and then always once a month, we suddenly sealed the whole school in late morning or the afternoon and staff had to list all attending in their lessons. These lists were then sent to the housemasters and woe betide the boy absent without his housemaster's permission.

Fourth-year boys who were not staying on into the fifth and sixth years began before the first mid-term to present a major behaviour problem. This we had to solve within the tribe and quickly. I decided to make them all lance-corporals. Accordingly, lists of duties were prepared for some forty boys a day, and since each house was on duty one day in six, responsibilities were thus found for all fourth-year boys. Large marshal and deputy-marshal badges were purchased in ornate house colours and issued to fourth-year boys by me on the day they returned from the October mid-term. Gates were given names from the humdrum to the exotic – Dustbin Alley, Headmaster's Gate, Chelsea Gate, Chittagong Gate, China Gate – and boys were told of their responsibilities to see that there was good behaviour near them and no boy slipped out at morning break to the tempting world outside.

The fourth-year boys were transformed. They now belonged and had specific responsibilities. Not only did the duty house fourth former stand by his gate and post, but boys from the other five houses who were allocated on the other days to that gate also stood alongside to ensure that all was well. Every day I went round with the duty housemaster to speak to the boys on duty and all was sweetness and light.

The fame of Highbury Grove was partially made by geography. Many of those who lived in our area of Islington were in radio, journalism and television, and a high percentage sent their children to our school. Their parents pretended it was because of the music or the classics, which were very good, or the art, but they had already checked the academic results and the university intake before they came to see me.

Every lunch I ate in a house room and invited the housemaster and his house staff to join me before lunch for a glass of sherry in my study with any visitors who were in the school that day. The school became very civilized and the staff felt that they belonged. I taught the sixth form for general studies, visited most classrooms every day, walked the school, met visitors and attended all organization meetings. I was the ninepin of the country dance and I enjoyed it immensely.

The three separate schools had 40 per cent more boys than the combined school with 50 per cent more in the top ability groups because of the original three-form entry of Highbury Grammar School. Once, however, we had the first of our fifth-year intakes through in 1972 we had an overall GCE pass rate almost equal to that of the three schools with a 25 per cent increase in A and B grades. In addition, we had 23 grade ones in CSE examinations which counted as 'O' level passes. A further 450 passes in CSE were gained at 2–4 grades.

The sixth form results showed a similar improvement. In 1966 the three schools had seventy 'A' level passes, including five A grades. In 1972 from an intake which was of relatively low ability, because of parents opting for other grammar schools in the last year of Highbury Grammar School, we scored seventy-six passes, including ten 'A' grades. Some twenty boys a year were by then going on to university and a dozen were going on to other forms of higher education which could lead to degrees.

11

The Winds of Change

*

I had finished my thesis; the school was in good heart and I soon turned my restless energies to other fields. I had left the Labour Party in 1964 and up to the end of 1967 I was in the political wilderness.

We all need beliefs to give meaning and purpose to life. Until my middle twenties I was convinced that socialism would build a more prosperous and more just society. I no longer believed this to be the case, and the failed policies of the Wilson government strengthened my change of view. I now accepted that we lived in a world that was not perfectible. The most that we could do was to make life tolerable by strong defence, firm internal law and order and the maximum use of the market in economic affairs. My study of the nineteenth-century Liberal free marketeers had changed my economic views. I had always been in favour of strong defence and firm law and order. With my changed economic views I was now akin to an American conservative Republican.

We all knew by the mid-1960s that the so-called New Civilization in Russia as portrayed by the Webbs was a myth and that Communist Russia was a dictatorial force at home and abroad, neither prosperous nor a purveyor of liberty. Fritz von Hayek in his *Road to Serfdom* portrayed socialism as the waiting-room for authoritarianism. By 1968 I began to think that Churchill had been right when he quoted from Hayek's book in his 1945 election broadcast. By 1968 I also noticed that socialist governments made decisions to bolster their short-term popularity and not the long-term industrial improvement of their countries.

In 1968 we had seen the Labour Government expenditure cuts, the increase of taxation, the failed prices and incomes policies, a failed National Plan and the devaluation of the pound. There was little socialist vision left. Moreover, as a schoolmaster I was dismayed by the growth of the permissive society. I believe freedom comes from the acceptance of necessary restraints and inhibitions, preferably voluntary but, if need be, compulsory. In the 1960s we had seen swinging London, pop art and music, football stars no longer models for the young and the growth of soccer hooliganism. I opposed the abolition of capital punishment, the legislation for easy abortion and the homosexual reforms. I was horrified that drug taking with cannabis and LSD was becoming part of popular culture. These so-called reforms were supported more from the left than the right and they had nothing in common with the Methodist nonconformist self-help socialism of my father or the socialist beliefs of my early years. They certainly did not encourage me to rejoin the Labour Party. Nor was a Liberal Party, permissive in personal conduct and corporate in economic affairs, one that would have appealed to Henry Ashworth.

There was also one other very decisive factor: the Labour Party's move to a compulsory secondary school comprehensive school policy, which I opposed from the beginning. I believe that the purpose of schools is to give all children the skills of reading and writing and arithmetic, a body of knowledge in history, geography, science and religion, the habit of sustained concentration and a taste of high culture in the arts. I thus judged the success or failure of comprehensive schools on whether by putting all types of scholars in the same school more would reach higher educational standards. The advantages of large comprehensive schools with their wide range of courses and easy internal transfer of pupils were obvious, but I was still to be convinced that these advantages exceeded the downside of size and the difficulties of teaching at secondary level across the whole ability range. I also wished to know what such large comprehensive schools would achieve with the least able and the most able pupils.

In my first two years at Highbury Grove, I had already begun to see the downside. Highbury Grove was a good school and it knew what it was doing. This certainly was not so in neighbouring comprehensive schools with which I had contact. The change to comprehensive education in such schools seemed to be an excuse for slack teaching and for the use of the classroom to advocate social revolt. A new type of headteacher along with young politically motivated classroom teachers were arriving in London and using pupils as puppets for the extension of their political ideas. The new comprehensive schools had no tradition or structure and thus were vulnerable for take-overs. Maybe if I had still been teaching in Lancashire I would not have met such social revolutionaries or the slackness of many teachers, but I was in London and I did meet them.

I was prepared to support controlled experiments comparing the achievements of typical comprehensive schools with their bipartite equivalents. Instead of such an approach the Labour Party, in search of a programme, seemed to have a developing hatred of the grammar schools. Hatred is never a successful emotion in social change, as it clouds the mind. The Labour Party and the Liberal Party switched the secondary education of this country over to comprehensive education on 'salvation by faith' and not by 'works', a view I have never shared in education or in religion. I sometimes suspect the Labour Party took up this crusade because of its need for something new to offer the electorate, its economic policies having so obviously failed. Interestingly enough my father, who always saw the grammar schools as ladders of working-class mobility, shared my view of the new educational policy of the Labour Party.

Anthony Crosland, following his circular 10/65 of that year, promised to destroy every grammar school in England, Wales and Northern Ireland. This promise was made long before there was any proper assessment of the long-term effects of the change to comprehensive education.

In the late 1960s Highbury Grove was virtually under siege from parents – many working-class and immigrant – wishing to put their children there because of the slack discipline and poor results in certain nearby comprehensive schools whose low standards did not seem to worry Labour politicians at all. One year thirty boys from one primary school had to be rejected by Highbury Grove under the formula we were given by ILEA for entry because they lived closer to another comprehensive school, about whose academic results and discipline the least said the better. This primary school had long sent boys to Highbury School and their parents were determined to continue the link. They kept their children out of school for several weeks until a leader of one of the far-left parties in the area threatened political action and I was summoned to County Hall and asked to take all the thirty boys, which I did.

Next year thirty other parents from various schools refused to send their children to another comprehensive school of low aims and achievement, and they set up an alternative school in a local hall for several weeks, financed by themselves and with books and equipment donated by a friend of mine – the head of a well-known public school. Again, when this situation began to gain publicity, I was asked to take all the boys into Highbury Grove.

One problem with the move to comprehensive education at this time was that it was happening when standards were collapsing all around, when primary-school teachers were being coerced to adopt ineffective discovery teaching methods and when there was increasing pressure for so-called classroom democracy.

One day Harry Greenway, whom I first met in 1961 when we were both living in the Oxford University Settlement in Bethnal Green, came into the head's study at Highbury and asked me if I was ever likely to be active in politics again. He had known me as a supporter of the Labour Party. I dismissed this question immediately by replying that if I were, it could be in his own party. My reply surprised me as much as it surprised him.

The May 1968 local government elections in London were approaching and in Waltham Forest, where I lived in Chingford, the Labour Party had detailed plans to move to a full comprehensive system on a two-tier level, a system I have never favoured. These plans were opposed half-heartedly by the local Conservative leadership, but with more effectiveness by an *ad hoc* group of local parents led by the Greater London Conservative councillor for the area where I lived. I was approached by him to give assistance and to speak at a public meeting, which I did. The hall was packed, with people standing. The audience included all local groups including the Labour leader of Waltham Forest Council, the chairman of East Walthamstow Liberal Group and the chairman of the Waltham Forest Communist Party. It was a lively meeting and was even reported in *The Guardian*. I made clear my opposition to two-tier comprehensive schools, whatever the year of the break. I favoured eleven to eighteen schools, if one was to have comprehensive ones.

Meanwhile, my elder daughter had joined the local Young Conservatives and informed me one evening on her return that the following evening there was to be an open Chingford Conservative meeting. I decided to go, was warmly welcomed and joined the Conservative Party. I then told Harry Greenway what I had done. He informed Conservative Central Office and I was made a member of the National Advisory Committee on Education for the party.

As soon as I joined the Conservative Party I went up to Lancashire to see my father and mother and informed them of my action. Father simply replied: 'In our family we have always done what we believe. You must do the same.' Mother was rather confused and took a little more time to adjust.

Father by now had returned to wide reading, especially of philosophy. On education he opposed compulsory comprehensive schools and as Chairman of the Rossendale Divisional Executive under the Lancashire County Council he fought, alas vainly, to keep Haslingden Grammar School which I attended as a boy as a selective school.

However, he fought successfully to preserve the Bacup and Rawtenstall Grammar School, which still exists in its own right. Father had always seen the grammar schools as ladders for working-class opportunity, although he sometimes mused upon what it would do for the leadership of the Labour Party if there was no real working-class leadership in the next generation. It was a wise thought.

I was coming to the conclusion that the comprehensive school was in favoured areas a grammar school with a CSE stream, and in downtown areas it often turned itself into a secondary modern school with few taking worthwhile examination passes. Able boys in the downtown areas would, under such a system, have little chance of a first-class education. Labour's move to the comprehensive school, like so much of socialist welfare, enhanced the life opportunities of the middle classes who knew how to pull the levers of the one-armed welfare state bandit, yet depressed the life opportunities of the genuinely deprived groups. The rich could buy houses in the catchment areas of the best comprehensive schools, while the bright boy in the downtown area had little chance of educational mobility once the grammar school ladder was removed. I was aware that in my own area at Highbury local estate agents showed on maps the catchment area of Highbury

Grove, and house prices within it could be 10–20 per cent higher than in other areas.

My relationship with my father surprisingly came much closer after we were in different parties. He took my change of party in his stride and began to take a great interest in my political career. He did not mind my changing party, but he still hoped that I would stay in education as against full-time politics. As I moved to national politics, he read the newspapers with greater interest and changed his first newspaper to the *Daily Telegraph* so he could follow my writings and my speeches.

Yet my home town was aghast. I remember two unpleasant experiences. I always rang my father and mother every day and visited them for five days every main holiday and at half-term. I took work with me and wrote and read while with my parents. On my first visit after my change of party was announced locally I saw one of my Labour friends whom I greatly admired. As I approached, he turned his back on me. I put my hand on his shoulder and said his first name and he turned and said, 'I did not think you would speak to me now that you have joined the Conservative Party.' He actually believed this and it hit me like a whiplash. One other Labour leader in Haslingden whom I had always liked wrote an unpleasant letter to the local Lancashire papers, to which I had to reply. Sadly we never met again.

12

Political Immersion and the Black Papers

*

I was soon approached by the Chingford Conservative Party to stand for the 1968 local elections and was selected for the ward in which I lived. I began to write letters to the local press on local issues and I organized a 100 per cent canvass of my ward, largely done by my own family.

In 1968 there was in London, as elsewhere in the country, a huge swing from Labour to the Conservatives. Labour previously had thirty-four seats in Waltham Forest as against fourteen held by the Conservatives and the Ratepayers. In 1968, forty-four Conservatives and only four Labour councillors were returned. Labour was at the height of its unpopularity. The Ratepayers failed to win a seat. My ward returned three Conservatives and I was second with 3,095 votes, seven behind the top Conservative and 1,722 ahead of the leading Ratepayer candidate. Labour was far behind.

I sat on the Conservative front bench at the town hall and chaired the Establishment Committee. I also served on the Education, Finance and General Purposes Committees. In addition, I was elected by all the London boroughs to chair the London Boroughs Management Services Unit.

My father and mother came to stay with me in London for the last time in 1968 and they attended a Waltham Forest Council meeting. They heard me speak and were then given drinks by the mayor. They were delighted – Father said little but his face showed total contentment and his eyes twinkled. A special treat for him on his visits to Chingford was that our garden backed on to the grammar school playing-fields and every summer afternoon he could watch the cricket there.

After a year I resigned from the Management Services appointment because of the time required to keep control of it. I had always opposed the 1964 change to larger boroughs in London since they would, to my mind, lead to further bureaucracy and full-time councillors, and, with their larger areas, I did not feel that this was really *local* government. My father entirely agreed with me and when the rest of England was reorganized under the 1970–4 Conservative Government, he led in Haslingden the opposition to the creation of one council for the whole of Rossendale.

The first meeting of the Conservative Group in Waltham Forest agreed that the comprehensive school reorganization plan would go ahead. I helped, however, to gain certain changes, including the early transfer to the 14-plus schools of bright pupils, the enforcement of ability group teaching in all schools, the limitation of minority subject teaching to certain schools only and regular assessments of the working of the changed system.

Over the next three years of Conservative control of the borough I spoke regularly in committee and full council on educational issues, on the need to sell council houses to sitting tenants, and on opposition to giving a grant to Essex University at the time of student unrest. I also applied to go on the parliamentary candidates list for the Conservative Party and was interviewed and accepted. Lists of vacancies for candidates were distributed to all on the list and as a candidate I indicated the seats in which I was interested. I applied for a number of seats, both Conservative-held and Labour-held, and awaited replies. The first came from Eccles in my native Lancashire, a seat with a 9,257 Labour majority but winnable within the political climate of 1968. After two interviews they offered me the candidature, which I accepted. I returned to London the following day to find in my post an invitation to be interviewed for a safe Conservative seat, but the die had been cast.

At the Eccles interviews I used a technique I repeated time and time again. I read the local papers for the previous few years, and as well as obtaining a knowledge of local issues, I memorized the names and photographs of local leading Conservatives. When I attended my first Eccles interview, which was by a dozen or so people, I already knew half of them by name and I also knew their occupations and interests.

For the next eighteen months after my selection on 30 October, I regularly visited Eccles at weekends and on all school holidays. Every week I would have at least one or more letters, news items or photographs in the two local papers in the constituency. The following week there would be up to one and a half broadsheets of the local papers filled with letters from 'Regular Reader', 'Fact Finder', 'Voice in the Wilderness', 'Anti-Tory' and even 'Neutral' attacking my views, along with named Labour members, only to be replied to in the following week's papers by Conservative supporters.

My father and mother were pleased I was fighting a Lancashire seat, since I stayed with them each night when I was in Lancashire. Father watched with wry amusement my political activities. In March 1969 I addressed a Conservative public meeting in Haslingden at the Haslingden Conservative Club. This was the first time I had ever entered its portals! By now the whole town of Haslingden had accepted I had changed parties and was looking at me as a local lad who might make good.

By then I was also extending my writing. I wrote a chapter on 'The Threat to Tradition' in a book *Crisis in Education*, published in 1968 with a number of other authors who bridged the whole political and educational spectrum. This chapter showed my educational views at that time regarding comprehensive and secondary school reorganization. I wrote:

> My experience in small secondary modern schools convinces me that the tripartite system was not a good one ... there was considerable waste of average-plus talent under the tripartite system. . . . Yet I fully recognised and still recognise that the grammar schools had considerable success to their credit. The academic tradition of public, direct grant and grammar schools enabled academic excellence to be fostered, the first degree course to be completed in three years and our university failure rate to be the lowest in the world. . . . It was essential that comprehensive schools maintained and if possible strengthened the academic tradition, whilst offering it to an increased proportion of the age group.

I then put down the conditions for the success of comprehensive schools:

They must be large enough to carry large fifth and sixth forms with a wide variety of courses. They must have a full share of the top ability groups otherwise an economical sixth form with a wide variety of academic subjects is impossible. They must be truly comprehensive and not neighbourhood schools. . . . Finally, they must be developed as educational and not social organisations.

I laid down what I thought comprehensive schools should achieve: I believed that 40 per cent of the pupils could aim at the General Certificate of Education, 40 per cent at the Certificate of Secondary Education and 20 per cent would need definite help to achieve full literacy and numeracy.

I also warned as to what would happen if the mooted comprehensive reorganization lowered academic standards: 'Should comprehensive education spread further and should there be a drop in academic standards then more parents will opt to public and private schools. As the public schools become more academic and less socially selective then parents will pay for academic success.'

When I read this chapter again twenty-five years later, I find there is nothing with which I disagree. Schools are for schooling – the passing on of learning – and they must be judged on educational not social grounds. The tripartite system wasted a great deal of talent in unimaginative secondary modern schools. The comprehensive school needed to be large to provide the necessary variety of courses. If such schools enhanced the educational achievements of children, they would be a success; if not, the changed system would be a national handicap. I was certainly correct in forecasting that the end of the grammar schools would be a lifeline to public and private schools, since more and more parents would buy their children's education if there was dissatisfaction on academic grounds with the standards of education in the new comprehensive schools.

I well remember in the early 1960s a public school headmaster saying to me that the public schools would die out in his lifetime. Comprehensive schools, introduced by the Labour Party with Liberal Party support, with in many cases emphasis on social and not educational aims, gave the public schools a new lease of life. They became the equivalent of the priest holes at the time of the persecution of the Catholic religion helping the old faith to be maintained.

The switch to comprehensive education came at a time when academic values in themselves were being challenged. The retreat from schooling being for schooling was at its height in the late 1960s and was part of an anti-academic movement challenging old-established values and institutions. I was becoming more and more concerned about the collapse of structure in our society and in our schools – the cement that holds everything together. Events in Paris and the United States triggered off a student revolt against all values, standards and social and moral inhibitions. It was as if everything had to be torn down and destroyed and then a purer, wiser, more compassionate society would naturally arise. Taken to extremes we were back to Rousseau's view of the noble savage, with additions from Freud, Piaget and Froebel in the classroom. Young teachers and grandfather Beatles joined a movement challenging traditional teaching. There could not have been a worse moment for changing the structure of secondary school education, since the change to the comprehensive school opened the door to all kinds of innovations which had nothing to do with secondary school reorganization itself.

This anti-education movement was nihilistic and I was convinced as a practising schoolmaster that it would be the young who would suffer most. In the end, there would be nothing to revolt against as the adolescent youth flexed his intellectual muscles – the ultimate deprivation. Every year I informed my new sixth formers that now was the time for them to revolt but they must never win, otherwise the game was over!

Was the comprehensive reorganization inevitable? I do not think so. The limitation on the number of grammar school places was its death-knell. I always held that 40 per cent of children could approach academic excellence. If the number of grammar schools had been doubled, there would on one side have been far more parents available to defend them; and on the other side, fewer indignant parents joining the pro-comprehensive movement because their children had not been selected for grammar school education. The attempt to preserve the grammar schools by making them more selective was totally destructive.

The 1944 Act also ended the opportunity of those who failed

the 11 plus (as I had) to join local grammar schools as subsidized fee payers.

The 11 plus was now final, and it was the parents of average plus children who failed the 11 plus who now became the officers of the anti-grammar school lobby instead of being the fee-paying supporters of the grammar schools.

My concern was the preservation of culture and good academic education wherever they existed, irrespective of whether this was in a tripartite, a bipartite or a comprehensive system. I was first and foremost an educationalist concerned for high standards, as I still am.

In March 1969 I discovered that I was not alone in my views. This was when Professor Brian Cox and Tony Dyson, both distinguished literary figures who edited *The Critical Quarterly*, published the first 'Black Paper' on education. It was the first effective public reply to the growing fashion of so-called progressive and permissive school education and the growing left-wing interference with intellectual freedoms. The *Black Papers* became nationally renowned when Edward Short, then the Labour Secretary of State for Education, described the new publication as 'one of the blackest days for education in the past hundred years'. A copy of this first 'Black Paper' had been sent to every Member of Parliament.

This critique of the deteriorating education scene had articles from leading educational and literary figures like Kingsley Amis, Robert Conquest, the headmasters of St Dunstan's College, Abingdon School and Prendergast School, Bryan Wilson and Warden Sparrow of All Souls, Oxford. Edward Short's outburst made everyone, including me, rush out to buy a copy. Giving publicity to one's opponents is always a grave error. I was so impressed by the contents of the *Black Paper* that I wrote immediately to its editors and soon took a train to Manchester to visit Professor Brian Cox in his book-lined study at Manchester University. I felt elated, like the Old Testament prophet who found that he was not alone. I was as impressed by Brian as I was by the publication, and Tony Dyson, his co-editor, soon visited me at Highbury Grove and I met another first-class intellect on our side of the battle.

The first *Black Paper* made the case for intellectual rigour and structure and tradition. Alas, Mr Short's outburst made it party political and this was damaging for the debate, for the country and particularly for the Labour Party. Many of the *Black Paper* writers had voted Labour – indeed Cox and Dyson had done so in 1966. It began to seem that only the Conservative Party was prepared to defend standards of excellence. Labour seemed to have sold out before the battle and, with rare exceptions, the Liberal Party – once the defender of intellectual freedom and thought – did not even recognize the growing threats to these freedoms.

The *Black Papers* ensured that there was a debate and allowed barriers to be built against the destroyers. Eight months later the second *Black Paper* was published and there was a huge radio, television and newspaper coverage. The opponents of the *Black Papers* were often emotional, aggressive and spiteful. It was as if we had challenged a long-held and much respected religious truth. It is difficult after so many years fully to recall the anger these publications aroused amongst the progressive educational lobby. The reader can perhaps gain an insight into my mind at that time when I quote from my article in the second *Black Paper*, entitled 'The Essential Conditions for the Success of a Comprehensive School'. I accepted the grave defects of the tripartite system and the need for extended courses in secondary modern schools. At the same time, I made clear that comprehensive schools would be very different according to their catchment areas, adding: 'It is a pity that the advocates for such schools did not look at the map and note that the Duke and the docker lived in different areas.' I then listed five conditions necessary for the success of a comprehensive school. These I gave because many local authorities were bringing together schools of little or no distinction in difficult buildings far apart, with unsatisfactory staffing and calling them comprehensive schools. Comprehensive schools are more difficult to organize than specialist schools because of the spread of ability and their size, and to handicap them further by using inadequate buildings was to load the dice decisively against them. The five conditions I listed were:

1. Basing the new school in an established area on a well-respected existing school;
2. Erecting special buildings on the one site;
3. A balanced ability intake;
4. A school of at least 1,400 pupils;
5. Good staffing both in qualifications and with senior teachers

of sufficient ability and confidence to be able to take decisions yet delegate responsibility.

I added:

Class teaching in a comprehensive school also demands great versatility. Unlike other professions a class teacher has to become the non-specialist. To take a fast 'A' level GCE group and then transfer to a remedial group or a group of fourth year rebellious leavers is to ask a great deal from a teacher. The staff who joined the early comprehensive schools were zealots who were prepared for this but it is only the most skilled and dedicated teacher who can achieve such teaching with complete satisfaction, irrespective of where his specialisation lies.

All this seemed to me sensible advice and was helpful to the proper organization of comprehensive schools, but I was attacked as if I were advocating the burning down of all comprehensive schools and the tarring and feathering of anybody who spoke in their support. From now I was daily involved not only in running my school and in my political activities, but in a battle to save schools and education from the lowering of standards as well as from total anarchy in many cases. It was very dangerous to be listed as a *Black Paper* man, since one had the nerve to indicate certain emperors had no clothes, and this is never popular!

The fact that the Labour Party in search of a programme was in favour of total comprehensive reorganization on one side and took a neutral stand on the growing student nihilist movement on the other convinced me that I had made the right decision in joining the Conservative Party. If I had not joined a year earlier, I would surely have had to join the Conservative Party as an educational refugee in 1969.

My new political theme was the superiority of the free society with a capitalist base over a communist or a socialist society. I emphasized the need for limited government along with the necessity of firm law and order and good education, including the continuance of the direct grant schools. I attacked wages and prices policies, nationalized industries, high taxation and the compulsory comprehensive education policies of the Labour and Liberal Parties.

I also attacked the proposed local government reorganization into bigger units following the Redcliffe-Maud Report. I even referred to the proposed local government reorganization when I gave an address at the Haslingden Grammar School speech day in 1970. This was the last time my father heard me speak in public and he agreed entirely with my speech, which pleased me immensely.

A year went by before I said in Eccles that there was no evidence that larger local government units were more efficient than smaller ones and, even if this were the case, people had a right to oppose such reorganization if they preferred smaller units. I added that people identified more with small local government councils and, the larger the population of a local council, the fewer people voted.

The launch of the second *Black Paper* also brought me into contact with Ralph Harris, general director of the Institute of Economic Affairs, which has played such a great part in reviving the study of free-market economics in Britain. Ralph Harris wrote an article on the Enfield situation where there had been a celebrated legal case opposing the compulsory comprehensivization of the borough. In the *Black Papers* I met my educational allies and in the Institute of Economic Affairs I found, with Ralph Harris and Arthur Seldon, my economic allies. The year 1969 was a good one.

The Labour Party did quite well in the local elections of May 1970 and Harold Wilson decided to go to the electorate. I heard the news while sitting in a small park at Westminster where I was reading before attending an evening meeting. The following day I applied for leave of absence from ILEA, which they granted me with their then usual courtesy and generosity. I went off to Lancashire, staying with my parents and spending the whole day in Eccles and Swinton, the twin townships that made up the constituency.

I am sure that all candidates desiring to turn over a large majority hope that a miracle will happen and that huge numbers of voters will meet their road to Damascus and amaze the nation by allowing the candidate to be elected. Away from the constituency this seems impossible, but when knocking on doors with one's supporters all things seem possible.

My book *The Ashworth Cotton Enterprise* came out half-way through the election. It was very favourably received with a long review in the *Daily Telegraph* by (Peter) T.E. Utley and I simply quote two sentences from this review:

> If the Conservative Party really believes in free enterprise, and if it wishes to convert that abstraction into terms of flesh and blood it could do no better than abridge and distribute Rhodes Boyson's brilliant study of Henry Ashworth, the great Lancashire cotton magnate of the last century.... Mr Heath should embrace Dr Boyson with as much delight as Churchill embraced Dr Hayek in 1945.

I knocked on doors every afternoon and evening and I had a small band of enthusiastic workers, including Bob Dunn, now Conservative MP for Dartford, who sat his degree finals in the morning, canvassed with me in the afternoon and revised for the next examination in the evening. I exhausted myself on the day and then went to the count. I hoped I had won for my party workers' sake. I heard there was a swing to the Conservatives, but was it enough? It certainly was not! I had a swing of 4.7 per cent and cut the Labour majority from 9,257 to 5,455.

There was one slightly amusing anecdote from the 1970 election, regarding my sideboards. I was clean-shaven when I was selected for Eccles in 1968 and grew my sideboards in 1969 after a half-joking agreement with my sixth formers that they would cut their long hair provided I grew sideboards! By the time the agreement expired at the end of three months, they were part of me and I have retained them ever since. The chairman of the Eccles constituency, however, objected to the sideboards and I cut them off for the election. This desperate act certainly did not seem to have increased my vote and I grew the sideboards again immediately the election was over.

The local council elections of 1968, 1969 and 1970 indicated the state of political opinion in the constituency. In 1968 and 1969 council elections in the two boroughs of Eccles and Swinton and Pendlebury gave substantial Conservative majorities on average-sized polls. The April 1970 county council election produced a narrow Conservative majority on a low poll, but the 1970 council elections in the constituency recorded 2,400 more Labour than Conservative voters on an average poll, and Lancashire always believes with considerable truth that there is a heavier Labour poll in high-voting general elections than in local elections. The front page of *The Swinton and Pendlebury Journal* of 14 May 1970 had on its front page: 'Labour's Election Boost!' Only two Conservative councillors were elected in the seven wards contested.

The local papers gave me good obituary notices – I believe I deserved them, since I had for eighteen months helped to fill their papers. *The Eccles and Patricroft Gazette* of 25 June 1970, wrote:

And so there came to a close a campaign which had been fought with exceptional intensity over a period of not just a few weeks, since the dissolution, but for some 18 months or so. In fact, since the Tory candidate, Dr Rhodes Boyson, came upon the scene. . . . There is no doubt that Dr Boyson made a considerable impact on the town. In Dr Boyson, Lancashire-born headmaster of a London comprehensive school, the Tories felt they had a candidate who would be the first to top the poll for the Party since Robert Carey won as far back as 1935.

My opponent, Mr Lewis Carter Jones, fought a good campaign. He let me fill the papers with views to which his supporters replied, while he made the occasional magisterial speech to his supporters, widely reported in the local press, especially bringing to public notice his efforts on behalf of his constituency and the handicapped in debates in the House of Commons. There are distinct advantages in being a sitting candidate for any MP who uses the opportunity properly. I did, however, attack the Labour and Communist candidates for using the captive audience of the counters on election night to deliver political speeches instead of just thanking all those who helped to organize the election.

The Swinton and Pendlebury Journal reported what I said at the count: 'Dr Boyson said that he trusted that he would continue to enjoy the friendship of hundreds of Conservative voters and thousands of electors in the Eccles constituency.' This was a fitting comment at the end of a vigorous but finally unsuccessful campaign.

We saved money in the campaign to order huge posters to be put up all over the constituency on voting day: VOTE BOYSON TODAY. When we got up in the early morning, the billposting firm had got them all wrong and throughout the constituency the posters read: VOTE SON BOY TODAY. This was certainly a depressing start to the day, but it saved the constituency money since we, of course, never paid for them. I doubt, however, that this lost me the election!

The following day I got up early, caught the first train to London and retook charge of Highbury Grove. The Son Boy election was over and I returned a month later to the north to meet my workers and to tell them that I would give them all the help I could but that I would not be fighting that seat again. This was a sad parting, but I am still in touch with many of the party workers there. A lifetime of trying to win an impossible seat was not my ambition.

13

Fighting the Nihilists 1970–1974

*

When I walked back into my study at Highbury Grove I knew I would very likely be there for the next five years. Part of me was very disappointed, as I would have liked to have won Eccles, but it would have been a super-marginal, very difficult to hold at a future election.

Part of me, however, was happy to be back at Highbury Grove. I always enjoyed schoolmastering and slipped back easily into the routine. Highbury Grove was my aircraft-carrier in which I could sail and from which I could regularly fly to other tasks. The debate between traditional versus progressive education took up much of my time, and with my school and council activities I was certainly fully occupied.

I also had a new activity. Ralph Harris had suggested that in order to propagate the ideas of the free market within the rule of law we should form a book club on the lines of the Left Book Club of the 1930s. We thus set up the Churchill Press and the Constitutional Book Club to publish such titles, and I became the chairman of a venture I found very satisfying. Ralph Harris, Ross McWhirter and I, with Joan Delderfield as secretary, were its leading lights. We decided to publish six books a year for a subscription of £2.50. These books would also be sold in bookshops at £1.50 hardback and 75p softback. Titles included *Right Turn*, *Goodbye to Nationalisation* and *Education's Threatened Standards*. The best-selling book was *Trousered Apes: A Study in the Influence of Literature on Contemporary Society* by Duncan Williams, but the most influential was *Rape of Reason: The Corruption of the Polytechnic of North London*. This latter book was written by Caroline (now Lady) Cox, John Marks and Keith Jacka. The first two had been Labour supporters, and the third was once a Communist. Mrs Thatcher, when Prime Minister, quoted from this book at a Conservative Party Conference.

Right Turn, the first book (a collection of essays which I edited), was well received and extensively reviewed. Alan Walters in the *Financial Times* commented: 'The dramatic emergence of what might be called the New Right – arguing tightly, logically and with great powers of persuasion – is eroding the grand consensus of socialism.'

The Economist, reviewing *Down with the Poor: An Analysis of the Failure of the 'Welfare State' and a Plan to End Poverty*, wrote:

> The thinking right went to sleep around 1960 with the exception of the unrelenting Institute of Economic Affairs. The publication of the black 'Papers on Education' was the first signs of reawakening. . . .
> . . . *Down with the Poor* is a further expression of the same philosophy. . . . It contains effectively argued essays on education . . . on student loans; and on the quagmire of high cost and limited availability that now engulfs the rented housing sector in most cities.

The controversial title *Down with the Poor* was a quote from Bernard Shaw.

Nevertheless the venture never took off commercially. It seemed that the jibe that the right does not read was true. The Left Book Club in the 1930s had 57,000 members. The Constitutional Book Club had 1,200 in the first year, but we needed a membership of 3,000 to be viable. Its influence, however, via the press, radio and television reviews of its books was much wider than its circulation. It thus played a necessary part in preparing the ground for the Thatcher years and it was particularly influential amongst the young in the universities and polytechnics. The first book came out in the summer of 1970 and the last book in 1973.

One of the Constitutional Book Club's claims to fame was that in July 1971 *Down with the Poor* was the second most read non-fiction book in the Lancashire town of Bacup, in the Rossendale Valley, a town that had provided one-third of the pupils of Lea Bank School when I was the head!

I also co-edited with Brian Cox the third *Black Paper*, to which I contributed an article, 'In Defence of Examinations'. I claimed that 'The present opposition to examinations arises more from the pressure for an uncompetitive egalitarian society than from any technical inefficiencies in examinations themselves.' I then gave four reasons for having external examinations.

1. The Teacher. Examinations test not only the knowledge acquired by the learners, but also the teaching efficiencies of teachers and teaching methods. Without examinations inefficiency of teachers can continue almost unnoticed for a lifetime, to the severe and permanent disadvantage of their pupils.
2. The Students. Examinations also act as a great stimulant to pupils, giving measurable and achievable goals at which to aim.
3. Protection of Students. Examinations also, of course, protect the individual pupils against teacher prejudice and misjudgement.
4. Equality of Opportunity. Examinations ... help the under-privileged students most. ... If external examinations were abolished on the lines suggested by Mr Short and Mr Wedgwood Benn, then the bright boy in the deprived neighbourhood school would be severely handicapped, while the dull boy in the privileged middle-class school would profit most.

The election of a Conservative Government earlier in 1970 and Margaret Thatcher's withdrawal of the compulsory comprehensive circular 10/65 with her circular 10/70 meant that the danger of a total destruction of our educational system had disappeared, at least temporarily. No more *Black Papers* were then issued until another Labour Government was elected in 1974.

I gave evidence to the Bullock Committee on Literacy on 6 June 1973, attacking the cult of reading readiness – that pupils should be taught to read only when they ask, since this discriminated against the boy or girl from the poor home who could not read as against those who came from literate homes and could already read. I warned that 'The more modern and well-equipped the infant school, the more time must be spent in justifying the expenses of a hall, gymnasium equipment, a playing field, sand and water facilities, radios, television sets and tape recorders.' I added: 'Recent research certainly seems to indicate that there is no relationship between smaller classes and improved literacy and numeracy; indeed the reverse seems to be true . . . It would appear that it is simply the calibre of the teacher and the method of teaching which is important. Reduced sized classes have been used to introduce the ineffective "discovery methods".' I ended: 'Standards can only be improved by agreed national standards of achievement for the average and below-average pupil being stipulated nationally and checked by HMIs or by national examiners.'

In an article in the *Daily Telegraph* on 12 April 1972 I made clear my advocacy of a national curriculum. The article was entitled 'Bring Out Your Illiterates' and I quoted from the Plowden Report: 'We have considered whether we can lay down standards that should be achieved by the end of the primary school, but concluded that it is not possible to describe a standard of achievement that should be reached by all or most children.' I accepted that 'Standards cannot be laid down for all children, but it should not be difficult to lay down standards in writing, spelling, comprehension, composition, numeracy and basic knowledge of geography, science and history to be expected by average eleven year olds. To fail to lay down such standards meant that every teacher in every school can "do their own thing".'

I always opposed the idea of one examination at 16 plus, believing in at least two levels of examinations with overlapping grades. I told the Conference of the National Council for Educational Standards: 'I do not believe what the NUT [the National Union of Teachers] assert, that there can be one examination at 16 plus which will satisfy all pupils from IQ 70 to IQ 170. Such one examination will be the ultimate bore to the bright boy and the ultimate insult to the dull boy.'

I had written in the *Daily Telegraph* the previous year:

What is required at 16-plus is not one examination for all as advocated by the Schools Council and the National Union of Teachers, but either over-lap grades between the GCE 'O' and CSE examinations or more common syllabus bases. No one 16-plus examination can possibly be suitable for pupils whose ability varies from the potential Oxbridge open scholar to those bordering on the ineducable. Any such examination would either be an insult to the very intelligent or the ultimate depressive to the academically non-gifted pupil.

I advocated national tests at seven, eleven and fourteen, these being minimum hurdles which all could jump. I also advocated that 40–60 per cent of pupils should be offered courses in trade or technical schools at secondary level. I defended streaming, instancing that among a sample of a hundred fourteen-year-olds there was likely to be one with a mental age of eight and another with a mental age of twenty, and how could such be taught in the same classroom without individual tuition? I was also concerned about the intellectual level of teacher recruitment, since in September 1972 only 40.5 per cent of entrants to colleges of education had two 'A' levels, 31.2 per cent had no 'A' levels and 40 per cent had even failed 'O' level mathematics.

I had developed a consistent theme: an improvement of educational standards would arise only from an increase of parental choice of school or the enforcement of basic national standards of teaching achievement.

I can still remember my horror when I read Richard Crossman's article in *The Times* of 25 April 1973. In this he said he had, 'no doubt that an ever-increasing number of young parents would be happier if a wicked socialist government compelled them to give up freedom of educational choice and accept compulsory state schooling for their sons and daughters'. That from a party which claimed to represent ordinary men and women! I suspected that such a statement could bring even my father to wonder if he was in the right party.

I began to express support for a variety of specialist secondary schools of the kind found in Eastern Europe and America. I also came out in favour of Timothy Raison's five-year contract for heads and teaching staff.

I continued to warn against the dangers of the neighbourhood comprehensive schools, whose standards and aspirations would be set by the area. I saw the educational voucher as the equivalent of the sale of council houses enfranchising people to freedom and bringing choice to more families. In 1970 I wrote in an appraisal to the Institute of Economic Affairs publication *Education: A Framework for Choice*:

> Such a system of educational vouchers would transform the educational scene. Schools and parents would no longer be at the mercy of 'progressive' but unrealistic idealists who gently levitated over the school desks, since they would have to

provide the type of education the parents considered most suitable for their children. . . . The vouchers would make the parent consumers influential in school education the way no ballot box could equal. . . . Moreover, parents enfranchised by the vouchers would grow both in dignity and responsibility by the exercise of choice.

In 1973 I wrote in a book I edited, *The Accountability of Schools*, to which Professor Brian Cox, Professor Arthur Pollard and Leon Brittan also contributed: 'Vouchers should be seriously considered as part of Conservative policy.' I always considered that schools are social as well as educational institutions. Schools are tribal and the tribe must be worth belonging to. I was quoted in the *Chingford Guardian* of 4 May 1973:

As adults identify with a football club, political party, golf club or working men's club [boys and girls] will identify with a successful school. A school should be lively, the teaching should be interesting, there should be a great variety of sport, music and other activities. . . . If the school is not worth identifying with, boys will form a thug gang inside the school and march with their own uniform colours, with scarves and boots, to fight and cheer in the crowd of their chosen football club. This is what happens when we fail to channel properly the energies of vigorous youngsters.

That quote is as true today as it was then and will be just as true tomorrow. Human nature has been static since the Garden of Eden, whether one is a creationist or an evolutionist, and as Edmund Burke made clear, if people do not identify with society's 'little platoons' they will create their own platoons at war with society.

I was also concerned about the security of children within the family as against those who advocated children's rights which would break up the family. I wrote an article about this in the *Daily Telegraph* of 31 July 1971. The security of the child in the family is even more important than the security of the pupil in the school, and any intervention with the family from outside is very dangerous and should be tolerated only in the last extremity. An ineffective parent is almost always better than an effective social worker.

I attacked the extension of sex education in schools as an affront to the family, decency and privacy. Children mature at different ages and cannot receive sex education as a class. I wrote in an article in *The Sun* on 25 July 1971: 'If you give a class of 13-year olds a sex lesson, it will be the right time for six of them, 18 will be bored stiff and you will harm the other six for the rest of their lives. . . . Children are being conned into thinking of sex as a package on a self-service shelf. I find it sad that sexual details should be presented cold on a slab.'

As regards Highbury Grove, I had taken the headship of this school as a comprehensive, but I had to fight ILEA all the time to try to get a full comprehensive intake. In the ILEA area more than 15 per cent of the age group went to voluntary and county grammar schools, many long established with fine standards and traditions. The voluntary grammar schools were beginning to leave central London and ILEA was slowly contracting the intake of its own grammar schools, but the continued existence of these schools seriously diluted the academic intake of the London comprehensive schools. Highbury Grove could easily have recruited a full comprehensive intake, since we were regularly oversubscribed in every ability group, but ILEA prohibited this. We were allowed to take only 25 per cent of pupils from the top three ability groups who made up 40 per cent of London's children, and this fact was communicated to the junior schools and to the parents. As long as ILEA retained grammar schools, it should have organized most of London into grammar schools and secondary modern schools, with comprehensive schools introduced only into areas where they could take a proper comprehensive intake. Highbury Grove did well – very well – but it was a continued battle with ILEA to be allowed to take something approaching a comprehensive intake.

In 1972 ILEA had ninety-four comprehensive schools, fifty-two voluntary and county grammar schools, fifty-seven general secondary schools and one technical school. On this balance it could have organized some thirty proper comprehensive schools, whereas it ran so-called comprehensive schools with appropriate courses and staffing but without the necessary intake of able pupils. ILEA's ruling meant it was easier for an able boy to obtain entry into a grammar school than into Highbury Grove.

Yet Highbury Grove's popularity continued to embarrass ILEA. I have a housemaster's note of a divisional meeting in 1971 where the divisional officer said: 'Let's name names – junior heads should not give advice which encouraged too wide an area for Highbury Grove. We have got to accept that some schools are more popular than others. Parents hear of Highbury Grove and they feel frustrated if their boys cannot go there. Junior heads should therefore be especially careful to avoid "misleading" advice about going to Highbury Grove. They should stick to the "safer" areas of recruitment.'

In the same year I received a letter from the divisional officer, a very capable and helpful man. He wrote:

> I am still seeing parents who, however much they may have misunderstood, quote a clear impression gained by them from the school that you would have been only too pleased to take their boy but 'authority' in the shape of the Divisional Officer directed you otherwise. We must know between us that if a school with 240 year places has well over 300 applicants, and you have offered places to 240+, it is not open to either of us to offer hope to more or to give them the impression that advice given by a 'faceless bureaucrat' was specific for particular children. Far better, surely, to say that the school is full and for what reasons.

That was a well-constructed letter, but the school was not full in groups 1, 2 and 3 to make it truly a comprehensive school. The answer was for ILEA to let us take our true comprehensive intake in competition with the grammar schools.

In the same year, 1971, the local junior school heads were advised by ILEA: 'The very heavy oversubscription to Highbury Grove . . . it is hoped that the advice given in this letter will help you to give an indication of the areas from which admission to this school is very doubtful indeed. . . . Choice of this school should be actively discouraged for boys living. . . .' So much for parental choice.

In the early years of Highbury Grove, with the appropriate housemaster in each case, I interviewed every applicant, since I fully believe in parental choice of school. Parents also like it. By 1973, however, I was not allowed to see parents until the divisional officer had decided which boys I was going to take. Before this I had taken boys according to the ability groups I was allowed to recruit, according to family connections, the distance from the school and their enthusiasm. The boy who replied that he wished to come to Highbury Grove because the boys wore more school badges than any other school was in, as was the boy who replied he had heard that in the technical department he could build a spaceship.

The problem of the intake of Highbury Grove was aggravated in the early 1970s by a decline in the reading ability of the potential intake. These were the days of reading readiness – don't ask children to read until they ask and some never did – open-plan chaotic classrooms, the retreat from phonics, the freedom from the 11-plus examination control and all the claimed glories of progressive education. Of our 240 11-plus intake in 1971 some forty-seven had reading ages below nine. A year later this figure rose to eighty-seven and I then said at a Cambridge conference that 'A popular and oversubscribed school in north London had one in eight pupils who cannot read three-letter words!' This was in a heavily oversubscribed school with a good cross-section of middle, working-class and immigrant families. In both 1972 and 1973 the average reading age of our intake was 2.3 years below what it should have been.

Another problem of the early 1970s was the increase in teacher militancy in London. I remained a member of the National Union of Teachers until 1969, when I resigned in protest at the NUT in London calling strikes literally at the drop of a hat, which made the running of a school very difficult and seriously handicapped working mothers. I considered this union action especially unfair since ILEA, whatever its faults, was prepared to give the maximum salaries allowed under the Burnham scale. I noted in 1972 that one-third of my teaching staff were under the age of twenty-five and two-thirds were under the age of thirty-five. There was no way on the teachers' national salary scales that a married male teacher could buy a satisfactory house or flat in London. Thus stability of staffing and the appointment of mature, experienced teachers was almost impossible. Teacher turnover in London at that time was 30 per cent a year.

To add to my problems, Labour-controlled ILEA then indicated to me via my chairman of governors, the formidable Evelyn Dennington, CBE, that ILEA was in favour of all the staff meeting regularly to discuss the running of individual schools in the form of school councils. We already had an elected teacher governor and a staff association which met irregularly and I had no intention of running Highbury Grove like a revolutionary commune.

Pressure increased, however, inside the school for a school council, made up of all teaching staff, including part-timers and supply teachers, to meet regularly. The more militant staff also wanted these meetings to be in school time. There are occasions when one has to bow to the wind and buy time and this was one of them. I agreed that such a school council should meet twice a term in school time and, when they requested the attendance of my two deputies and myself, that we would attend.

In the autumn term of 1973 we had two such meetings, both of which I attended part of the time. Most of the sensible hard-working staff were silent while, with the notable exception of one very good teacher, those whose classrooms often resembled a scene from the French Revolution held forth with their views on discipline. We had the usual calls for all staff to have the same number of free periods and the demand for the end of special allowances. Such demands were supported by some of the weaker heads of departments until I pointed out that there was nothing to stop such heads of departments sharing their allowances amongst all assistants every month. That had a sobering effect upon many heads of departments present.

Early in the January 1974 term another staff council was called to discuss school discipline and report to the full council. The second deputy took the lead and I played little or no part in it. Two or three days later the following missive arrived on my desk from the school secretary of the National Union of Teachers:

RESOLUTION OF THE NUT BRANCH MEETING ON
MONDAY 14TH JAN. 1974.

1. That
   THE NUT BRANCH AT HIGHBURY GROVE REJECTS THE PROCEEDINGS AND CONCLUSIONS OF THE STAFF CONFERENCE ON FRIDAY 11TH JANUARY, 1974 BECAUSE IT WAS <u>UNDEMOCRATIC FROM START TO FINISH.</u>
2. We take note of the following facts:
   a) <u>THE STAFF BODY HAD NO SAY IN DRAWING UP THE LIST OF TOPICS</u>
      The question of punishment was put in the forefront in an arbitrary way. This rigged the proceedings from the start.
   b) The staff as a whole were not consulted about how the discussion groups should be composed.

c) The staff as a whole had no say in choosing the chairmen and secretaries.

d) The proposed *discipline committee*, which the deputy head mentioned at the end of the meeting, showed up the undemocratic nature of the whole proceedings.

   i) The staff as a whole were not consulted about it.

   ii) There was no election of members.

   iii) At least some of the appointed members were not informed before the list of members was read out by the deputy head.

3. As a result, the whole proceedings were dominated by an authoritarian structure, and an authoritarian spirit.

4. THE NUT BRANCH THEREFORE CALLS FOR THE WHOLE CONFERENCE TO BE RECALLED, AFTER BEING PREPARED IN A DEMOCRATIC WAY.

I decided that it was time for action and we had better have a full showdown. My first deputy had retired at Christmas and Laurie Norcross had only just started at the school as second deputy. Mr Heath's troubles with the miners could bring a general election at any time and I did not want to leave any problems for my deputies or my successor. So that evening I made a set of notes and called the staff together at 9 a.m. the following morning.

I made clear that the school was not a workers' co-operative but a teaching institution where each had his or her job to do. Mine was to see that standards were kept high, that all staff did their jobs and that the parents and governors were satisfied with the progress of the boys. The deputy heads, the heads of departments and the housemasters also had their jobs to do – to run their houses and departments efficiently while the individual teachers were responsible for the progress of their classes. If heads of departments and heads of houses did not believe in their responsibilities, for which they were paid, I would welcome their resignations before the end of the day. I made it perfectly clear that I was not prepared to alter the organization of a successful school at the call of what were often transient and ineffective staff. I added for full measure that it was quite likely that I would be leaving the school in the near future and that if any staff wished for individual testimonials or signed references they could write to my home and I would prepare them after, of course, checking from whoever was then in charge of the school that there had been no change in their behaviour or teaching standards since I had left. I added that any member of staff who conscientiously objected to the way the school was run could ask me for a testimonial, which I would provide for him by 4 p.m. that day. The meeting lasted ten to fifteen minutes, no one asked for a testimonial and that was the end of the school council and the revolutionary commune at Highbury Grove in my time.

14

I Enter Parliament

*

By 1971 our two daughters had gone to university and Vicky and I divorced. I later married Florette MacFarlane, who had been known to me as a very capable teacher at the Robert Montefiore School and as a history researcher in her own right. Her general views were the same as mine and she was very interested in politics.

From 1972 I began to look for a winnable Conservative seat. I was interviewed by a number of constituencies and almost always finished in the final short list. I began to suspect that one-third of the members of these selection committees wanted me as their Member of Parliament, another third wanted me in Parliament but for another seat, while a final third preferred that I should remain a headmaster! It seemed that I was to be ever the brides-maid and never the bride. I had a feeling that my outspoken views on education, law and order and the economy made people very divided about my suitability as their local candidate. By the end of 1972 I had decided that, if I were not successful in obtaining nomination for a winnable seat in the next few months, I would look for other career opportunities. By then I had spent seven years at Highbury Grove and was ready for a new challenge in education or politics.

It was then that I was invited for interview by Brent North – a reorganized seat under boundary changes. I decided that in future interviews I would not research the make-up of the constituency, but would simply attend and give my views as plainly as ever and see what the result was. I thus approached Brent North in a fresh frame of mind. A hundred people had put their names in for the seat and there were three sets of interviews: the first, a long list at the Churchill Club in the Kenton Road; the second, a shorter list at the Century Hotel in the constituency; and finally, a short list of six at a meeting for all local party members who wished to attend at Copland School just outside the constituency. The final six, apart from myself, included Sir Eric Bullis, MP for Wembley North, which was being reorganized; Sir Ronald Russell, treasurer of the 1992 Committee and MP for Wembley South, which was also being reorganized out of existence; Michael Howard (the present Home Secretary); Michael Brotherton (who became MP for Louth, 1974–83); and Christopher Ward, who had been an MP.

Lots were drawn for the order of speaking at the final interviews. Counters were recruited by the constituency agent, Peter Golds, largely among Conservative agents but also including friends of Peter, one of whom was John Major. I was drawn to speak last, which is an advantage. I had noted from numerous governors' staff appointment meetings that everyone remembered the first and the last candidates. The first because everyone was fresh at the beginning of the meeting, the last because the meeting was coming to an end.

21 February, 1973, was a good day for me. We launched a book at Churchill Press in the morning, where Jeremy Thorpe spoke brilliantly; in the afternoon I recorded a television programme with Kenneth Allsop; and in the evening I dined with Florette in Wembley and walked down to Copland School some twenty minutes before my interview. As we passed the Triangle in Wembley we noticed that one of the corner shops, which was empty, had just been repainted over the door with the name BOYSON. Who this person was I do not know, since two days later another name was painted over it. There were then only two Boysons in the London telephone directory – one was mine and the other an owner of an art gallery in south London – so the surname coincidence seemed a happy omen.

All the candidates and their wives were put in Room 13 which, if one were superstitious, would undo the BOYSON omen, but it could mean that none of us would be selected! The tension was intense. We were plied with biscuits and threatened with tannic acid poisoning from numerous cups of tea. There was very little talking.

The meeting was attended by 500 constituency party members. It was chaired by Mrs Nina Talmage, a capable and wise woman who had been elected chairman of the new constituency of Brent North. She was a well-known magistrate and ex-mayoress of Wembley. All candidates spoke for an allotted time and then answered questions for a similar period before they withdrew to the silence of Room 13. I was of course the last in and voting commenced as I left. Agreement had been reached that the bottom one or two candidates would be dropped in each progressive ballot until one candidate had an overall majority. There was no over-all majority at the first vote. Sir Eric Bullis gained most votes and I was second. The two bottom candidates were then dropped and I took the lead. When two more candidates were dropped, in a straight fight I polled 289 to Sir Eric's 215.

I shall always remember the long wait in Room 13 before the result was announced. After a silence which seemed as if it would never be broken, we heard the sound of a single person's feet approaching and then the opening of the door. It was Mrs Talmage, who said 'Dr Boyson'. I thought I was being recalled for another interview and Florette asked, 'Shall I come too?' The decision, however, had been made. The name Boyson might disappear from the Triangle shop but it would certainly now appear on the ballot papers of Brent North at the next general election.

Most of the counters and the senior constituency officers then went to the home of George and Betty Boobyer for a celebration drink. George was then a fine photographer at Harrods, and he and Betty soon became close friends with Florette and me. Eventually he became my constituency chairman.

I rang my father when I arrived at George Boobyer's. Father always went to bed at 10 p.m. and it was now long past 11 p.m. There was a long wait before Father came downstairs and picked up the telephone and I informed him that I had been selected for the winnable seat of Brent North. Father simply said, 'Tha' could have waited till the morning to tell me that', and put the telephone down. I wonder if he even passed the message on to Mother before going back to sleep!

The next day we were taken round the constituency by Peter Golds. We called on Mrs Talmage's ladies' section and felt greatly at ease with everyone. The people of Wembley are good folk with whom it has been a pleasure to work.

I was asked to dinner the following week at the House of

Commons by Sir Ronald and Lady Russell and over the next year attended all local events to which I was invited. I was very sorry when Sir Ronald died in 1974 just after the general election.

The *Evening Standard* reported that I 'enjoyed the dislike of left-wing educationalists and the devotion of hundreds of Islington parents'. The local newspaper carried the headline 'Tories Pick Hard-liner' and noted: 'He brought cheers from the audience at Copland School, Wembley, when he urged the return of corporal punishment, the tighter control of immigration and the clamp-down on pornography. He called for the return of law and order to the streets of Britain and more help for victims of criminal attacks rather than for the attacker.'

My father was really very pleased that I had been selected for a winnable seat and told all who called upon him of my success, but he was physically weakening and going out more rarely and then only to council meetings.

At Easter 1973 I stayed with my parents as usual and one evening, when talking to my friend Chris Aspin, Father made clear that he hoped to live long enough to know that I had entered Parliament. Alas, this was not to be; Father weakened further and his bed had to be brought downstairs, where he spent more and more time in it. His doctor told me that he was worn out and the end was near.

I was with him on 15 May, and intended to return to London that evening. I bade him farewell and he asked me to look after my mother and then I caught the Ribble bus to Manchester. I rang Mother from Piccadilly station before I boarded the train and she told me Father had died. I took the bus back to Haslingden. I was sorry I was not there at the end, but we had said farewell and I had seen him within an hour of his death.

The funeral was on 18 May at Manchester Road Methodist Church, where Father worshipped during the last ten years after the closure of King Street Methodist Church. His death marked the end of an era. His contemporaries were largely dead, the cotton industry locally was dying, the mill chimneys were smokeless or destroyed and his beloved Haslingden Town Council was about to disappear and become part of a larger borough. Towards the end of his days he regularly recalled the old Roman curse, 'May you outlive your friends.' He had, with only one or two exceptions, outlived those who had known him in his prime.

I was very sorry he did not live to see me in Parliament. The

Rossendale Free Press reported: 'He was gracious enough to bemoan the fact that he would die with the unfulfilled ambition of seeing his son in the House of Commons.'

After the funeral I returned to London with Florette. I walked up Nevin Drive on a clear, starlit night. I looked up and felt a huge rush of emotion as if Father was telling me that he was now at peace. He had led a full life. A half-timer in the mill at the age of ten, he was a legend in the town and finally became above party. He remained a trade-union secretary until he was seventy-eight and was still a town alderman when he died.

Alas, Father destroyed all his notes. I remember one adult Sunday school class he took when I was on leave from the Royal Navy. It was one of the most remarkable and scholarly talks I have ever heard. He kept his books but destroyed all his notes. His books had no notes in, apart from pound notes. He was a Lancastrian suspicious of banks, although he used them. We had to go through all his books to find the pound notes he had put in them to cover his immediate reserves.

I have probably painted my father in too dark colours, but part of me always saw him as the large, taciturn and withdrawn character I knew as a child. He had a strong sense of humour, but only in his later years did he show it to the full as he mellowed largely, I think, because of his close relationship with my children. Chris Aspin reminds me of Father laughing as he recalls the meeting at which a councillor suggested they had paid too much for the horse that pulled the corporation cart; and that next time they should buy a second-hand horse. Similarly I recall at a time of full employment after the Second World War his fury over anyone who remained voluntarily unemployed, and when he saw people gathering by the railings near the Commercial Hotel he called out to ask whether they would like hot water piped through the railings so that their voluntary unemployment would be made more pleasant!

Almost a year later, in the coal crisis, I was in my study at Highbury Grove when the telephone rang and my agent informed me that the starter's whistle had blown and the general election was on. That evening I addressed a parents' meeting at Highbury Grove, which was as I wrote four weeks later in *The Times Educational Supplement*, 'Strangely unreal. I spoke as usual yet seemed to listen to my own words as if I was hearing them for the last time.' That same evening I also spoke at a prearranged meeting at Harrow County School, probably the best grammar school in the country, which was threatened by a Conservative council with being turned into a comprehensive, and then I joined my agent to plan the election campaign.

Strangely enough I have less recollections of my first general election than any of the others. I remember it as cold, bleak and strange. This also describes the Conservative election campaign. Mr Heath had already – in the view of many, including myself – sold out to the miners after introducing an incomes policy which, as usual, never worked. I fought the election, however, as well as I could on Who Rules – the miners or the Government; on the need for law and order, including the return of capital punishment and the retention of corporal punishment in schools; on the need for sound education and the preservation of the green areas of Wembley from socialist house building. I recall that the Liberal candidate fought a tough campaign and I took out a writ against him from the High Court regarding one of his leaflets which I considered totally misrepresented my views.

In the early hours of March 1st my vote was declared:

Dr Rhodes Boyson	(Conservative)	25,700
Mr James Goudie	(Labour)	17,759
Mr Fred Harrison	(Liberal)	12,537
Mr Alan Smith	(National Front)	1,570
Conservative majority		7,941
Poll		80%

I was pleased by my own poll but was very concerned that we had lost our government majority. I was driven into central London for radio and television interviews without having had any sleep. I then returned home and went to Highbury Grove to ensure that everything was running smoothly there.

I wrote in the next week's issue of *The Times Educational Supplement*: 'School was the most traumatic experience of all – a school that was no longer mine. I still haven't really realised that 19 years of headship is now at an end and I shall be joining the House of Commons as a new boy.' This was certainly brought home to me when I received a telegram inviting me to attend a meeting of the 1922 Committee in Room 14 on 5 March. I really was a Member of Parliament.

15

The Battle for the Highbury Grove Succession

*

On the Monday after the general election I arrived at Highbury Grove as always, took the morning assembly and spent the day in the school. I attended the school regularly until Parliament was called and I swore the Oath of Allegiance to the Queen in the Commons chamber. Parents contacted me regarding the future of the school with which for eight years my name had been identified.

Before the general election I had mentioned informally to ILEA that, because there was no chance of a headmaster replacement until Easter or September, I would be prepared to stay on until a new headmaster could take over to ensure continuity. I now put this suggestion forward officially, but my offer was immediately rejected. What I had in mind was that, with or without pay, I would attend Highbury Grove from 8.30 a.m. to 1.30 p.m. until a new headmaster was appointed. The last thing I wanted was a long interregnum, which would damage the school. ILEA had other ideas. I suddenly realized that ILEA was glad to be rid of me and that while I had made Highbury Grove successful and well known, my views and the school achievements had showed up the failure of so many ILEA policies and initiatives. ILEA wanted a trendy image; I wanted schools for schooling. I even began to suspect that ILEA would be content if Highbury Grove ceased to be oversubscribed and faded into obscurity. The Conservatives on ILEA raised my offer at County Hall but ILEA just threw the book at them. The parent governor wrote letters to local and national newspapers condemning ILEA for not accepting my offer.

ILEA's attitude was to reap the whirlwind. Highbury Grove may have been led by me, but its success was due to immense parental involvement, certainly unsurpassed to my knowledge by any other school in London. The parents did not want any change of direction in the school and were determined to have none. Five of the governors had children either at the school or had children who had attended the school during my headship. ILEA was to be hoisted by its own petard of consultation – in this case real parental consultation by real parents with real children and not by trendy and extreme left-wing activists who represented no one but themselves!

The headship was advertised and twenty-five applied. A short list of seven was drawn up by ILEA to be submitted to the school governors for them to choose three to go forward to a final interview at County Hall. The governors, with an overwhelming Labour majority – only two being known Tories – refused to interview the seven because they believed that they would change the disciplinary arrangements of the school, ban the cane, end streaming and close the remedial department, all on bogus social arguments. One parent governor said, 'Frankly I felt that they might be what you call trendies.' Another governor said, 'We want to appoint a disciplinarian to replace [Dr Boyson] so that the standard will be maintained' and 'The governors are not a bunch of softies and we will not have a candidate steam-rollered upon us'.

The situation was unprecedented. The chairwoman of ILEA's staff and general sub-committee condemned the action of the governors as 'highly offensive and improper'. The governors refused to back down and threatened to take ILEA to court over the issue of governors' powers.

The press had a field day, with regular reports in the London and national newspapers and mention even in leading articles. One day Ronald Butt, who had visited the school during my headship, wrote a long article in *The Times*. The same day I contributed an article to the *Daily Mail*, and there was also much news coverage regarding events at Highbury Grove in other national newspapers. Even the boys joined in. The *Evening Standard* interviewed boys inside the school and photographed them, putting their comments, names and photographs prominently in the paper. All the boys came out for corporal punishment, including those who had received it. One who had received it said it had prevented 'too much mucking about'. One said they were sorry to see Dr Boyson go – 'He was a good geezer.' Another said, 'We respected Dr Boyson. You always knew where you stood.' One said, 'I would rather be here than at one of those trendy places where kids can do anything. It really is a good school.' Another boy, referring to me, said, 'He was really a nice bloke, he always worked for the kids', and another added, 'Everyone used to do as they were told when he was about. We respect him.'

ILEA began to realize it was creating more problems for itself and offered a new short list from the twenty-five who had applied. This would include Mr Sharr, the acting headmaster, and Mr Norcross, the second deputy. ILEA had been very badly advised to omit these two deputies from the original list, since it was the custom in London always to put them on at least the long list. By now, however, the governors had got the bit between their teeth and by eleven votes to two they demanded a new national advertising campaign, which was eventually agreed by ILEA. On this occasion Mr Sharr, who was then aged sixty-three and due to retire in two years, did not apply but supported the application of Mr Norcross, who was eventually appointed, the governors making him their favoured candidate for the last three in the final short list. This was a great pleasure to me, since I had considerable respect for Mr Norcross and I supported his application when he was appointed second deputy. He was to remain at Highbury Grove until August 1987 and protected its outstanding features as well as its popularity with parents.

Meanwhile, in the summer of 1974, the total parental commitment to the school was again shown in action. In July there seemed to be a plot by at least one teacher on the staff – presumably one of the teacher council enthusiasts – along with certain third-year boys and the National Union of School Students – to undermine the school. Leaflets were distributed in the school attacking corporal punishment and school uniform and proposing a strike, but the plot failed owing to the quick action of Mr Sharr and the parents who, at their own request, ringed the school to stop anybody leaving. Indeed, one housemaster had to go back for written permission from Mr Sharr before he was allowed to leave the school with a small group of boys on an official visit.

16

My First Parliament

*

It was a great day when on Monday, 11 March 1974 I attended Parliament to hear the Queen's Speech and to be sworn in as a Member. I came to the Members' entrance and fortunately encountered John Page, whom I had met at educational meetings and for whom I had spoken at the general election. John took me up to the Members' lobby and introduced me to two essentials for the peace of mind of an MP – the loos, labelled 'Members Only', and the Conservative whips' office. Since a number of Labour MPs had lost their Conservative pairs in the general election, I was quickly paired with Ronald Brown, brother of the legendary George Brown.

In that first week I attended all debates to get the feel of the chamber. I had decided to wait for some three months before I made my maiden speech. The House of Commons is house-proud and does not warm to someone with a known reputation outside the House who presumes the House shares this outside opinion.

The Queen's Speech was debated for a week and Friday, 15 March was allocated to front-bench opening and closing speeches on education and the social services. On Thursday, 14 March I received two messages. One was from Mrs Thatcher, asking if I was speaking on the Friday, and the other from Mr Prentice, then Secretary of State for Education and Science, asking the same question. Never one to refuse a challenge, I replied 'Yes', and approached the whips, who made arrangements with the Speaker for me to be called on the Friday morning. Never again would I be guaranteed to be called on a set day and time unless I became a government or shadow minister. Florette was still teaching as deputy headmistress of a large mixed London comprehensive school and she was amazed when later that Thursday evening I informed her I was speaking the following morning. I gave her the gist of the speech and spent a slightly troubled night.

I was called fourth on the Friday morning after the two front benches and Martin Flannery, another ex-schoolmaster and a newly elected Labour MP. A maiden speech is not interrupted and should not be too controversial or political. I paid tribute to my predecessors as Members of Parliament for Wembley North and Wembley South and then launched into a carefully crafted speech, setting the themes to which I would return at greater length over many years. I said: 'But my experience, certainly in London and many other areas, and alas what I have seen in America and read about in Eastern Europe convinces me that comprehensive education is not the great answer it was thought to be.'

I warned the House of the challenge of the super-selective schools in Russia from which, '80 per cent go on to university'. I then took up the theme which had been mine since my first headship: the need for parental choice and involvement. This was a matter which at that time scarcely touched the educational policies of either major party. I said: 'It is fascinating how readily we talk about participation yet make little reference to the parents, the people most concerned with the education of the children.' I predicted that parent power would be the power of the seventies – it certainly has become that of the 1990s. I concluded: 'We are likely to go one of two ways. Either there will be an emphasis on national standards because of disillusionment with standards in many schools – I should not be surprised if the Labour Party goes in that direction in the next ten years – or there will be more parental choice, which in itself will monitor schools.'

My prophecy of national standards and parental choice as future themes was correct, but I did not expect that both would eventually become distinctive features of Conservative policy and that the Labour Party would simply be a brake on their development. This is probably one of the major reasons for the long years in opposition of the Labour Party.

Sydney Irving, Labour MP for Dartford, followed me and said: 'I am glad to follow the hon. Member for Brent North [Dr Boyson] who has been a controversial figure in education. He held himself very well in hand this morning, making a highly competent maiden speech in the best tradition of the House, which I think we all heard with great interest.'

After listening to other speeches I travelled up to Cheshire, where I was speaking at a dinner, and rose early in the morning to read the following in the *Daily Telegraph*'s Peterborough column, presumably written by the redoubtable Bill Deedes, still then a Conservative Member of Parliament, and under the heading 'With honours': 'Dr Rhodes Boyson will have got a good degree from his examiners, certainly a First, for his maiden speech to the House of Commons yesterday. . . .' No piece of print in any newspaper has ever given me such pleasure.

I was also fortunate at the time of my entry to the House of Commons to be one of the two lead speakers in Robin Day's *Sunday Debate* for three consecutive Sunday evenings on the subject of children and discipline. Life was very good.

Two months later, on 1 May, I spoke again in the House at greater length. Again I referred to highly specialized schools in the Communist bloc and then said: 'It is a tragedy that the comprehensive school in this country became, at a certain point of time, a political issue. It does not naturally belong to either the Left or the Right. . . . But the comprehensive school has been accepted by one side and has become almost a dogma, a doctrinaire or millennialistic system. . . . I cannot accept, after two thousand years of education, that a new method for the education of children has been discovered which is far different from and better than the previous system.'

I warned the Labour Party that in London and other big cities the comprehensive schools were not giving a grammar school education to more pupils, but they were 'becoming non-academic schools'. I also warned the Labour Party that 'The neighbourhood ghetto schools will deprive the working-class child much more than he has been deprived since state education came in in 1876.' I was also aware that the Conservative Party had no clear policy on comprehensive schools and added: 'I think it must be said that on the Conservative side we have never had a policy for comprehensive schools. It really seemed that they were all right if they happened slowly.'

I compared the people who were destroying good schools through forced secondary school reorganizations to those who destroyed stained glass at the time of the Reformation and I again appealed to the Labour party 'to move to a system involving more parental choice of schools'.

On 5 July 1974 I said: 'I also believe that there are more ways of educating children than in school. At the moment there are more women teachers outside our schools than in them. Many children could be taught at home as well as in school if we laid down standards which were to be achieved at certain ages. We might see the blossoming of a fourth television channel devoted purely to education in the home for those who preferred home tuition to that available at school.'

In the short Parliament of 1974 I also asked for a full enquiry into the sixteen- and eighteen-year-old achievements of children before and after comprehensive reorganization and the standards of eleven-year-olds under both systems, since the 11-plus test undoubtedly raised academic standards in the junior schools.

In the summer of 1974 I visited Israel for the first time with an all-party delegation and joined the Mont Pelerin Society at its annual conference that year in Brussels. I was fascinated by Israel and honoured to join the Mont Pelerin Society, whose members included Professor Hayek and Milton Friedman. Again this was through the influence of Ralph Harris of the Institute of Economic Affairs.

Soon we had, on 10 October, the second general election of the year and the return of the Labour Party with a very narrow working majority. I fought this election on the evils of inflation (then running at 20 per cent), law and order, and again the saving of the green areas of Wembley. I believe that we would have won the second 1974 general election if we had come out for capital punishment for murder after the Guildford bombings of 5 October that year, then attributed to the IRA.

By now I had also become involved in a number of local issues, including the right of patients to choose their own doctor. Some two thousand patients of one sick doctor strongly wished his substitute of three months to be appointed to succeed him, but the Brent and Harrow Area Practitioners Committee decreed otherwise. For months I fought for the patients' choice of doctor as I have always fought for the parental choice of school, but in this case we lost. I am sure it was my involvement in local issues that caused me to be the only Conservative in the ninety-two seats in Greater London who had a swing to him – however small – in the October election, compared with the February results. The 10th October results were:

119

Dr Rhodes Boyson	(Conservative)	24,853
Mr James Goudie	(Labour)	17,541
Mr Fred Harrison	(Liberal)	8,158
Mrs J. Cattanch	(National Front)	1,297
Conservative majority		7,312

Later that month my book *Oversubscribed: The Story of Highbury Grove* was published on the very day that the governors of Highbury Grove appointed Laurie Norcross to succeed me. I was also asked to review my own book in the *Daily Telegraph* – a rare privilege indeed. The book had other interesting reviews. Tim Devlin in *The Times* compared Highbury Grove with another Islington school, Risinghill, and wrote: 'If Risinghill is paradise lost so Highbury Grove is paradise regained.'

The review I liked most was in *The Times Educational Supplement* of 8 November 1974, by Tom Howarth, the high master of St Paul's School and father of Alan Howarth, who would become one of my parliamentary private secretaries in the House of Commons. Tom Howarth wrote:

As I read Dr Rhodes Boyson's *Oversubscribed: The Story of Highbury Grove* I felt a growing conviction that years and years ago I had heard exactly this tone of voice. The brisk, no nonsense style, the hatred of cant and bureaucracy, the phrase 'completely useless', the passion for tabulation, the fearless employment of the first person singular, the burning conviction of rightness, the virtue of making everything 'perfectly clear', the need for the head to be seen frequently in the classroom front line, the emphasis on leadership – this is the authentic voice of Monty in his early days, an equally controversial and criticised figure.

Tom Howarth had been a senior officer serving on the staff of General Montgomery in the Second World War. After visiting my school Tom had earlier written: '. . . he runs it with Napoleonic mastery'.

The first printing of my book soon sold out and a second edition was then issued.

17

Immersion in Parliament

*

From the time of my return to Parliament after the October general election I was fully involved in the life and activities there and enjoyed almost every moment I spent at the Commons. I attended and usually spoke at the weekly meetings of the Conservative Education Committee and was elected its vice-chairman, the chairman being whoever was the Opposition number one spokesman in education. This was Norman St John Stevas, who had replaced William Van Straubenzee in the summer before the general election. I had found myself in regular disagreement with Mr Van Straubenzee and I suspect he considered me at least partially responsible for his replacement.

The major question being asked by Conservatives in the new Parliament was, would Edward Heath remain the leader of the party? We had now lost under his leadership three out of four general elections – a record a soccer manager, let alone a party leader, would find difficult to justify. We had lost thirty-four Conservative seats in the February 1974 general election and another twenty in the October election.

The Executive of the 1922 Committee soon found themselves at odds with Mr Heath regarding the future leadership of the party, which they believed should now be an open question. Kenneth Lewis is reported to have asked at the 1 November meeting of the full 1922 Committee whether the leadership of the party was a freehold or a leasehold and a hunting season was open. The 1922 Committee showed clearly that while it was the job of the whips to support the leadership, it was an essential feature of the 1922 Committee to ensure the leadership was fully aware of back-bench feelings.

I was a humble foot soldier in this war of succession. Initially I favoured Sir Keith Joseph, whom I had known for some years, though I doubted if he had the right temperament for party leadership. I then worked for Mrs Thatcher. I simply wanted Mr Heath replaced. So did many others. Some opposed Mr Heath on ideological grounds, opposing prices and incomes and such policies, while others wanted him replaced because they thought he would never again have the full voting support of the British public, and the Conservative Party does believe in being in government. I had met Margaret Thatcher on a number of occasions since she had visited Highbury Grove in 1970 and made a very good impression even on staff and pupils who disagreed with her (and me) on comprehensive schools. Her work on housing and mortgages as the Conservative environment spokesperson before the October election had been impressive and attractive, but she really made her mark in the new Parliament in her work on finance.

After the October 1974 election Mr Heath had appointed Margaret Thatcher as number two on finance, and the Finance Bill was going through Parliament at the time of the leadership election. She was outstanding. I remember her verbal battle with Denis Healey on 21 and 22 January 1975. It was the first time I had heard the Conservative benches in full cry. She showed her mastery of facts, her political skills and her tremendous courage. Mr Heath had handed Margaret Thatcher a powerful weapon when he made her a finance spokesperson. She showed clearly that she could draw blood from the Opposition and that she had firm views on what Conservative policy should be.

I admired Airey Neave's campaign for Margaret. It was almost as skilful as his legendary escape from Colditz and his organization of Allied prisoners' escape routes from Europe. He was everywhere and heard everything. He had attained minor office when Mr Heath was Chief Whip, and then he had a mild heart attack and had to resign. According to the 1975 and 1978 biographies of Margaret Thatcher by Russell Lewis and Patrick Cosgrave, Mr Heath is alleged to have said to him, 'Well, that's the end of your political career.' Airey recovered and from that day plotted the fall of Mr Heath. Never make gratuitous enemies in life!

Airey Neave concentrated his attention on those who, for one reason or another, disliked Mr Heath either on personal or policy grounds. He also talked with others who, while not necessarily wishing to replace Mr Heath as leader, wanted to teach him a lesson and hoped that he would not win by too big a majority. To keep the latter members on his side, Airey regularly underestimated in public the number of Thatcher supporters. He spun a web around those who wanted Mr Heath defeated on the first ballot so that Willie Whitelaw could cruise to victory on the second. Airey's plans worked. On the first ballot Margaret Thatcher scored 130, Edward Heath 119 and Hugh Fraser 11. On the second ballot Margaret Thatcher scored 146, Willie Whitelaw 79, Geoffrey Howe 19, James Prior 19 and John Peyton 11. The face of British politics was to be changed at least for fifteen years.

On 17 April Brian Cox and I published the fourth *Black Paper*. In one week it became the sixth best-selling paperback, a first for an educational book. Some twenty thousand copies were sold in advance of publication. In our letter to MPs and parents at the beginning of the book we wrote: 'Five years have elapsed since *Black Paper* Three and it is again time to survey the educational scene. Expenditure has further increased, the pupil-teacher ratio has fallen, teacher training has lengthened, the school-leaving age has been raised, there are more in higher education; it is doubtful if there has been any advance in real terms.' We advocated national tests at seven, eleven and fourteen. We wrote:

The seven plus examination should cover literacy and numeracy and pupils should be expected to pass such a test before they proceeded to junior school. The eleven and fourteen plus tests should also cover a body of minimum geographical, historical, scientific and literary knowledge. Teachers could teach beyond these basic syllabuses and could introduce other subjects; but such syllabuses would ensure that all schools offered a reasonable education, which is not now the case.

We also advocated the introduction of 'specialist schools in science, languages and other subjects' and trials 'with the educational voucher', and welcomed the Conservative commitment to the election of parents as governors.

A further suggestion we made was that mini-schools, as in San José, California, should be introduced into the very large comprehensive schools, with specific courses for the basic three Rs, for fine arts and advanced mathematics and many other specialities. On higher education, we advocated quality before quantity with a new basic matriculation standard for entry of seven subjects at credit standard in the 'O' level examination including mathematics, a science and a foreign language.

This *Black Paper* again had weighty contributors, including Kingsley Amis, Professor of Education Geoffrey Bantock, Jacques Barzun, Ronald Butt, Robert Conquest, Professor Hans Eysenck, Bernice Martin and Iris Murdoch. We said at the press conference that launched the book that it would take twenty years to put British education right after the damage done to it by the academic and political trendies.

A second leader in the *Daily Telegraph* warmly commended the publication. *The Times* had a first leader with a clever heading, 'Black Mark for Progressives'. *The Guardian* wrote: 'A best-seller on education – and that is what *Black Paper 1975* is – cannot be ignored'; and the *Financial Times* commented: 'The time has surely come when the *Black Paper* argument must either be refuted, or else admitted.' Norman St John Stevas wrote in the *Catholic Herald*:

The *Black Paper* in particular offers a fundamental challenge to the educational orthodoxies which for so long have held undisputed possession of the field and about which there is now widespread doubt. I myself would not go along with all the proposals put forward in the *Black Paper*, but I think it is a healthy sign that there should be an alternative view on education and I hope it will lead to a general and independent debate.

In a Commons debate on 29 January 1975 I said: 'The problems are two-fold. One is the decline of an understood curriculum, by which teachers knew what they were doing in schools. . . . The second is the change in teaching methods in many cases which have not been checked before being spread like a fever throughout the country.' I added: 'The [discovery] method, so-called, is not as successful with the average teacher as the traditional method. The top 10 per cent of teachers succeed with any method and can excite children. The bottom 5 per cent would have a riot with a dead rabbit. In between the other 85 per cent can basically teach well in a structure in which they know what they are doing but not in which the curriculum has gone and the timetable has gone.'

In the same speech I again advocated more parental choice and power in education. I said: 'I believe that 95 per cent of parents are concerned about their children.... Families and parents now want a say in how their children are being educated, a matter which is basic to them. I believe that they are sufficiently mature to be able to do this. If not, we must have wasted a hundred years of state education.'

During a speech from the floor at the Blackpool Conservative Party Conference on 7 October 1975 I said: 'In the present situation the worst 30 per cent of the schools were the worst seen in England for a hundred years. Going to these schools was as destructive to the children as it had been for the chimney boys during the Industrial Revolution. Parental choice would not make all schools equal, but it would result in the closing of the bad schools and would strengthen the free society.'

On 27 November 1975 came the murder by the IRA of Ross McWhirter. Norris, Ross and I joined the Royal Navy on the same day and were boy seamen together at the land and sea training ship HMS *Ganges*. We met again in the 1960s, and Ross and I were both directors of the Churchill Press and the Constitutional Book Club. We met often – indeed, he was in my home two days before his murder. He was shot because he offered a £50,000 reward to anyone who provided information leading to the arrest and conviction of a terrorist for murder. His offer arose from a conversation with members of the French Resistance in the Second World War who maintained that very many Allied cells in France were broken by financial reward.

I was at a meeting at Brent town hall on the night of the murder. Florette telephoned me and I immediately went home. Alas, he was already dead. I appealed to the Government to double the £50,000 reward and take the terrorists on at their own game. The Labour Government refused. I also asked for a referendum on the return of the death penalty, a request in which I was supported by Margaret Thatcher. On the night of the murder I went on programme after programme on radio and television to advocate the death penalty for terrorism. It was the least I could do for Ross's memory. Roy Jenkins, the Home Secretary, said in the House of Commons the day after the murder: 'I have no respect for softness in present circumstances. I have no sympathy whatsoever with those who commit these bestial crimes. If they were shot in the act I would have no sympathy with them of any sort at all.' Yet he refused to bring back capital punishment.

I wrote in a letter to *The Times* on 3 December,

I feel that I must comment upon the statement of Mr Roy Jenkins on the murder of Ross McWhirter. He made this last Friday in the House of Commons.

The Home Secretary said, after indicating that he still was an abolitionist on capital punishment, 'I have no sympathy whatsoever with those who commit these bestial crimes. If they were shot in the act I would have no sympathy with them of any sort at all.'

Does this mean that while, according to Mr Jenkins, we cannot rely upon the State to revenge the deaths of law-abiding citizens by the return of the death penalty, yet if we carry a gun to shoot to kill against terrorist attacks we are good citizens?

It is such statements from abolitionists which will bring gun law, private armies and lynching into our streets and it is no wonder that the Police Federation itself has been moved to attempt to influence public opinion towards a firmer stand on law and order.

I prefer the rule of law enforced by the State, and it is the so-called permissives and abolitionists who will, according to Mr Jenkins's statement, cause its breakdown.

David Waddington was, in my understanding, the only home secretary of recent years who has supported capital punishment, and he was soon shunted off to Bermuda and we lost the Ribble by-election – which led to the replacement of Mrs Thatcher. The permissive lobby is certainly highly effective still in Britain! Indeed, I have no doubt that the so-called liberal establishment has in every field in my time increased the agony suffered by the law-abiding and brought the virtual collapse of law and order in parts of our society.

I was in 1975 one of the eleven, led by Ralph Harris, including Margaret Thatcher, Odette Hallowes and Norris McWhirter, who then set up the Ross McWhirter Foundation for the preservation of law and order. One of the others was Ross's MP, Anthony Berry, who was later to be killed in the Brighton bombing.

On 16 December there was a memorial service for Ross at St

Paul's Cathedral. Airey Neave, who was sitting near me, was also to be a victim of the IRA. The address was given by Lord De L'Isle, VC.

Three months later I revisited HMS *Ganges* with Norris McWhirter, just before it shut down. We saw the famous mast again and the covered way. How different it was from our first visit when we were run in at the double by a petty officer. This time we put Norris's car on the quarterdeck and were met by the captain. Times had indeed changed.

On 4 February 1976 there was the second reading debate on Labour's Bill to abolish all selection in secondary education and to end the direct grant schools which had been so successful. To my surprise and delight I received a note the previous week from the Chief Whip asking me to wind up from the front bench for the party at the end of the debate. I well remember that week's 1922 Committee meeting when the Whip read out the subject and front-bench speakers – Mr St John Stevas and Dr Rhodes Boyson. I would be front bench for a day before returning, like Cinderella, at the stroke of midnight to my previous condition.

I pointed out in this second reading debate that the Plowden Report concluded that, next to the academic ability of the pupil, the most important factor in his or her schooling success was the degree of parental involvement.

I learnt a great deal about parliamentary procedure in the thirty-five long sessions of the committee stage of this Education Bill – the longest time any Education Bill had spent in committee. I made clear my views on comprehensive schools in the committee. I said on 13 February 1976: 'My attitude is that we are not pro or anti any type of school. We are concerned with which system is likely to be more successful. We do not wish to be dogmatic.' The following day I quoted that 20 per cent of our intake to universities and 35 per cent of the total entry to higher education came from children from working-class background – the highest in Europe, as Mrs Shirley Williams herself had quoted in 1968. I added on 4 March: 'I sometimes wonder whether, when social historians write the history of our times . . . they will say that the only successful form of reverse discrimination was the 11 plus within our grammar schools.'

On 27 April, towards the end of the committee stage of the

Bill, I advocated that, as in Denmark, if sixty-nine parents wished to set up their own school, they should be entitled to be funded at the level of government funding which was given to all state schools.

At the report stage of the Bill I moved two new clauses. The first was that all schools should have to publish their GCE 'O' and 'A' and CSE results, their annual staff turnover and their literacy rates, and for secondary schools where their leavers went: to jobs, to further and higher education or to unemployment. Even more significantly, on choice of school the second new clause stated: 'On request from a local education authority the Secretary of State shall authorise the establishment of a schools voucher scheme devised and run by the local authority in question, on an experimental basis, for a period of time agreed by the Secretary of State and the authority. During this period of time the Secretary of State shall monitor the results of such an experimental scheme.' Peter Morrison, then MP for Chester and later the last PPS to Margaret Thatcher as Prime Minister, seconded the clause.

I argued that the voucher would fulfil four objects: it would get rid of the worst schools, it would strengthen the family, it would increase the variety of schools and it would improve general educational standards. I said: 'The voucher is a means of increasing the choice and control of schools by parents. This is the way in which the education system should go.'

I also suggested that, as in the United States, the voucher could be worth more in downtown areas, so that schools competed for deprived children instead of turning them down.

Margaret Jackson, Labour's Parliamentary Under-Secretary of State for Education and Science, quoted Mr Heath: 'The voucher system needs to be examined with a healthy degree of scepticism.' Nigel Forman was the only Conservative to abstain, while Mr Heath voted in favour, but the clause was lost by 303 to 266 votes.

Meanwhile, in April 1976, came the publication of the Bennett Report, which showed clearly the superiority of structured as against informal education in the primary school. Entitled *Teaching Styles and Pupil Progress*, it was an examination, under the direction of Dr Neville Bennett of Lancaster University over four years, of teaching styles in hundreds of Lancashire primary schools. The research showed clearly that formal classroom methods involving good class control, the teaching of subjects separately and using marks, grades and even punishments put children four to five months ahead in mathematics and two to three months ahead in English, compared with pupils taught by informal methods. An even more interesting conclusion of the Bennett Report was that pupils taught in formal classes were less anxious than those in informal classes.

In 1976 James Callaghan replaced Harold Wilson as Prime Minister. James Callaghan was always a man who had his ear to the ground. He decided that the Labour Party should recognize that Labour's existing educational policies were not vote winners for parents and the public. He used the opportunity of a stone-laying ceremony at Ruskin College, Oxford, on 18 October that year, to express his concern. He said: 'It is not my intention to become enmeshed in such problems as to whether there should be a basic curriculum with universal standards – although I am inclined to think that there should be. . . . To the teachers I would say that you must satisfy parents and industry that what you are doing meets their requirements and the needs of their children. There is no virtue in producing socially well-adjusted members of society who are unemployed because they do not have the skills. . . . I do not join those who paint a lurid picture of educational decline because I do not believe it genuinely true, although there are exceptions which give cause for concern.'

In the following months the Labour Government organized a series of conferences on education and Shirley Williams issued a green paper. This was a great disappointment. It began reasonably: 'There are legitimate grounds for criticism and concern. . . . A small minority of schools have simply failed to provide an adequate education by modern standards.' It added: 'The child-centred approach has deteriorated into lack of order and application.' Then it deteriorated. It affirmed that 'The comprehensive school is at the centre of the Government's policy on secondary education', and went on to throw doubt on the continuance of the GCE 'O' and 'A' level examinations.

I concluded an article in *The Spectator* on 24 September on this Labour green paper: 'The Green Paper does not live up to the promise of Mr Callaghan's Ruskin College speech. The end-of-year report could read, "A welcome return to the three Rs. Yet it is too dogmatic in approach and too self-opinionated in social subjects. Must do much better to live up to last year's promise."'

On Friday 19 November 1976 I was having lunch at home with Florette and two constituents when the telephone rang from Mrs Thatcher's office asking me to see her early that evening. I was then offered the number two slot in education in Mrs Thatcher's reshuffle of that day. Perhaps she felt Mr Callaghan was threatening to steal the Conservative education clothes and we needed a more robust educational policy.

Ronald Butt wrote in *The Sunday Times* of 21 November: 'Dr Rhodes Boyson ... is a remarkable figure whose arrival on the front bench is something of an event. Dr Boyson has an unflagging physical and intellectual energy, with a capacity to fill holes and an instinct for identifying the minds of ordinary people.'

I had a real problem that weekend. I had sent out earlier on the Friday morning a press release on the National Health Service for a speech I was to deliver on the Saturday evening. It was thus embargoed until late Saturday. In the speech I made clear that I considered that a National Health Service would never work, since demand would always exceed supply even if 105 per cent of the gross national product was spent on health. Such a speech from a front-bencher – especially one who had only just arrived – could cause widespread press comment and would be a gift to the Labour Party. What should I do? The views I expressed were the ones I believed and I certainly would not deny them. I thus decided to do nothing and feared I would have the shortest front-bench career in recorded history!

On the Saturday morning I was rung by Walter Terry, who drew my attention to the speech and to my Friday appointment to the front bench, suggesting that he should ring his press friends and ask for my press release to be ignored. I agreed and the Sunday papers carried no report. The press is often maligned, sometimes justifiably, but it was very kind to me on this occasion, unless of course it had already made up its mind that nobody would believe such a press release from a Tory front-bencher and would consider it a spoof.

Norman St John Stevas is alleged to have said on my appointment as his deputy that two dervishes could not perform on one mat. It was a splendid remark which I wish I had thought of first. Norman is very bright, learned, witty, industrious and artistically inclined. However, our temperaments are quite different. We also had a different educational emphasis: Norman was concerned for educational excellence, which he understands and fully appreciates. I was most concerned about the betrayal of the bright working-class child in a comprehensive school in the middle of one of our cities.

On 26 November *The Times Educational Supplement* reported my reaction to my new post to be 'characteristically succinct'. It quoted me as saying, 'Some people go into politics because they want office and some because they want to influence events.' I was reported also as saying, 'I don't care if I'm at the back of the party or the front of the party as long as things go the right way.' I added that I wanted 'nationally enforced standards at seven, 11 and 14 – not just talk about them'.

Before I was promoted to the front bench, I had already agreed with Brian Cox to co-edit another *Black Paper*. I explained this to Norman. This came out in 1977 as the last of the *Black Papers*. Patrick Moore, Max Beloff, Richard Lynn, John Marks and Caroline Cox were among the contributors. We welcomed the Ruskin College speech of Mr Callaghan and quoted *The Times Educational Supplement* that he had 'gathered his *Black Paper* cloak around him', but regretted that few if any in the Labour Party had followed his example. Advisers and colleges of education still trained teachers on the lines of the Plowden Report that 'finding out' was better than 'being told', as if these were alternatives. We also advocated that new teaching methods should be tried only in specially designated experimental schools which parents specifically agreed their children should attend.

This *Black Paper* also carried an article by Dolly Walker on the William Tyndale School, which had been one of my feed schools at Highbury Grove. Everything good and bad seems to happen educationally in the Islington area. This school was taken over by the trendies who totally fulfilled the chaotic informal methods advocated in many teacher training establishments. The working-class parents took their children away, reducing the roll from 213 to 96 in two years, and there was a special enquiry into the school. Children at this school were considered according to an internal notice to have 'inalienable rights – to do as they like, to learn or not to learn; to decide for themselves what to do and where to go . . . to hold no deference to authority and indeed to challenge it'. No wonder our society shows every sign of breaking up.

The *Black Paper* also again advocated that children should be allowed to leave school at the age of fifteen if they passed suitable leaving tests and had jobs to go to. Many newspapers commented upon this proposal, pointing out that it was Mrs Thatcher who raised the school-leaving age to sixteen. The *Daily Express* had the heading, 'Rebel Boyson Risks Sack from Maggie'. No message, however, came from No. 10! I have always considered that an early-leaving scheme for less academic pupils who attend school regularly, pass a basic literacy, numeracy and general knowledge test and have a job to go to would ensure that such pupils would have a higher academic standard at fifteen than they have now at sixteen. We give such non-academic pupils a five-year sentence with no remission for good conduct. We thus have tens of thousands of pupils playing truant from the age of fourteen to sixteen, living on the fringe of society and acquiring bad habits for life.

I had opposed the Schools Council since it was first set up in 1965. If an institution is established to suggest changes, it will continue to do so to justify its existence whether such changes are necessary or not. The fact that in its humanities project it considered the writings of Fidel Castro to be suitable for fourteen-year-olds made it, to use a left-wing phrase, 'an enemy of the people' as far as I was concerned. On 21 July I accused the Schools Council of what St Paul accused the Athenians: that they worshipped all things new.

There was also continued Schools Council and Labour pressure for one 16-plus examination. I still favoured three levels of examination, with overlapping grades. The first would be the GCE 'O' level examination for the top 40 per cent academically, the second the Certificate of Secondary Education for the next 40 per cent, and thirdly the bottom 20 per cent should have a new basic skills and knowledge certificate.

In 1978 Shirley Williams accepted the Waddell Report Committee proposal that there should be a seven-grade leaving certificate for the top 70 per cent, and she expected this to be introduced by 1985. Once again the lower ability pupils were ignored. Norman St John Stevas opposed this recommendation as reckless folly and a triumph of egalitarian doctrine over educational values. He later said that he was not opposed to a single system of 16-plus examination, but the progress towards it should be gradual and organic. Fortunately both Norman and I opposed the proposal to replace the 'A' level GCE gold standard examination by the suggested Ns and Fs.

I also opposed the introduction of sixth form colleges, except for a number of experimental ones. I considered that potential scholars needed the influence of skilled sixth form teachers in the middle school, that sixth forms were a training-ground in social responsibility, and I was very suspicious of non-academic sixth forms, believing these pupils should be in further education and technical colleges. I once said that the only advantage of non-academic sixth formers was to increase considerably the salary of the heads and senior staff because of the formula on which these salaries were based.

In 1977 I stated 'that to attract the non-academic sixth former coffee bars have replaced subject libraries and the bright lights of the noisy common room have replaced candlelight study'.

I did my share, while in opposition, of going round the university circuit preaching the merits of the free society. I became expert in dodging bags of flour and other missiles and I still have 'Boycott Boyson' posters from Goldsmiths College, supposedly one of our most distinguished teacher training institutions. One sentence of the poster I agreed with: my political views would generate a climate of intolerance which was not conducive to the development of progressive education!

Since religion has always been one of my main interests, I took part in a debate on religious education in the House of Commons on 19 March 1976. I gave two particular reasons for the justification of religious education in schools. First, more people worshipped in churches on Sundays than played football on Saturdays, so if sport was taught in schools, so should religious education. Second, I quoted from the Durham Report: 'Religious education is essential because we in England are heirs to the cultural tradition of the West. Christian faith is so interwoven with our history, art, music and literature that it would not be possible to teach these subjects in schools without some teaching about religious education.' I added: 'I think with sadness one must say that there is a lack of firm belief in the Churches themselves. Mass revolutions are made by the treason of the clerks and not by those always knocking on the door to come in. Many of our Churches, and some of our leaders, have turned the Churches into a sort of Rotary Club without the good dinners. They do not think in the sense of the propagation of the faith. If religious education dies, to my mind the Churches will have been more responsible than the National Foundation for Educational Research or the humanists and the do-gooders.'

133

Economically I always opposed government subsidies and wished to cut back the share of the national product going to government. I believed in small government but with full enforcement in the areas for which it was responsible. On 21 May 1975 I voted against any government financial assistance to British Leyland. I referred to the 'inverted funnel syndrome' whereby the more money was given to a company by government, the more money would then have to be poured in on the excuse of safeguarding the original government investment. I illustrated my speech by talking about my grandmother's mangle – a large two-cylinder machine used to squeeze water out of textiles after washing. I said: 'I remember as a boy my Grandmother had a mangle. I trust that right hon. and hon. Members know what a mangle is. . . . It was explained to me that the mangle turned only one way, and if my finger was put into it the only way to get out was by continually turning the mangle until I had gone right through. That basically is what we are doing now with the money. . . . Once turned in one direction it will never come back.'

How right I was. The joke was, however, that I was informed that the Labour minister replying had to have explained to him what a mangle was!

On 10 March 1978 I took part in a Commons debate on Labour's economic policies. I said: 'I do not believe that economic decisions are better made by 20 people in Westminster and Whitehall whichever side of the House they come from. Such people pay no penalty for the failure of their economic plans.' In this same speech I contended that it was a pity that the Labour Party had not lost the 1964 general election, which they nearly did. If they had done so it was very probable that, like the Social Democrats in Germany in the Bad Godesberg Declaration, they would have earlier accepted the economic free market provided there was fair and genuine competition.

In May 1978 my book *Centre Forward: A Radical Conservative Programme* was published by Temple Smith. In it I outlined a policy for the next Conservative Government of full-scale denationalization, lower government expenditure, the end of all trade-union privileges, floating the pound, lower taxation and the strengthening of law and order. The last two pages outlined a seven day re-creation of Britain programme as follows:

Day one, taxes would be reduced for all, with a top rate of
50 per cent. Day two, a declaration that government
expenditure would be cut by 5 per cent a year in real terms
each year of the five-year term of government. Day three, the
statutory monopoly of the nationalised industries would be
ended and existing nationalised industries would be both
offered for sale and opened to internal and international
competition. Day four, all exchange controls would be
repealed and a pledge made to let the pound continue to
find its own level. Day five would see the announcement
that the present welfare state would give way to a system of
topping up individual spending power by money or specific
vouchers to put the consumer in charge of all the welfare
services. Day six, increase police pay and numbers and
declare war on crime and the moral pollution of our cities.
Day seven, rest like the Creator and stroll in our gardens
apart from attending the funerals of socialist suicides for
whose widows we must care.

The cover of the book said 'It is not a bland book.' No one
ever called it one. The title derived from a conversation I had at
dinner at the Oxford Union before a debate. My game is soccer,
then even more than it is now a populist game, and the centre
forward was the 'striker' who scored goals. One of the young
men with whom I had dinner suggested the title. I liked it: it
was short and succinct. I also thought it would be a clever bal-
ancer to Sir Ian Gilmour's book *Inside Right*, published the previous year. I considered my views were the views of the majority
of the British public, especially those of the working classes. The
title of my book, however, was a mistake and confused people.
A simple, straightforward book should have had a simple, straightforward title.

Reviews of the book were many and varied. *The Times* headed
a long leader 'The Colossus of Rhodes' ending: 'Dr Boyson speaks
with a headmaster's confidence that his arguments are simple
commonsense and will be seen as such by all but stubborn dunces.
Should this not be the national Tory style?' A *Daily Express* leader
stated: '*Centre Forward* is a sharp-tongued attack on the idea of
the usual limp consensus.' Arthur Seldon, editorial director of
the Institute of Economic Affairs, stated that I was an 'intellectual
populist', while *The Sun* gave it a half-page review under the

heading 'Crack-shot Boyson Goes for Gold'. Hugo Young wrote a long review in *The Sunday Times* headed 'Vote Boyson and Make the World Flat' which began:

> Most Conservatives are smooth men, but Dr Rhodes Boyson is a hairy man. Mr St John Stevas is a very smooth man and, bringing out his razor, has fashioned a joke about dear Rhodes: he calls him the Colossus. What Dr Boyson calls Mr Stevas is not recorded, but it is probably like most of the things Dr Boyson says: blunt, impatient and imbued with astonishment at the failure of anyone else in the world to see that he, the great unbarbered Boyson, is right.

The following month, jumping up a number of steps at the House of Commons, I seriously damaged my left Achilles tendon and was in desperate pain for two months and in steady pain for another four. It was a time when I possibly made a number of misjudgements. One should be careful of making judgements when one is racked by pain.

In June my book was chosen for a Foyles luncheon by Christina Foyle, who had always been helpful and kind to me. My friend, Norris McWhirter, was in the chair and Lord Longford was to move the vote of thanks. I took as my theme my views on law and order as given in the book. My views might be acceptable to the audience, but they were anathema to Lord Longford, and Norris had to control a very bitter and public argument between Lord Longford and myself which reached the columns of the press the following day.

For almost two years I worked as number two to Norman St John Stevas. I enjoyed his wit and his scholarship. He opened debates and I closed them. We must have been a formidable pair, what Shirley Williams called 'the heavenly twins'. A minor war, however, broke out in September 1977 when I returned from a visit with Florette to Taiwan.

In Manchester the county secondary schools had become comprehensive in the middle 1960s, while the voluntary religious secondary schools, largely Catholic, remained bipartite, so one could compare over a number of years the improvement or deterioration of the two systems. Raymond Baldwin, a fine statistician and chairman of Manchester Grammar School governors as well as being a member of the Manchester City Education Committee, disclosed these comparative results in *The Times* of 20 July 1974, under the heading, 'Fall in Exam Standards in Comprehensive Schools' and commented: 'It was dynamite in the present battle between Conservatives and Labour in the country at large.' Baldwin released the 1975 figures in *The Times Educational Supplement* and sent the following year's figures to me. These showed a further deterioration in academic results in the county comprehensive schools compared with the voluntary bipartite schools.

I had referred to the Manchester City secondary school results in a speech to the National Council for Educational Standards as early as 9 November 1974. I referred to them again in a speech on the second reading of Labour's Education Bill on 4 February 1976, and asked an oral question regarding them on 8 June that year. The *Daily Telegraph* had published the comparative results of the Manchester schools on 22 July 1975, commenting: 'A-level examination results at a city's comprehensive school ... show a disturbing fall in standards.'

Twice in 1977 I again quoted the Manchester results. On 11 March I stated that between 1964 and 1976 the number of 'O' level passes in the county comprehensive schools in Manchester had risen by 44 per cent as against a 390 per cent increase in the bipartite voluntary schools. At 'A' level the increase was 12.5 per cent in the comprehensive schools as against 300 per cent in the bipartite voluntary schools.

All my life I have believed that parents should have full information on schools, including their examination results, so that they can make meaningful choices for their children. I do not like secret gardens. From the beginning of the move to comprehensive schools I regularly asked for comparative results at 'O' and 'A' levels before and after secondary school reorganization. As an ex-working-class boy myself, I have always been concerned about what happens to academically gifted working-class boys in downtown areas after reorganization. I was supported in the request for such information by Professor Brian Cox, Fred Naylor and Raymond Baldwin.

In 1978 I was given the detailed 'A' level results for all Manchester county comprehensive schools and the voluntary bipartite schools and Brian Cox suggested that I should disclose these at a Conference of the National Council for Educational Standards which we were having in London on Sunday 17 September, at the Pembroke Hotel. Since I had regularly referred to the Manchester results, I saw nothing exceptional in such a disclosure.

I pegged my comments on the 1978 'A' level Manchester results to the proposed Labour Government's Freedom of Information Bill, pointing out that Mrs Shirley Williams, the Labour Secretary of State for Education and Science, 'with the connivance of Labour-controlled educational authorities supports one of the biggest cover-ups in Britain – the refusal to publish the results of comprehensive schools for fear of the public reaction when they see the dismal failure of many comprehensive schools and the betrayal of the educational opportunities of very many able working-class children'. I then went on to compare the 'A' level results of Manchester's Labour-controlled comprehensive schools, which had been comprehensive since 1966–7, with those of Conservative-controlled Trafford, which were still bipartite. One Manchester comprehensive school in a middle-class area had 200 'A' level passes in 1978, while sixteen of the other 26 comprehensive schools had fewer than 30 single 'A' level passes each. Four of these schools had fewer than 10 single subject passes and another five had 10 or 11 passes. I continued: 'It is clear that there is total inequality of opportunity in Manchester's comprehensive schools. This particularly affects the working-class child who is often sent to schools with appalling academic attainments in which he will find little or no encouragement from his peers for serious study.' I accepted that there was a difference in socio-economic groups in the populations of Manchester and Trafford and between catchment areas in Manchester itself, but the comprehensive school had been introduced with the promise of giving better opportunities for working-class children, not to lessen their opportunities. It seemed to me that the comprehensive schools had been sold on a false prospectus.

I continued in my press release: 'Parents with bright or even average children should refuse in Manchester to send their children to the nine schools with 11 or less 'A' level passes.' After calling for the publication of all individual school examination results I ended with this challenge: 'If Shirley Williams and the Labour Party are not prepared to do this then we shall know that she and the Labour Party do not care a fig for academic standards and equal opportunity and social mobility, but prefer to condemn working-class children to inferior education so as to create Labour rotten boroughs in the middle of our cities. This would be a sad but true reflection.'

That Sunday must have had little or no other news, for all the Monday papers prominently featured my speech, the *Daily Mail*, the *Daily Express* and the *Yorkshire Post* also giving it sympathetic leading articles. From early Monday morning I was asked to appear on numerous television programmes and to speak regularly on radio on the subject of my speech.

Norman St John Stevas rang me, but I had already left. The Chief Whip rang and I sent round to him a copy of my speech. Many others, including Conservative MPs, rang to compliment me on the speech.

For a week the controversy continued, with news items and leading articles. The *Daily Mail* heading was 'Disaster Results of the All-in Schools'. One *Daily Express* article was headed 'The Schools That Fail', *The Times* had a heading 'Results in Comprehensive Schools Covered Up to Hide Betrayal of Opportunities', and the *Daily Telegraph* had one heading ' "A" Level Results Prove Grammar School Is Best'.

The Times of 19 April under the heading 'Mr Boyson's Remarks "Monstrous" Critic Says' wrote: 'Mr Boyson's critics have not explained, however, why the number of 'A' level passes in Manchester schools fell from 1,423 just before reorganisation to 999 last year.' In the second leader on the same day *The Times* stated: 'There appear to have been fewer 'A' level passes in Manchester after reorganisation.' The *Daily Telegraph* the same day headed its second leader 'Dr Boyson Unanswered'. Meanwhile I continued to appear on the media to defend and expound my views.

Not surprisingly I was savagely attacked by the teacher unions, by Labour leaders of education committees and rather more surprisingly by the Conservative chairman of the Association of County Council Education Committees and the Conservative chairman of the Association of Municipal Authorities Education Committees. I was defended by Manchester Tories and the Conservative leader of ILEA and by a huge post-bag of letters from parents. I had, not entirely innocently, pointed out that the emperor had no clothes and it seemed that the mass of parents were already recognizing this.

It had not even occurred to me that what I said was not party policy, whatever that policy was. I had regularly said it before. I realize I must have been a difficult number two to Norman St

John Stevas. I am a good number one in taking total charge of what is happening and gaining people's co-operation, I am a good sergeant or petty officer, but my temperament is not ideal for a number two. I had also joined Parliament not for office but to fight for the policies in which I believed, and I made this regularly known.

On 22 September *The Times Educational Supplement* defended the need for the publication of examination results under the heading 'No Reason to Withhold Information'. It added: 'Dr Boyson was unrepentant this week. The argument that the statistics might be misinterpreted was phoney, he said. Do we not look at public opinion polls in politics or publish balance sheets? People had a right to know what their schools were really like.'

On the same day Norman St John Stevas gave a speech to his Chelmsford constituency executive to clarify his views on the publication of examination results. He supported personal choice of school and accepted that parents must have access to their schools' examination results, which should be in the school prospectus. He added, however, that 'we do not favour the publication of league tables of results: we want to see the results placed in their appropriate social setting and in the context of the school and its problems'.

Norman St John Stevas's statement was attacked the following day by the *Daily Telegraph* in a first leader under the heading 'A Right to Know', 'as it epitomises the rationale of the non-competitive society'. The *Sunday Telegraph* of 24 September carried the statement, which I gave to all the press who rang me that weekend: 'I joined the Conservative Party and became an MP to fight the Labour Party and the collectivist take-over of the country and I shall continue to do so.'

On 25 September the *Financial Times*, under a heading 'Bid to Damp Down Stevas–Boyson School Examinations Row', wrote: 'The Conservatives were busy last night trying to diffuse another embarrassing split on education, this time over publication of examination results between Mr Norman St John Stevas and his rumbustious Number Two Dr Rhodes Boyson.' The next day the *Daily Express* gave a whole page to an article by George Gale under the heading 'Let the Exams Be The Test', and I even appeared in the Peter Simple column of the *Daily Telegraph*.

By then a *modus vivendi* had been arranged. Norman St John Stevas and I should issue joint statements, the first of which came out on 30 September in reply to an HMI report when we advocated regular national tests in the three Rs in infant and junior schools.

On 22 November I was attending a lunch at *Punch* when the Chief Whip rang and informed me that Norman had been appointed Shadow Leader of the House and that Mark Carlisle had replaced him and 'they' wished me to continue as the number two. I was disappointed not to have been appointed number one but realized the circumstances were unpropitious, to say the least.

The three-legged race between Norman and myself was now over and we went our separate ways. Mark Carlisle immediately invited me to a meal and I worked with him most amicably for two and a half years. We came from different wings of the party and we often disagreed, but always amicably, and agreed a joint conclusion. Mark was always very kind to me and I know that he later tried to have me promoted to the Home Office – not to get rid of me but because he thought I would be of more use to the Government there, as far as public opinion was concerned.

Mark Carlisle, in a speech in his constituency on 3 February 1979, said: 'There is no educational evidence for Mrs Williams' repeated and dogmatic assertion that comprehensives are the best available type of school. Figures published this week by Raymond Baldwin, member of the Manchester Education Committee, appear to show that the exam results at both "O" and "A" level achieved by children in Manchester City which has gone comprehensive are considerably inferior to those in nearby Tameside, which has kept its selective form of education. As he points out, these areas are reasonably compatible in social terms.'

So one chapter of controversy was ended, but it probably did me harm as far as political preferment, since other Shadow Cabinet and later Cabinet members probably thought that I was very difficult to work with.

The last months of the 1978–9 Parliament saw me heavily involved in opposing Labour's 1978 Education Bill. It was as if Mr Callaghan's 1976 speech had never happened. When I wound up at the second reading debate on 5 December I opposed Labour's plans for 'planned admission' limits for every school, since this would allow local education authorities to control the intake of all schools, ignore parental choice and practise social engineering.

I also advocated in the second reading debate that each school should prepare an annual balance sheet of their achievements over the previous year to be discussed by parents at a specially called annual meeting. The Bill was still in committee when the Labour Government fell on 28 March 1979.

The committee stage of the Bill, however, allowed me to raise issues of local parental choice of school. Before the disastrous Conservative London Government reorganization of 1964, Wembley's education was controlled by Middlesex County Council and schools were built throughout the county for the maximum convenience of pupils irrespective of the borough in which they lived. Brent and Harrow, under the 1964 reorganization, became separate education authorities, which meant for instance that a junior school could be in Harrow while the secondary school linked with it could be in Brent. Parents had thus to ask their new local education authorities for permission to send their sons and daughters to the nearest school if this was in another borough. Without permission the host borough would not take such children because there was no guarantee that the other borough would cover the cost of their education. Thus children could be forced to attend a school much further away from home simply because it was in the borough in which he or she lived after the reorganization.

There was a natural tendency for boroughs to keep all their children 'at home' wherever they lived. As far back as 1974 I had raised this matter with Reg Prentice when he was the Secretary of State for Education. I saw the Labour minister in charge of the 1978 Bill privately on this matter and I raised it regularly in the standing committee on the Education Bill. Here was a major issue of parental choice that I would be able to take up when, as I hoped, we had won the next general election. Why not give all parents freedom to send their children to whatever school they wished if there were vacancies there and if the parents were prepared to pay the travel costs?

I could claim to be the man who brought the Labour Government down on 28 March 1979. The date of the confidence vote was the date of the Ross McWhirter Foundation annual dinner. As a trustee I, along with other Conservative MPs, wished to be there but the whips said 'No'. The guest of honour, however, was Jo Grimond, the ex-Liberal leader, and his vote was required to bring the Government down. The whips then agreed that I and two other Conservative MPs could go along provided I guaranteed to return with Jo Grimond and my colleagues before the 10 p.m. vote. I thus went with Florette as the 'outside whip' and arranged for three large chauffeur-driven cars to be outside Haberdasher's Livery Hall where the dinner was to be held, at 9.30 p.m. One car should have been enough, but I dared not risk one or two breakdowns.

Jo Grimond spoke well and I had the greatest difficulty in catching his eye to ensure we were back before 10 p.m. I decided that I never wanted to be a whip!

I voted and sat behind the Opposition front bench to wait for the result. The whips said it was too close to call. When the Conservative whip stood on the Speaker's left to read the result, we knew we had won. We actually won by one vote and the House erupted on our side as the duty whip gave the score to the Speaker, while the Government side looked shell-shocked.

I met Florette and others in the central lobby and we went to Ian Gow's house for drinks and then home. Now for the election and, we trusted, victory. Ironically, it was while the 1976 Education Bill was in committee that Mr Wilson resigned as Prime Minister and was followed by Mr Callaghan. Now we had Labour's second Education Bill and we had a general election. I concluded that education bills were very dangerous.

My mother died early in 1979. She had continued living in the same house that my parents had had built in 1934 and had proudly done much of her own housework. We, of course, had asked her to come to London, but she remained active at home and people could check their watches every day against the time she passed their houses on her one-mile walk round the town centre. She fell off a chair dusting one of Father's bookcases and was taken to Rossendale General Hospital, where she died within a fortnight. The doctors said that she was worn out. I went up to visit her regularly and I was with her when she died, with my second daughter Diana and her husband. She knew she was dying but stayed alive until I arrived from Manchester, when she smiled and closed her eyes, confident in her religious faith and the Resurrection.

I came out of the hospital and looked across the valley to Grant's Tower in Ramsbottom, where the Grants had stood when they came from Scotland. They decided in biblical terms to pitch their tents there – in normal terms they decided to build their works below that spot. This moment is written up as the Brothers Cheeryble in *Nicholas Nickleby*. I stood now on the hills at the other side of the valley and by the hospital, which was the old workhouse about which I had written. I knew I was leaving the valley and a great sadness came over me. Mother's funeral was in her beloved Methodist church and it was the end of an era. Haslingden, the place that made me, with its nineteenth-century social and religious values, was no longer my home. I now belonged to Wembley and London.

18

Higher Education Minister

*

The 1979 general election was very exciting. I had feared the previous autumn that the Labour Party would still be returned to
power. Mr Callaghan, however, teased the British electorate with
the possibility of an election at that time, when it seemed that
the Labour Party had a real chance of retaining power. Indeed, I
was so convinced – as were many other people – we would have
a general election, that I arranged to change the day I was lectur-
ing at the Mont Pelerin Conference in Hong Kong to earlier in
the week so that I could be back in London for the Saturday,
which would be the date of my readoption meeting if an election
was announced. Florette and I were thus a couple of thousand
miles on our way home when the pilot informed his passengers
that Mr Callaghan had told the British electorate that there would
not be an autumn election. He had certainly fooled me.

The winter of 1978–9 was one of severe discontent with strikes,
disorder and concern on all sides and I became convinced that
the Conservative Party would now move into government whenever an election was called and that I had every chance of becoming a minister. I spoke all round the country that winter and
canvassed hard in my constituency and on the night of the general election attended my count. Brent is, for no justifiable reason, one of the slowest counts in the country and we learnt that
we would have a Conservative Government long before the Brent
result was announced at 3 a.m. that morning. A car had been
waiting for three hours outside Brent Town Hall to take me to

the television studio to comment upon the election results. The Brent North vote was:

Dr R. Boyson	(Conservative)	29,995
Mr J. Lebor	(Labour)	18,612
Mr A. Ketteringdam	(Liberal)	5,872
Mr G. John	(National Front)	873
Conservative majority		11,383

My vote had risen from 47.9 per cent of the poll to 53.8 per cent. Labour took 0.1 per cent more of the poll than in October 1974, the Liberal vote fell from 15.7 per cent to 10.6 per cent, and the National Front poll fell from 2.5 per cent to 1.6 per cent. The local paper heading was 'Boyson Romps Home for a Top Tory Job'.

There followed almost three days of silence before the telephone rang. I did go out on the Sunday afternoon to an event in my constituency, where everybody seemed as concerned as I was as to whether I would have a post in the new government. Mrs Thatcher rang on the Sunday evening asking me to be a Parliamentary Under-Secretary at the Department of Education and Science. I had hoped to be a minister of state and I was slightly disappointed and asked who the other ministers were. Mark Carlisle would be the Secretary of State, Baroness Young was the Minister of State and Neil Macfarlane was to be the other Parliamentary Under-Secretary of State. Ralph Harris was disappointed that I was not appointed to an economics ministry. He thought my background would have been ideal for the Employment Department. It is also never an advantage to be in a ministry where the current prime minister has served.

Early the following morning my private secretary rang from the Department and asked me when I wished to be picked up. 'Immediately,' I replied, and the ministerial car was on its way taking me to my office and to meet my personal staff. Later I met Mark Carlisle and the Permanent Secretary of the Department. A decision had already been made that I should take responsibility for higher education, while Lady Young would cover schools and Neil Macfarlane further education and science. I felt that I was being marginalized and that the Department did not want me in schools. With hindsight, however, I can see that Lady Young, who was the Minister of State and with whom I worked very well, might have made her preference for schools clear when she first saw Mark Carlisle. However, I was disappointed and I said I would consider the matter until the morning and talk again. Politics is less predictable than school-mastering.

That first evening I saw my chairman, George Boobyer, with his wife Betty, and George made clear that he wanted me to be a minister – any ministry, even of frogs and tadpoles – and so did my party workers. That was it. Brent North had chosen and sup-ported me and on this I must support them. I informed Mark Carlisle the following morning that I would take the responsibil-ity for higher education.

Recently I turned up a cutting from the *Sunday Telegraph* of 13 May 1979, written by the late Patrick Hutber. It states:

> I am delighted that for all his outspokenness, Dr Rhodes Boyson has safely finished up inside the Department of Education. It has to be admitted that when Norman St John Stevas was Shadow Minister of Education his relationship with Dr Boyson, then his deputy, was not without its colourful side and, one suspects, the occasional strain.
>
> My happiest memory in this respect comes from the previous year's Tory Conference at Brighton. I was standing in the middle of the foyer of the main conference hotel talking to Dr Boyson when Mr St John Stevas appeared in the hotel doorway. He rushed towards us crying 'Rhodes, we must have a conversation' and then, without pausing for a second passed straight by, climbed into the lift and disappeared.
>
> Rhodes watched him go and then said thoughtfully, 'I suppose that was the conversation. You know, it was the longest talk we've had all year.'

Education, the journal of the local educational authorities, com-mented:

> Dr. Rhodes Boyson, MP for Brent North, whose birthday it is today, will not be showered with presents by the LEAs. His championship of educational vouchers and the publication of

examination results have caused the local authorities to be wary of him to say the least. The critical stance he adopted towards administrators in his recent book *Centre Forward* and his call for a £1,000 m. cuts in education a couple of years ago have not enhanced his reputation with the LEAs.

I have, however, still got the June 1979 edition of *Pipilon*, the student paper of the Polytechnic of North London, then fairly notorious, which has a full front-page photograph of me with a conclusion inside: 'All in all the appointment does not bode well for institutions such as ours.' This article included an apocryphal story of how at Highbury Grove I maintained discipline: '... he extracted a false white Father Christmas beard from his desk, donned it and said, "See how you have aged me, boys. Go and sin no more"'. I wish I had thought of doing this!

The *British Student* newspaper called me on 18 May 1979 'the notorious student-hater'.

Then in June the *National Student* wrote:

Worried student union leaders heard through the grapevine that the Education Secretary Mark Carlisle ... had given him [Dr Rhodes Boyson] the job to keep him away from the school system. ... His apparent contempt for student unions and avowed intention to stop Britain becoming a semi-Communist slum island ... combined with a predilection for loans as opposed to grants and a wish to see students sign good behaviour pledges before being admitted to a course did not make him a particularly favourite appointment with students.

My views on universities and higher education have always been clear: I would give generous scholarships to the most able students to study whatever they liked to keep and extend learning, while making the majority of students take full-price, interest-free loans which would ensure that they studied subjects which society required so that they would be able to take jobs to repay their loans when they left higher education.

We were in financial crisis in 1979 and I was prepared to make and support cuts immediately and met my officials on this matter as soon as I joined the Department. The area chosen was overseas students, one that proved highly controversial with the established university community. The number of foreign students in Britain had increased rapidly from 29,000 in 1967–8 to 87,000 in 1977, some 20,000 of whom were in non-advanced courses. These students were heavily subsidized by the British taxpayer.

Anthony Crosland, as Secretary of State for Education and Science in the 1966–70 Labour Government, had levied a differential higher fee for foreign students from the academic year 1967–8. Between that year and 1979 this differential fee was increased five times, four times by a Labour Government, but the number of foreign students continued to increase. In 1976–7 the Labour Government increased the foreign fee by 30 per cent, yet 11 per cent more foreign students enrolled. The following year the fee was put up by another 60 per cent yet 4 per cent more enrolled and the Labour Party then fixed a quota for foreign students which itself was exceeded.

In 1975 the Committee of Vice-Chancellors had itself suggested that fees for overseas post-graduate students should be raised further to discourage our economic rivals from sending students to this country to be trained cheaply so that they could compete more effectively against us later in world markets. I was well aware that some 20–25 per cent of foreign students came from countries with a higher standard of living than Britain, and that many of the others came from families abroad whose incomes would far exceed that of the average British family. The four countries sending most foreign students to Britain were Malaysia, Iran, Iraq and the United States, countries not without considerable financial resources. It is also of interest that three out of these four countries have had, to say the least, poor relationships with Britain over recent years despite the claim that the reception of foreign students helps economic and political relations. This blanket subvention from the British public to foreign students seemed to me to be totally unjust to those British taxpayers who were not privileged to have a university education themselves. I thus declared that I did not believe that the British taxpayer should continue to be the milch cow of the world.

As a first step in 1979 we increased the fees for overseas students by one-third and from 1980 we charged economic fees for the appropriate courses. In 1979 there was a fall of 8.5 per cent in the number of new foreign students enrolled, followed by a fall of 7.5 per cent the following year, but the number enrolled was still more than the quota fixed by the Labour Party for that year. There were still well over three applications per student enrolled and to my mind the British first degree was, and still is, because of its short length and generous staffing ratio, probably the best buy in first degree courses anywhere in the world.

At the same time as we introduced economic fees we set up the (Boyson) bursaries which would fully fund 1,500 able overseas post-graduates at a cost of £3 million a year, and we gave £800,000 to the universities to cover hardship cases among overseas students. Many other students would also continue to be funded by the British Council and through overseas aid.

The London School of Economics and the new City University immediately used their initiatives and recruited far more overseas students at economic fees and used the system to their advantage.

Surprisingly, I had a fairly good press. *The Economist* of 22 September 1979, commented: '. . . the case for increasing fees, apparently to cover costs, is a good one on economic as well as educational grounds'. *The Observer* of 12 October the following year under the heading 'Boyson Beats Dons' defended our decision.

Yet the Labour Party, in its usual cowboys-and-Indians attitude to British politics, opposed the changes, as did the Liberal Party.

I was, however, totally astonished by the great and often unpleasant opposition I received from parts of the university establishment, which had long vision to see any injustice abroad while having no consideration for the British taxpayer at home. The ivory towers shook with uncontrolled anger at the restrictions on their doing good with other people's money. Anthony Bottomley, Professor of Economics at Bradford University, described the university state of mind at that time in a paper he sent to me:

> In an engaging letter to *The Times* . . . the Master of Balliol
> and others pointed out how unreasonable it is for Dr. Boyson
> and his average taxpayer to deny them and their
> undergraduates the society of as many interesting foreigners
> as they may care to invite. Needless to say, no mention was
> made of how these eminent academics might, in their turn,

try to put their own house in order or otherwise question the undoubted quality of their own lives in order to help pay for foreign students who are so essential to such cultural development.

While this fracas was on I went to speak one evening at the Oxford Union. Word spread in the university and crowds had gathered in the streets and I had to be taken in by a police escort. Everyone – dons, students, including some foreign students – wanted to talk about foreign student fees with a degree of blind prejudice I have rarely encountered. It was a wasted evening, with no finesse, humour or sense of proportion.

I had made it clear from the beginning that I believed that universities should exist for the preservation and extension of learning, while the polytechnics should exist for the training of the technically qualified graduates needed in commerce, industry and government. In an article I wrote in *The Guardian* I even questioned whether we could in Britain afford to fund forty-five universities to remain in the world league and asked whether, like many of our soccer teams, they would fall below world standard. I queried whether some of the universities should not just become teaching institutions. The continuance of a staff-student ratio of 1:9.3 in universities and of 1:8.5 in polytechnics – the lowest in the world – would obviously have to be looked at. Lord Todd himself said in his presidential address to the British Association in 1970: 'I do not believe that this type of university education is appropriate for such a large proportion of the age group.'

Anthony Crosland had seen the polytechnics as providing an ever-increasing number of 'vocational, professional and industrial-based courses'. Yet in 1979–80 65 per cent of full-time students in polytechnics and 83 per cent of part-time students were reading arts and social sciences. This was a much higher proportion than the 49.6 per cent reading arts and social sciences in the universities. I certainly became alarmed when I found that the Social Science Research Council was funding 200 doctoral students in sociology and 230 in planning. I was also concerned about the growth of 'liberal arts courses', some of which seemed frivolous in nature.

I also found that only 59 per cent of sociology doctorate students completed their research within six years and only 10 per cent completed their research in the normal three years. I had completed a doctorate in four years while I was working as a headmaster of a large comprehensive school, so this information did not endear the subject or its students to me!

There had been a rapid increase in the 1970s in all fields of higher education. I did not want to reverse this trend, but to keep the numbers the same while we examined whether the courses were the ones we needed both for the preservation of learning and for the needs of our society.

As far back as 1969 the Labour Party had, when Shirley Williams was a minister in the Education Department, prepared a paper called 'University Development in the 1970s' which discussed loans, students living at home and made many other suggestions which would control the level of higher education expenditure.

The press continued to be far more sympathetic to my endeavours than the university establishment. The *Weekly Education Review* wrote on 30 August 1979: 'Yet if we really face a choice between Robbins and Boyson, can there be any doubt that Boyson must win. If he treads softly, he might find friends in unexpected places.' By temperament, however, I do not tread softly, nor did I particularly welcome the action of one university Association of University Teachers which sent me a wreath of deadly nightshade!

Nevertheless from the time that I arrived at the Department I made contact with all representative bodies, including the Association of University Teachers and the National Union of Students. The first lunch I had with the senior officials of the Association of University Teachers was at the Charing Cross Hotel, then still owned by British Railways. All was sweetness and light until we reached the sweet and cheese course. I am always a cheese man, strongly preferring British cheeses. This time, however, I was brought a selection of fifteen cheeses – all non-British. I immediately sent for the *maître d'hôtel*, questioned him as to whether the British taxpayer was the owner of the hotel and the subsidizer of it and then asked him why he was not serving British cheeses and said that I would sit there until he found a selection of such cheeses for me. The conversation regarding the future of the universities then came to an end amid a degree of embarrassment amongst the AUT officers, some of whom found that they had urgent engagements elsewhere. I stayed until they brought me between six and eight British cheeses for my choice. I wondered whether there was something in common in the attitude of the university establishment to foreign students and the Charing Cross Hotel's attitude to British cheeses!

Long-term, however, I reached a reasonable and indeed pleasant relationship with the Association of University Teachers, and after we reached one pay settlement the general secretary wrote to me: 'Having reached a pay settlement, I am writing to express my appreciation of the work you did to make this possible.... You can rest assured that we are aware of your part in helping to resolve a difficult situation.'

I also developed a 'respectful' relationship with the two National Union of Students presidents I met regularly – Trevor Phillips, now a noted television star whose brother attended Highbury Grove, and David Aaronovitch, then a Communist but also, like myself, a Manchester history graduate. David was reported in the press as saying 'I am a fan of him [Dr Boyson] in a personal sense, we have a number of things in common.... The bloke is very forthcoming and blunt and these are the qualities which are lacking today.' Before his re-election as president in 1981 David was even attacked by a delegate as wanting to live 'in a cosy world drinking tea with Dr Boyson'.

On 5 January 1980 I addressed 600 delegates of the NUS and spoke firmly in defence of the Conservative Government's policies. I said I wanted no defence cuts and: 'I will differ from many of you here that I have no desire to become part of the Russian colonial empire.' I also said in reference to overseas students 'to keep the doors open to all-comers at the present subsidized fees is out of the question'. I made clear that 'The politics of some student unions, of sit-ins, academic disruption and demonstrations will do absolutely nothing to help the student image.'

At this meeting Trevor Phillips exercised his authority against a minority of interruptors and he wrote to me later: 'I think that all but a small minority of the delegates found it an interesting and stimulating session; and the small minority privately felt the same secretly, but their peculiar brand of politics prevents them from admitting it.... I think that you bore the flames admirably and, whilst not agreeing with all that you said, gave as good as you got.'

I tried to help the National Union of Students on the prompt payment of grants and on welfare services and met them regularly. I also made it clear that I wanted the replacement of the parental contribution, if necessary by loans. *The Guardian* reported in March 1981: 'Tee-shirts have been swapped for ties and jackets. Jeans are out for the regular visits the NUS leaders make to the Department of Education and Science for their meetings with Dr Rhodes Boyson.' I also kept close contact with the officers of the Federation of Conservative Students.

I have always been sceptical of the funding of university sabbatical officers. In 1979 there were 170 funded by student unions, probably a higher figure than the number of Conservative agents in the country.

In December 1980 the Plymouth Polytechnic had, without inviting me, a 'Rhodes to Ruin' Dance and the 1980 NUS Conference passed two resolutions against the votes of most of the national executive that: (a) Rhodes Boyson hates students, and (b) In the words of John Cooper Clark 'If work was any good the rich'd do it.'

I continued to consider, however, that something had to be done about the spiralling costs of student unions. Every year the decision as to the amount that was paid per student to the student union was made by the head of the university institution and the president of the local union. This was a formula for continued increases, since it was the local authorities who then had to pay the fixed fees and this system was criticized by the Public Accounts Committee in 1978 for its 'open-endedness'. We thus changed the system from 1981 to one in which the amount of student union subvention was charged to the higher education budget for each institution so that the amount going to the student union came from its own allocated fund. This made higher education institutions much more responsible, since the more the student union received, the less could be spent on other university activities.

I did suffer a number of serious student union disturbances. The worst was at King's College, London, when a hundred students from the London School of Economics broke up a Conservative meeting I was addressing and police had to be called. Fortunately, most of the medical students from King's College, who wished to question me regarding medical grants, fought back gallantly against the yobbish intruders until the police arrived.

The other serious event was at Essex University, where I spoke in a hall with the curtains closed and my speech was regularly interrupted by another smashed window and a chanting crowd of students outside.

Compared with these two events, Bristol University was fun. I was attacked with a bag of flour, two tomatoes and an egg, all of which I avoided, and the egg (hard-boiled) was cleanly caught by the chairman and kept by him as a memento of the meeting. A letter I received from the chairman afterwards congratulated me on 'calmly continuing answering a student's question whilst you dodged the missiles which were the culmination of boos, hisses and constant interruptions'.

The Observer considered at that time that I was 'as popular as Attila the Hun'. I thought that a slight exaggeration. I was certainly the main character in a three-page Christmas story in *The Times Educational Supplement* of 19 December 1980, in a take-off of Scrooge.

From the time I arrived in the Department I turned my mind to how we could introduce a loan system for higher and further education students. I thought and think that paying (or borrowing) one's way through college is part of the work ethic itself. The compulsory parental contribution had to be paid by some 76 per cent of parents and was deeply resented by many of them. Some 7 per cent of parents refused to pay any of it at all, and since it was not legally compulsory, such students could not go on to higher education. Many of the other parents did not pay the full amount. I considered that it is not tenable to allow people to marry and have sex at sixteen, to vote at eighteen and yet to make university students automatically dependent on their families until the age of twenty-five, if they go on to higher education. The only exception to this was if a student had maintained himself for three years, but this was a long break from the educational cycle.

I visited the United States and Canada and saw ministers, officials, university administrators, students and banks to see how the loan system worked there. I also visited Sweden and modelled the report for the Cabinet sub-committee largely on the Swedish pattern. People had some twenty years to pay back their loans; they paid nothing back in the years in which they earned below the average income; and there were also bonuses for quick repayment and the interest rate was kept low. The fact that no one paid anything back until they earned the average income ended the negative dowry argument – that a husband would have to pay for his wife's back loan if she were at home with a child. I was also impressed that a higher percentage of working-class children went to university in Sweden than in Britain.

I suggested that the student grant should remain but that the loan would replace the parental contribution and over a period of years would be increased to replace also part of the grant element. I thought this would be popular in the country. This would, however, save government money only in the long run. Indeed, the replacement of the parental contribution would have cost the Treasury £100 million in the first year.

Mark Carlisle was very supportive of the scheme I drew up, and the Federation of Conservative Students, then under right-wing leadership, was very enthusiastic, and the press was generally in favour of some form of a loan system. I then took the scheme to a Cabinet sub-committee. Mark Carlisle briefly introduced the topic and left the explanation to me. Sir Keith Joseph, Industry Secretary, who I had hoped would support my scheme, said nothing but looked at his watch. Lord Hailsham was very much against my scheme and within a few minutes it was consigned to the grave. Ah well, the end of another chapter. It could, however, have been helpful in creating the climate to allow the later introduction of the present loan system. But I was disappointed, as were the officers of my Department who had given me every support. I saw then and see now no equity in a system where the person who leaves school at the age of fifteen or sixteen has to subsidize the education of those going on to university, who can increase greatly their future income by way of their university degrees.

However, I was able to help the University of Buckingham, which had been formed largely through the efforts of Lord Harris. The Labour Party was suspicious of it and many parts of the educational establishment also considered it a cuckoo in the nest. Nevertheless, its licence had been accepted as the equivalent of a degree by many higher education institutions and we brought it within the grant system at a cost no greater than were the grants to students in the public universities. Its two-year intensive course is very attractive. The University of Buckingham is also very interesting because its capital cost per person was only half that of the new state universities, and its teaching costs are less than three-quarters of the average state university costs.

I have always been sympathetic to adult education. I remember as a child being taken to workers' education classes in politics, history and literature by my father during the school holidays. I knew what it meant to my father – books came before food.

Moreover, I had been a WEA youth lecturer when I left university. I thus, as a minister, supported adult education despite being described as a 'malevolent Triffid' at one adult education conference. I ensured that in 1980 we put up £500,000 additional government money in the Adult Literacy and Basic Skills Unit.

As for the Open University, I originally opposed it, believing it to be a Labour Party gimmick. Bit by bit, however, I changed my mind when I saw the dedication of the students and how economic such courses were compared with residential university degree courses. As the higher education minister I regularly visited the Open University, attended a couple of its summer schools and talked to students. I was also impressed by the fact that 49 per cent of the students were studying science, technology and mathematics courses.

I fought very hard in 1981 to keep down the increase in fees at the Open University and *Education* Column One paid tribute to my efforts: 'So this is by way of recording a vote of thanks to a man who clearly believes in pulling one's self up by one's bootlaces.'

In the same year I put a scheme to a Cabinet committee to offer part-time students of the Open University interest-free loans, but it was rejected by the Treasury. I received the following letter from the vice-chancellor of the Open University when, in September 1981, I gave up my higher education responsibility: 'I thought I should write to thank you for all your help while you were responsible for higher education, including the Open University. You may not have agreed with everything we put forward, but you always listened to our case and were as helpful as you could be in these difficult economic circumstances. Please accept our best wishes for the future.'

Two final points regarding the training of teachers. First, I find it quite farcical that in Britain teachers are allowed to teach any subject or any age of child irrespective of what they have studied and what their specific qualifications are in. I believe a teacher's certificate should, as do licences for heavy goods vehicle drivers, include restrictions, lay down what level and what subject a teacher should be able to teach. This is the case with most other countries. Yet if there had been such a rule at the time I joined teaching, I would not have got my first job as a head of department in a secondary school when I had actually trained for junior school teaching. There must, however, be exceptions to any rule! Second, I have always supported a general teaching council, about which Mrs Thatcher was far from enthusiastic, and a staff college to train staff for promotion.

One final point. I have always considered that no teacher should be appointed or promoted until the interviewing committee has seen him or her take a class. After all, a soccer manager never buys a player until he has seen him play. I remember to my discomfort a brilliant interview by a drama specialist, whom I appointed, and the only dramatic event he ever achieved was at his interview! Put him with pupils and one had an unintended bear garden in every lesson.

19

In Charge of Schools

*

Dramatic changes at the Department of Education and Science left me the sole surviving minister in September 1981. At my own request, however, I moved to take the responsibility for schools. Sir Keith Joseph became Secretary of State, Paul Channon moved in as Minister of State responsible for the arts, Bill Shelton came in in charge of further education, and William Waldegrave took over higher education. I had hoped to be rated up to a full minister of state in the reshuffle, but Paul Channon's arrival meant that we already had one *in situ*.

I was sorry to see Mark Carlisle go. He was good to work with and genuinely concerned for educational standards. Nevertheless Sir Keith brought a breath of fresh air intellectually into the Department, and ministerial meetings became rather like post-graduate seminars. Bill Shelton and Paul Channon were excellent colleagues and Bill, with his intellectual honesty, immediately decided that there was not really a job in further education but it was a just reward for his work as the whip in Mrs Thatcher's leadership campaign. William knew higher education well and I had plenty to do in schools.

I have a copy of the long minute I quickly prepared for Sir Keith Joseph outlining the financial and educational choices in the Department. Finance could be saved by charging for nursery schools as recommended in the note of reservation in the Plowden Report. Loans for higher education costs could be introduced alongside generous grants for the most able scholars. Student grants themselves could be cut to cover home grants only, with the extra costs of studying away from home being carried by the students themselves. Uneconomic village schools could be subsidized by local residents up to average pupil costs in their counties. The Schools Council could be shut down.

Educationally, I wrote that I was still very suspicious of the GCE 'O' and CSE merger. Instead, I again suggested that there should be more overlap of grades and syllabuses between the two examinations so that pupils could easily transfer from one to the other. In addition, I advocated a leaving certificate examination for the bottom 20 per cent ability groups who, to my mind, were, and are still, the most neglected group in British school education. I also advocated externally marked basic tests for all pupils at seven, eleven and fourteen in English and arithmetic to ensure that all schools were doing their job properly.

I considered that selection of pupils by ability and interest should also be made acceptable again. We were suffering in education from egalitarianism not socialism. We could in the beginning return to partial selection on the Eastern European pattern, with schools specializing in languages, mathematics, science, arts – even sports.

On teacher training I recommended the B.Ed. should become a specific primary school qualification, while secondary school teachers should take a degree in the subject they intended to teach before they took their university post-graduate, one-year training.

Looking back at the list I must say it is a pity it was not accepted; certainly the British educational system would be now in a better state if it had been.

Although I had originally wished to have the schools portfolio in 1981 and was still very pleased to move to it, I soon realized that the climate of opinion in the schools part of the Department was totally different from what I had met in higher education. Officials would argue with me – quite rightly – in higher education, as on loans, but they would then accept my view and try to make it work once our internal debates were over. There was no rigid orthodoxy in higher education and when I, for instance, lost out on loans at the Cabinet sub-committee, some of my officials certainly seemed more upset than I was. They had loyally supported me even if they had originally held strong objections to my scheme.

In the schools section, there was an accepted official orthodoxy on almost every item. Comprehensive schools were the wave of the future, the Schools Council was an opinion leader and the one examination at the age of sixteen was considered inevitable. There was a departmental view on almost all issues that could be changed only with the firm, specific and continued backing of the Secretary of State. There was a continuous verbal battle between this branch of the Department and myself, with Sir Keith, as it were, chairing the fiery debate and often the next meeting starting from where we began at the previous meeting instead of where we ended.

I had first met what one could call the doctrinaire views of this part of the Department while I was still involved in higher education. A committee had been set up, chaired by Neil Macfarlane, comprising people from the Department and from local authorities, to consider the advantages of tertiary colleges as against sixth forms. After a year it became obvious that this committee was likely to report in favour of tertiary education – all the post-'O' level pupils should be in a tertiary or sixth form college.

The Guardian reported on 14 November 1980 that the report would conclude: 'We think that there are indeed powerful arguments in favour of educating 16–18 year olds in fairly large groups and are clear that a scatter of small sixth forms offering an inadequate range of options of indifferent quality at a high cost must be avoided. Thus in many areas sixth form or tertiary colleges may be the best solution both educationally and financially.'

I have always regarded the British sixth form as one of the glories of British education. It allowed us to have the shortest first degree course in the world and it trained sixth formers in leadership and maturity. I was particularly worried that the rigour of the academic sixth form would disappear in a mixed cultural sixth form or tertiary college.

I was joined in my reservations by Lady Young, the Minister of State in charge of schools, and we made our views known to the Secretary of State, the Permanent Secretary and indirectly to the Prime Minister, who I believe also expressed her doubts about tertiary education.

Three days after *The Guardian* report the committee gathered for what was intended to be the last meeting and the report was amended to give greater emphasis to the good work being done in many sixth forms. The emphasis of the report was toned down, but the concluding paragraph was still very much in favour of tertiary education: 'Some would say that educational merit, demography (i.e. falling pupil numbers in secondary schools) and financial constraints point inescapably to the adoption nationally of a break at 16.'

At a further meeting on 9 December another draft was discussed, and the publication of the report was delayed until 1981. The new draft stated: 'Many sixth forms have inevitably been set up in the belief that it is better to provide a separate institution specifically designed for the older adolescent student. They are seen by some as a preferred way to achieve the agreed objectives of academic standards and personal growth. We take no position on this.' This wording proved too bland and the committee took five hours redrafting it. The final version, agreed a week later, stated that sixth forms would continue in some areas, which implied that in other areas there would be a move to sixth form or tertiary colleges. The merits and demerits of both sixth forms and tertiary colleges were then noted. So is public policy made.

Watching this committee I knew in my own mind why I supported sixth forms. I do not believe that there is a need for a huge sixth form or a wide spread of subjects, which are certainly not required by higher education itself. The core sixth form subjects are English, history, geography, one or two foreign languages, Latin, mathematics, physics, chemistry, biology and two or three other subjects at the choice of the school. I considered my own sixth form experience very satisfying despite the fact that the upper and lower sixth numbered together less than thirty pupils, and indeed to save staffing the upper and the lower sixth were taught together.

School reorganization took up much of my time in my new post. There was a decline in pupil numbers and pressure to close the small village schools. This worried me, since I saw the village school as essential to the continuance of traditional British village life and feared its disappearance would be fatal to many villages. Unlike the Department, I did not believe that a one-teacher school with the occasional parent or village member coming in on their specialities was unviable, and later research supported my view. Two such schools were kept going by local money helping to pay for an extra teacher, until I was advised that this was illegal. I ignored this advice. One was a primary school in Oxfordshire, where parents and the village community pledged to raise two-thirds of the extra teacher's salary.

There was certainly increasing pressure from the growing number of Labour local authorities to complete secondary school reorganization. Most of these schemes were accepted, but some – like the Bacup and Rawtenstall Grammar School in my native valley – were saved. I spent some three half-days a week seeing delegations for and against comprehensive reorganization.

While I was in charge of higher education I also took full responsibility for taking the 1980 Education Act through the House of Commons. This allowed all parents to state a choice of school and to go to an appeals tribunal on which the local education authority had a majority of only one if they were refused their choice. The Act also stopped local education authorities cutting down the intake of popular schools. Parents were to be given full information by individual schools on all aspects of their life, including the form of discipline, examination results, internal course choices and what sports were played. In addition, parents could choose schools outside their local authority and, provided there were vacancies in such schools and their children were accepted, their local authority had automatically to pay the recoupment costs. The 1980 Education Act thus put schools into a market and was the real forerunner of the grant-maintained school.

This Act also brought in the assisted places scheme. The 1974–9 Labour Government had ended the direct grant schools – ladders of academic opportunity for so many children from poor homes. The Labour Party wanted a 100 per cent comprehensive system which, because of the low standards of many inner city schools, would condemn tens of thousands of children to full or semi-illiteracy and full or semi-innumeracy. The ex-direct grant schools had largely gone independent, with the exception of certain of the Catholic schools which had joined the state system.

The assisted places scheme is, to my mind, superior to the direct grant scheme, since it subsidizes the pupil and not the school, so that full or partial remission of fees goes only to pupils from economically poor families.

The scheme began in 1981 with the ex-direct grant schools and certain independent schools opting to accept such pupils. Originally we had envisaged some 15,000 pupils in each year group being aided, but because of the dire economic circumstances this number was cut back to some 5,500 a year. Indeed, I suspected that the Department did not like the scheme and thus tried to have it dropped. Originally the Department used the excuse that it would cause the Bill to be guillotined – which in my opinion would have to be done in any case because of the great difference between the Conservative, Labour and Liberal policies in the whole field of education. The extra cost of the scheme was only a net and not a total cost, since the assisted place pupils would have had otherwise to be totally funded in the state system and the cost of state education in many local authorities was for day pupils, already high, particularly in the cities.

The direct grant school scheme has been a great success, with four to five applications for every place. The income scale level allowed 30 per cent of parents to send their children to assisted places free, 43 per cent of parents would receive some help, while 27 per cent would still have to pay full fees. Only one-sixth of assisted-place pupils came from families whose income was 50 per cent above the national average. Pupils came from families in all walks of life: the children of bus-drivers, agricultural workers, postal workers, nurses, milkmen and the unemployed. The scheme opened the doors of some of the most academically distinguished schools in our country to able pupils from the least affluent homes. It was and is good value for money and also it is one of the few schemes of reverse discrimination that actually work.

I have always supported the educational voucher and I hoped, once Sir Keith became Secretary of State, that we could make progress in this direction. I had, however, invested in my previous post so much time and energy preparing a loan scheme which came to nothing that I made up my mind there was no point in spending endless hours in meetings on the voucher if it was not going to get anywhere.

Between 1979 and 1981 the voucher had been raised in parliamentary questions by a number of Conservative MPs. On 11 December 1979, in a written reply to a parliamentary question asking what plans the Government had 'to extend the voucher system in education', I replied: 'My right hon. and learned Friend [Mark Carlisle] has at present no plans to do so. He will watch with interest the progress made by the Kent education authority, which intends to mount trial voucher schemes in primary and secondary schools in the next few years.' In similar answers over the next two years there was a clear indication of little government or departmental enthusiasm for the voucher.

Sir Keith called an early meeting to discuss the educational voucher after taking up the reins of his Department. He said he was already tempted to see how open enrolment under the 1980

Act would increase parental choice before going further. I made clear that I considered that the voucher should be allowed to be used in the private sector only if it was for full cost. I felt strongly that, since private schools were in a market, they should be more efficient than state schools, and that if parents were allowed to top up the voucher in private schools, the whole scheme would be destroyed by the Labour Party claiming we had introduced the voucher only to save the independent schools and to subsidize the rich.

Sir Keith indicated his interest in the voucher at the 1981 Conservative Party Conference. He then stated on 29 October, in a parliamentary reply: 'The Government has long been committed to doing everything possible to advance parental choice and parental influence in our school system. . . . However, as I said at the recent Party Conference, I am intellectually attracted to the idea of eventually increasing parental power even further through a voucher system. . . . It is now for the advocates of such a possibility to study the real difficulties to see whether proposals can be developed to cope with them. There would be no question of more than an experiment in a limited area as a first step even if a practical scheme does arise.'

The Department drew up a 2,250-word submission on the difficulties of the voucher, which was replied to by Marjorie Selsdon's Fever (the Friends of the Educational Voucher in Representative Regions), by the National Council for Educational Standards and by fourteen distinguished scholars, including Professor Milton Friedman, Michael McCrum, the master of Corpus Christi College, Cambridge, and ex-headmaster of Eton, Professor Sugarman, Professor Coons and Lord Harris of High Cross. No departmental reply was given to these submissions.

I put in a paper in March 1982 on parental choice of schools as follows: 'I do not believe that we should limit our consideration of alternatives to state provision of education to the voucher scheme alone. The free society depends on alternatives being considered. This consideration must include the right of parents to set up their own schools as can be done in Denmark and Holland and other countries. . . .' I had visited such continental schools and sent minutes to Sir Keith describing them.

In February 1983 it was reported that a Cabinet committee under William Whitelaw had given the green light to the voucher despite the opposition of the Department of Education and Science.

Nothing happened, however, and after the general election of 1983 Sir Keith announced at the Conservative Party Conference that the voucher was dead. It was interesting that Margaret Thatcher revived it in her speech at the Conservative Conference in 1990, a few weeks before she fell! Is there a curse on the voucher? One thing is certain: the voucher was never full-hearted departmental policy.

It was ironic that the 1979 general election affected the future of Highbury Grove and again brought the school to national attention. The population of Islington was falling and, while Highbury Grove continued to be heavily oversubscribed, other schools were half empty. It was no surprise that ILEA decided that some form of closure or combination of schools in that area was necessary. ILEA was counting on the planned admission limits in Labour's 1979 Education Bill to control the intake of popular schools in the area, but this hope collapsed with the general election of 1979 and the fall of Labour's Education Bill.

I suspected that ILEA would take advantage of any reorganization to close Highbury Grove, with its traditional type of discipline and good academic results, which showed up the lack of achievement of other local schools that espoused the progressive philosophies which fitted the views of County Hall. When I was shown a report from one ILEA inspector involved with the Islington reorganization, my fears were substantiated. This report warned against the danger of attempting to assess the quality of a school since 'The quality of a school was ephemeral and notoriously difficult to measure' and he 'would discourage it as a basis on which to plan'!

ILEA was too crafty to suggest that Highbury Grove should just be closed. Instead it suggested that it should be combined with Philip Magnus School. These two schools had little in common in discipline, curriculum and organization, but if the two schools were combined, then all staff would have to be reappointed to the new school and Laurie Norcross and the senior staff of Highbury Grove would, to my mind, not be reappointed but made redundant and Highbury Grove would die. On 27 September 1979 ILEA issued a Section 13 notice to close Highbury Grove School in July 1982.

Yet once again the machinations of ILEA were defeated by the largely Labour governors and parents of Highbury Grove, who believed in the value of the school for their children. The press –

the fourth estate – was also of great help. The governors, the parents and the staff rejected the ILEA plan, and the governors and staff of Philip Magnus School similarly rejected the plan for its closure. A petition of almost 26,000 signatures was collected at Highbury Grove and over 600 pupils and parents marched on the Department of Education and Science, the staff being prohibited from taking part. The *Daily Telegraph* wrote that Mark Carlisle 'must step in to stop the madness' and it reported that 'leading Socialists and Liberals are now joining Conservative MPs in a behind-the-scenes battle to persuade ILEA to change its mind and keep open the highly successful Highbury Grove which Dr Boyson left five years ago'.

Christopher Booker wrote in defence of Highbury Grove in the *Daily Mail*. Ronald Butt in *The Times* commented that for ILEA Highbury Grove was the 'educational face' which 'doesn't fit' and added: 'What we have here is the blatant politicisation of education. To the ILEA it is a partisan matter because they are determined that though they want good academic results, they must always be subordinated to their over-riding wish for social engineering.'

Mrs Thatcher said in the House of Commons: 'The former headmaster, now Under-Secretary of State for Education and Science, has been one of the more successful headmasters of a comprehensive school. Many generations of children have cause to be grateful to him.' A friendly Labour MP warned Mrs Thatcher not to say anything to pre-empt a government decision on what was an extremely delicate matter, but the Prime Minister continued: 'Nothing will stop me from saying that a previous headmaster was an extremely good headmaster.'

I had already accepted earlier in the year an invitation to be the guest of honour and speaker at the Highbury Grove speech day of 1979. My nostalgia was heightened by the threat to the school and it was a very emotive evening, with all the pupils, parents and staff wearing badges 'Keep HG HG'. I said at the prize day: 'Local education authorities should not consider popular schools an embarrassment but an honour, and if some schools have to shut because of a fall in child population it should be unpopular schools.'

The *Daily Mirror* reported on 14 November: 'A HORRIBLE thing happened in the House of Commons on Guy Fawkes night. Rhodes Boyson, the Tories' junior Minister for Education, lost his temper. "The schools which Inner London are trying to keep open," he bellowed, "are in most cases the schools to which no one wants to go." "Name them," demanded Labour MPs. "I shall name one," said Boyson. "Islington Green had only two 'A' level passes that year from 800 children. That school is being kept open. A school nearby [Highbury Grove], with 40 'A' level passes is being closed."'

Apart from this emotional outburst, I took no part in the battle of Highbury Grove Act 3 other than putting forward an internal minute on the history of the school. I knew, however, that if the Secretary of State and the Minister of State decided to let the merger go ahead, I would have to resign as a minister. I did not mention this to them because it would have been too much like blackmail, but no other course was open to me. I had not entered politics and the House of Commons for office but because I had a set of views. Highbury Grove was the living embodiment of those views in education, and if a Conservative Government closed that school, I could not remain in that government.

As is my wont, I had been to a morning religious service in my constituency and I was preparing for lunch that Sunday when the telephone rang. It was Lady Young, who wanted to talk to me about Highbury Grove. My heart stood still – this is it! She quickly came to the point: the Department would not, on educational grounds, allow its closure.

The day the decision was announced there were educational questions in the House. Harry Greenway said: 'May I congratulate my hon. Friend on the Department's decision this morning regarding Highbury Grove School, which is a good decision about a good school.'

Laurie Norcross remained at Highbury Grove School until 1987, but he had to fight a continual battle against ILEA and left-wing parents and governors to preserve the standards of the school. He was warmly supported by the National Association of Schoolmasters/Union of Women Teachers. There should be a sequel to my *Oversubscribed: The Story of Highbury Grove*, charting its history since 1974 until the resignation of Laurie Norcross.

Once I was put in charge of schools, I tried to save other good secondary schools – grammar, secondary modern or comprehensive – when other reorganizations were put to me for recommendation to the Secretary of State. In this I was helped by Stuart Sexton as educational adviser, whose leg work round the country and whose considerable knowledge of education were invaluable to me. As an illustration, let me describe what happened on the Manchester reorganization.

In January 1981 Manchester published proposals to reorganize every secondary school in the city. Over the next ten months a war was waged with memos and counter-memos, meeting after meeting, private notes, public notes, even unofficial press briefing. The full battle order of the top civil servants was mustered against me. I was supported much of the time by Sir Keith, and Stuart Sexton and Fred Sylvester, MP, brought me information from Manchester.

Manchester's secondary schools had gone comprehensive some years earlier. With some exceptions, the old grammar schools continued as eleven to eighteen comprehensives – that is, retaining their sixth forms – while all the rest were eleven to sixteen comprehensives, with no sixth forms. Some of the sixth forms in the eleven to eighteen schools were still good, offering 'A' levels for university entrance and three of them had retained their full academic ethos. These three schools thus attracted the more academic pupils and therefore the numbers in their sixth forms pursuing 'A' levels held up better than the others. Two of these three more academic schools were also single sex schools, and this had an added attraction for parents wanting single sex education, notably the Muslim and Sikh population of Manchester.

However, there were too many secondary school places for the number of children and this surplus was projected to get worse as the years went by. The perceived poor quality of many of the schools was attributed to their having to waste money on surplus places. This, of course, was by no means the full story. The Manchester City Council also wanted 'open access' sixth forms; in other words, any pupil should be able to stay on into the sixth form regardless of aptitude or ability, not necessarily doing 'A' levels but to repeat 'O' levels or CSEs, or to do nothing in particular. The 'academic' schools were quite rightly not catering for these non-'A' level children. The current fashion was that children were adults at sixteen and ought to grow up in the more adult atmosphere of a mixed-sex egalitarian college in which 'A' levels were a minor concern.

So the Labour City Council proposed to close several schools, to lop off the sixth forms of all the eleven to eighteen schools and to create sixth form colleges in the premises of the closed schools. Such proposals had to be published by the local authority, two months elapsed for objections to be registered, and the Secretary of State then had to come to a decision. Not surprisingly the departmental officials recommended that the whole package should be approved.

At an early stage it became clear that the quality and popularity of most of the schools were poor and that for them the package of closures and amalgamations made sense. There was little point in trying to defend them. However, three schools, all in the south of Manchester, were good, very good in the terms of the rest of Manchester: Parrs Wood, Burnage and Whalley Range. The sixth forms at two other schools, Chorlton and Wilbraham, were also far better than others in Manchester and deserved retention.

The Secretary of State had powers to approve proposals, to reject or to approve with minor modification. It was soon evident to the departmental officials that Sir Keith was likely to approve the whole package, with the exception of the three 'good' schools, or possibly the five 'good' schools. All their efforts were therefore concentrated upon why he could not exempt these schools from the general reorganization.

The officials held that the schools were not full to capacity and provided figures to prove this. Therefore, argued the officials, these schools were not as popular as was claimed. However, Stuart Sexton came back with figures to show that the 'good' schools were actually oversubscribed, but that parents' choice had been refused by a strict zoning policy in order to reduce the numbers at the more popular schools and to boost the numbers at the failing schools.

The officials then said that the 'A' levels were nothing like as good as those in the best schools of the country. Stuart Sexton showed that they were still far better than those for the rest of Manchester.

The next argument was that the 'A' levels in the 'good' schools were so good that if these sixth forms were retained, they would deprive the proposed sixth form colleges of the necessary talent of sixteen- to eighteen-year-olds. The officials could not have it both ways: either they were good or they were not good. I took the argument to mean that they were so good that they merited retention, and that the sixth form colleges, compared with them, would be largely non-'A' level institutions.

The officials returned with the argument that the parents did not support retention of these 'good' schools and their sixth forms. Again Stuart Sexton had to dig out the figures from Manchester. These showed that 93 per cent of the parents of children at Parrs Wood favoured the retention of its sixth form; similarly 93 per cent of parents at Burnage favoured retention of the sixth form, and the Whalley Range figures were practically the same. A further factor was the single sex argument. Burnage was a boys' school with about 35 per cent 'Asian' pupils, including a high proportion of the sixth form being 'Asian'; Whalley Range was a girls' school with 29 per cent 'Asian' and 17 per cent 'West Indian' pupils, again with a higher proportion of 'Asian' girls in the sixth form.

Manchester claimed that the Muslim parents had been consulted and had agreed to single sex schools. I did not believe this for a moment. Stuart Sexton and I then made a trip to the Adelphia Hotel in Liverpool, where in the daytime we examined school closure proposals for that city and in the evening, by prior arrangement, we met representatives of the various Muslim and Sikh organizations from Manchester, all of whom confirmed that for them it was essential that the single sex schools should be retained, with single sex sixth forms, and they brought with them a petition to back up this claim, which they followed with a written submission to the same effect.

By now the departmental officials were on the defensive. Sir Keith asked, 'What would happen if I reject the proposals?' The officials' reply was: 'Manchester will make as much political capital out of such a decision as possible, and they will refuse to submit further proposals and wait for a general election and a possible change of government. Meanwhile, many of the Manchester schools will have surplus places with all the extra expense that this incurred.' An observer might think that the departmental officials were very shrewd in judging what Manchester would do, or alternatively might consider that Manchester's response had been worked out jointly by the Department and the Manchester officials. Thus Sir Keith was placed in a very difficult position: he wished to preserve the best schools and the best sixth forms, yet he had pressed Manchester to get rid of surplus places.

The departmental officials then brought in the legal tack. Since those days there have been several legal challenges to decisions of the Secretary of State, but at that time such challenges were comparatively rare and generally thought best avoided. It was considered that while the Secretary of State could modify proposals before approval, any such modification could be only minor. A major modification, amounting to substituting the minister's own proposals for those of Manchester, was considered to be beyond his powers. To exempt three schools from the whole package of twenty-five Manchester schools could be too much, would probably be challenged by Manchester in the courts, and the Secretary of State would most likely lose. The Department's own legal advisers supported the departmental opinion.

Stuart Sexton first suggested saving all the five schools with good sixth forms, and then put forward a compromise for saving Parrs Wood, Burnage and Whalley Range only. The officials considered this too great a modification and suggested only two should be saved – possibly the two single sex schools.

All this time the little platoon of politicians had beaten off the big battalions of the officials when the Department brought in the big chief himself, the Permanent Secretary, who rarely attended departmental meetings with ministers. He sent a minute, 'I rarely intervene in Section 12 proposals', but then went on to say he fully supported the arguments put forward by the Department. Those were of course the arguments for not saving the 'good' sixth forms.

Sir Keith was then convinced that he could not legally modify these proposals, as he wished to do, and rejected the whole scheme. Within months the Manchester City Council resubmitted exactly the same proposals, and they were then approved by the Secretary of State. Such prolonged periods of trench warfare between departmental officials, local education authorities and Stuart Sexton and myself were exhausting.

There had been increasing interest in the return to a core curriculum for all schools since Prime Minister Callaghan's Ruskin College speech and circular 14/77 under the Labour Government announced an intention to provide a 'desirable framework for the school curriculum'. Thus *A Framework for the School Curriculum* was issued by the new Conservative Government in January 1980. Compared with later attempts to develop an over-tight curriculum, one sentence in the 1977 circular stands out:

The Secretaries of State do not seek to determine in detail what the schools should teach or how it should be taught:

but they must have an inescapable duty to satisfy themselves that the work of the schools matches national needs. This task cannot be undertaken from the centre alone. The Government must bring together the partners in the education service in the interest of the community at large; and with them seek an agreed view of the school curriculum which would take account of the range and needs of local development. . . . The school curriculum is not, and should not be, either static all the time or uniform throughout the country.

Interestingly enough, *A Framework for the School Curriculum* discussed only English, mathematics, science, modern languages and religious education.

It is a pity that later Conservative ministers did not keep to this broad-brush approach, which is surely the one within the Conservative tradition, instead of laying down all the detailed curricula and examination methods, which brought conflict with teachers and parents.

On 5 March 1981, while I was still concentrating on higher education, I summed up in a Commons debate when I reminded the Members present of the need for a basic curriculum, especially in English and mathematics.

Later that year, in July, in another debate in the Commons, I stressed what schools were primarily for: the teaching of literacy and numeracy; the giving of a body of necessary knowledge; the teaching of the skills to earn a living; and awe in the presence of beauty and truth and all the verities.

I remained suspicious of the Schools Council. If a body is set up to suggest changes it will obviously do so to justify its existence. I blame the Schools Council for the introduction of the GCSE. I was still far more concerned to set up a leaving examination for the least able 20 per cent, which would guarantee to employers basic literacy and numeracy and correct habits of work and thought. Some 12.2 per cent of sixteen-year-old pupils were leaving without a single GCSE or CSE graded pass. As before, I suggested early leaving for low ability pupils who achieve sufficient marks at an examination at fourteen and fifteen.

When I started teaching in 1950 we had a national curriculum and I acquired a copy of the 571-page *Handbook of Suggestions for Teachers* (1944 edition, price 3/6), and later acquired a copy of

Primary Education (1959 edition, reprinted in 1965). We then had an accepted national curriculum, but it broke down in the 1960s. It would have been better to have returned to this historic curriculum and adapted it, instead of creating an entirely new model, which was far too prescriptive. It was a classic example of reinventing the wheel while making it too big.

Mark Carlisle had already announced, however, on 19 February 1980, that 'the separate grading systems of GCE "O" and CSE must be incorporated in a single consistent system of clearly defined goals, while the GCE "O" levels are retained'.

When John Tomlinson, chairman of the Schools Council, suggested in March 1980 that pupil profiles would replace 16-plus examinations within ten years, my fears for the future of reputable examinations were increased. The following year the president of the NUT came out against the 16- and 18-plus independently marked examinations.

It was while I was in charge of schools that the European Court of Human Rights ruled in February 1982, by six votes to one (the British judge), that the existence of corporal punishment in British schools failed to respect the parents' 'philosophical convictions' and thus violated Article 2 of the convention. Brent Council had banned the use of the cane in its schools in 1979 and other local authorities, including ILEA, followed. I had used and authorized corporal punishment in all of my three headships, believing it was necessary among tough boys to ensure full discipline and learning. I used it in response to verbal or even physical attacks on teachers or other pupils and for downright disobedience and destruction of property. I often gave a pupil the choice of the cane or increased written work and pupils nearly always chose the cane. Occasionally, I put tough boys who had seriously broken school rules in my chair, told them to describe what they had done and then asked them what punishment they, if they were the headmaster, would give. Never once did they suggest a punishment less than I required and I usually had to tone down their recommendations.

I also usually saw a caned boy later in the day or the following day and threw a bridge to him by suggesting we had a table tennis or badminton game, to ensure that our relationship would remain a friendly one. Boys (and I) much preferred the cane to bitter sarcasm in front of a class, particularly if it was a mixed sex or ability class.

It was ironic that the European judgement came at the time of the Toxteth riots in Liverpool when one primary school had to be shut for a fortnight because of continued disorder.

I immediately attacked the European judgement, warned of its consequences and argued that there would have to be two sets of schools: the first with no corporal punishment because of the 'philosophical convictions' of the parents, and the others with caning because of their parents' 'philosophical agreement' with it. Indeed, the Brussels dissenting judge argued: 'There may be very strongly held beliefs on such matters as the segregation of the sexes, the streaming of pupils according to ability or the existence of independent schools, which could be claimed to have a religious or philosophical basis.' Full acceptance of the court's judgement, as it applied to other school issues, could totally break up the British school system. I said that the judgement would 'open the floodgates and bring chaos in schools throughout the country'. A fortnight after the judgement I linked the growing crime figures with the withdrawal of caning in schools and said: 'Without discipline, there is no learning, and the disciplinary methods of any school, including the use or non-use of corporal punishment, should be a matter to be decided by the staff and parents of the school.'

The Society of Teachers Opposed to Physical Punishment reported me to the European Court for alleged incitement of local authorities to ignore the court's ruling and, with the usual charity of such one-issue minority pressure groups, they sent a letter to Mrs Thatcher advocating my sacking as a minister. Mrs Thatcher sent them a vigorous reply ending, 'I totally reject your criticism of Dr Boyson.'

Sir Keith Joseph sent a memorandum to schools drawing the attention of headteachers to the ruling, without further comment. The National Association of Headteachers advised their members to continue caning, while the vast majority of parents and a considerable majority of teachers regretted the court's ruling.

The ruling was, however, the beginning of the end of school caning. In July 1982 the Church of England condemned corporal punishment as 'institutionalized violence' and called on all its schools to abolish it. Corporal punishment in Scotland was abandoned in state schools in 1984 and on 22 July 1986, on a 231 to 230 vote, the House of Commons voted to end corporal punishment in English and Welsh state schools.

The withdrawal of corporal punishment from schools has had three damaging effects. First, schools unable to control male youths were and are happy to let them play truant and become apprentice criminals, the height of male crime being now at the age of fourteen. Second, boys who are not properly disciplined in school now consider they can do exactly what they like outside and they have given us our disgraceful international reputation as a nation of football hooligans. Third, the pride of a British teacher was, unlike those in Europe, *in loco parentis*. He or she was a parent substitute with the responsibilities and the powers of the parent, not a mere classroom instructor. This glory of the British schoolmaster has now been whittled away and the British teacher, modelled on the public school housemaster, has sadly disappeared in many state schools.

Alas, the anti-caning lobby will not be satisfied until they have taken away the glory also of parenthood, with the right of the parent to smack for misbehaviour. The 'do-gooders' – or rather the 'well-meaners' – never do good, but they will create a selfish, ill-disciplined nation with the need for ever more social workers, who would be unnecessary if we could restructure the family and the school so that both are able, and preferably encouraged, to do their job properly.

My time as schools minister also coincided with the rise of peace studies in schools. I have always been suspicious of political education in schools, apart from descriptive civics, and in the early 1970s I objected to the Conservative Party organizing sixth form political conferences. The early 1980s, however, were ones when impartial school standards of tuition were threatened by politicized teachers linked with the Committee for Nuclear Disarmament. Neil Kinnock suggested in 1982 that every school should have a teacher responsible for peace studies. Avon and Nottingham and other local education authorities supported and organized such studies.

I called peace studies appeasement studies and suggested that parents should remove their children from 'Ban the Bomb' classes and schools. I said: 'These are the people whose 1930 equivalents would have left us unprotected against the Nazis and would leave us unprotected against colonial Soviet aggression. The teaching of unilateral disarmament is an open invitation to the Soviets to take control of the world by threatening nuclear war.' I was flattered when an edition of *Socialism in Education* stated that I was 'making it very difficult for people outside London to raise issues like Peace Studies'.

In oral questions in the House of Commons on 22 June 1982 I attacked Avon's syllabus, which suggested that violent systems include 'capitalism, communism, fascism, imperialism, totalitarianism and institutional violence'. I quoted further from Avon's syllabus: ' "Books, leaflets, posters and any available teaching material related to the field of peace studies will be on sale. In addition, it is hoped to stock appropriate badges, car stickers, postcards, envelope labels and the like." ' I then commented: 'That would make schools look like a Labour Party rally in Trafalgar Square on a wet Sunday afternoon.'

Britain can be glad that we had a prime minister and a Conservative Party determined to defend our freedoms and who, by agreeing to have Cruise missile bases in Britain, gave a lead to Europe which convinced the Soviets they could not militarily win, and thus helped crack the Soviet empire.

In 1982 I also looked at the books and leaflets recommended for classroom use by the Health Education Council and the Schools Council. I was horrified. I found some of the books unpleasant, even repulsive, with all forms of deviance accepted as normal. In one book, bestiality, incest, paedophilia and mutual masturbation were treated as normal. I put four books on the banned list and met the Health Education Council to express my disapproval of many others. I also made the point that in an age attracted by the 'discovery method' of learning, pupils will want to 'discover' in action what they are 'taught' in the classroom. It is no accident that the number of illegitimate births rocketed in line with the increase of sex education given in schools. I urged parents to withdraw their children from sex education classes in school to which they objected. I am delighted that this withdrawal is now supported by the Government. Yet press reports in March 1994 indicated the grave dangers of sex education in class and the unsuitability of some of the material used by the Health Education Authority. The battle for reasonable standards in this area goes on.

I regularly drew attention to the fact that because of the move away from properly disciplined class teaching, from a set body of knowledge and from selection by ability, an increase of 68 per cent in real expenditure on education per pupil in the previous twenty years had brought no improvement at all in the standards achieved. On 7 May 1982 I said that, owing to the move to the so-called family groups, team teaching and other innovations, the children 'seem to be less disciplined, less able to concentrate and pay attention, less able to apply themselves to something different as well as, in certain cases, less well-rounded in reading, writing, spelling and all the essential basics without which the secondary school cannot hope to build'.

I always held that permissiveness in morality was as destructive of educational as of moral values and I said in Loughborough on 5 February 1982 that this had created a 'pathless desert for many of our young people who are denied the refined moral wisdom inherited from the past'. I added that, if in school children were not taught the difference between right and wrong, 'they will grow up value-free, seeing life as an amoral hedonistic existence of egoistic exploitation'.

It was in 1982 that I put in writing my three tests of a good school. First, the children's heads should be at 90 degrees in the classroom; if they were further forward they could be going to sleep, if they were further back they were probably in revolt. Second, the absence of litter in the school; and third, no graffiti in the lavatories. I later added a fourth test: that pupils should come out of school slower than they went in and parents should be warned against schools where the staff knock the children down rushing out of school at the end of the afternoon.

In 1983 the Assessment of Performance Unit submitted two reports to ministers in the Department which said it all. These reports showed clearly that the unfavoured small schools were more successful than the favoured large ones, that schools which gave homework had higher standards than schools which did not, that larger classes had better standards than smaller classes, since with large classes teachers had to use class teaching instead of individual work and that the best results were in Northern Ireland. In Northern Ireland we still had grammar schools and because of the troubles children were kept in at night. So much for the destructive theories of progressive education, which were always introduced for bored teachers and not bored pupils!

While I was a minister I paid considerable attention to religious education, with little help from the clergy and ministers of religion. I always stressed that religious education should be taught by believers and that children should first learn about their own religion before being taught about other religions. I was particularly alarmed to find that 29 per cent of religious education lessons were taken by teachers with no qualifications in the subject. I made clear on the floor of the House of Commons that the 1944 Act said specifically that 'in every county school and in every voluntary school the day shall begin with collective worship on the part of the pupils of the school', and I added: 'I wish to make it perfectly clear that this is the law on religious education and the school assembly and that we have no intention of changing the law, but every intention of seeing that it is upheld.'

Knowing of the shortage of religious education teachers, I was shocked when I visited a religious voluntary college to find more students were reading sociology than religion. This did not seem to worry the resident clergy there – indeed, until I raised the matter with them, they did not seem to have noticed.

Sir Keith Joseph must be warmly commended on his decision in 1983 to make all Her Majesty's Inspector's reports, including those on individual schools, into public documents open to all. This put an end to education's secret garden.

Answering oral questions in the House of Commons one has to be on one's toes. A little original humour usually helps. On 23 October 1979 Mrs Ann Taylor, the Labour education spokesman asked: 'Is he [Dr Rhodes Boyson] aware that one local authority that is giving children practice tests in the 11-plus examination has been obliged, because of the cuts, to use old papers containing questions in pounds, shillings and pence? As the children taking these tests were aged 3 when this country converted to decimal coinage, what effect does the Minister consider that that situation is having on their educational standards?' I replied: 'What better way is there to include history and mathematics at the same time? That, presumably, is what is known in schools as integrated studies.'

The year 1981 saw the rise of the Social Democratic Party. I was immediately affected since my pair, Ronald Brown, joined that party, as did his brother George in the Lords. Fortunately, at least one Cabinet minister's pair also joined the SDP, so we were allowed to continue pairing, apart from on Northern Ireland business in which they voted with us.

I spoke at both the famous Crosby 1981 Shirley Williams by-election and also the Warrington by-election where an SDP candidate also stood. Crosby was fascinating. I spoke along with the Conservative candidate and Malcolm Thornton, now the MP for

Crosby. The school hall was full and most seemed Conservative voters, yet we could not satisfy them. Someone from the audience would ask a question, one of us would answer, the audience nodded in agreement yet a few minutes later someone else would ask almost the same question, to which the audience listened to the answer again and seemed satisfied and a few minutes later this scene was again repeated. They wanted to be with us, but they did not believe us. I had never had an audience like it and I returned to London convinced that they would reluctantly vote Social Democrat.

I publicly attacked the SDP as 'a colour supplement with nothing inside', and asked, 'Can the Social Democrats in reality offer anything more than a milk and water version of Mr Benn's and Mr Foot's full-bloodied socialism?'

I suspected from the beginning that the Social Democrats were too like a research seminar in a country house to change the face of British politics. They needed a down-to-earth leader who could shift the working-class vote and neither Roy Jenkins nor Shirley Williams could do this. David Owen might have done so if he had been given full leadership from the beginning. His first speech in the House of Commons was magnificent in the face of Labour hostility, especially from the Tribune Group. It was a wasted opportunity to reorganize the left in British politics – a reorganization then, as now, desperately needed for the health of British politics.

The years 1979–83 showed the 'loony left' in Brent and the Greater London Council at its height and ensured me an increased majority in 1983. Brent raised its rates by 38.5 per cent in 1979, 39 per cent in 1980 and 47.6 per cent in 1981, far above the rate of inflation. The number of staff employed went up from 7,722 in 1971 to 11,527 in 1979, and another 1,000 were added in 1980. I attacked the yearly increase and asked the Government to introduce local referenda whereby the local electorate had a chance to vote 'yes' or 'no' to any rates increase ahead of inflation.

In 1979 a new mayoral car was purchased in Brent which cost, with its extras, £40,500, and the mayoral garage had to be extended to take it. Most people become confused when millions of pounds are spent, but all could understand the folly of a £40,500 mayoral car. The same year Brent staff were given a day off to protest against government cuts. The libraries were used for nuclear disarmament exhibitions, and an advice centre with two barristers and one solicitor was set up to advise children from the age of five with family problems!

In 1983 advertisements for Brent teachers stated: 'Applications are welcome from candidates regardless of sexual orientation.' Presumably paedophiles could apply for primary school teaching in Brent. In 1983 Brent headteachers refused to comply with a Brent Council 'request' to encourage pupil involvement in the extreme National Union of School Students. No wonder that Brent got the name of being London's barmiest borough and 'The People's Republic of Brent'.

Labour Brent also had the worst maintained schools I have ever seen and attempted to cut grants to Catholic and Jewish children who had to travel more than two miles below the age of eight and three miles from eight upwards to the nearest denominational schools. I considered this against the spirit of the 1944 Act. There can be no choice of school without the ability to get there. The only clause I did not take through in the 1980 Education Act when it was in committee was one restricting travel grants to pupils. I absented myself from the discussion and just came back for the vote, and my then parliamentary private secretary James Pawsey (a Catholic), refused, with my agreement, to vote for it. I was glad when the Lords struck this clause out.

Brent also tried to cut back the intake to popular schools despite the 1980 Act enshrining parental choice. It delayed, too, the sale of council houses to sitting tenants. By May 1980 more than a thousand council house tenants had applied to buy houses in Brent, but not one of these had been sold and I persuaded a minister at the Department of the Environment to threaten that the Department would take over the sales directly if there was further delay. Brent also had a boarding-school, in Hampshire, which was then costing £40,000 per pupil annually – ten times the cost of Harrow or Eton.

The local elections in Brent in 1982 brought a hung council: 33 Labour, 30 Conservative and 3 Liberal councillors were elected and, despite the Conservatives polling 13,000 more votes than Labour, the Liberals elected a Labour mayor which kept Labour in control. My electorate did not like this.

The Labour Greater London Council became similarly unpopular with many of my constituents. There were the high rate rises – 93 per cent in 1982 – and grants made to organizations not greatly favoured by my constituents: English Collective of Prostitutes,

Lesbian Line, London Gay Teenage Group, Bush New Collective and the £35,000 expenditure on the celebration of the hundredth anniversary of the death of Karl Marx.

Following my attacks on the GLC, Ken Livingstone suggested that the supporters of cheap fares should attend my meetings. I immediately replied that he should knock on all the doors in my constituency and explain the need for a 93 per cent rate increase.

I had thus no worries when the 1983 general election was announced, and I spent the first two days in Dublin at a European conference where I developed an admiration for Garret Fitzgerald, the Irish Taoiseach.

20

Social Security Minister

*

I spoke all over the country in the 1983 general election. I was confident that the popularity of Mrs Thatcher's government, along with the unpopularity of the Labour Party in Brent and in London, would ensure my return to Parliament. There was also little evidence of the popularity of the Social Democrats in Brent in the 1982 local government elections. The general election result was:

Dr R. Boyson	(Conservative)	24,842
Ms S. Jackson	(Labour)	10,191
Mr T. Mann	(SDP/Alliance)	9,082
Conservative majority		14,651

My majority went up by 3,268 votes and my percentage of the poll rose from 53.8 per cent to 56.3 per cent.

I was rung by the Prime Minister the following Monday and asked to go to the Department of Health and Social Security as the Minister of State for Social Security. I was pleased at the opportunity to widen my experience and to gain promotion to a full minister of state. The Secretary of State was Norman Fowler, the Minister of State in charge of health was Kenneth Clarke, while Tony Newton was Parliamentary Under-Secretary in my part of the Department, with John Patten being the Parliamentary Under-Secretary for Health and Lord Glenarthur the Minister in the Lords as a Parliamentary Secretary. I suspected from the time I met

Norman Fowler in the Department that he possibly considered I was a Thatcherite plant in the Department. He and Kenneth Clarke were very close friends and ate together regularly.

The press found my appointment interesting. *The Guardian* commented:

> Dr Rhodes Boyson, a figure who looks as though he might have walked straight out of *Hard Times*. . . . There are two possible readings here. One is that Dr Boyson's crusading style will return the spirit of the workhouse to our land; the other that daily confrontation with the immediate facts of life will moderate even Dr Boyson's initial prejudices.

The *Sun* stated I was expected to be 'the scourge of the scrounger'.

I was surprised that no one immediately picked up that my master's degree was gained by work on the Poor Law in northwest Lancashire from 1834 to 1871, part of which had been published, and that I had edited and contributed in the book *Down with the Poor* for the Churchill Press. This book was a set of essays on how to dismantle or rather pass beyond the welfare state. A week later *The Guardian* did carry a letter with a cartoon ending, 'Not only down with the poor, but out!' This letter quoted a number of paragraphs from my article in the Churchill Press book, such as: 'A state which does for its citizens what they can do for themselves is an evil state: and a state which removes all choice and responsibility from the people and makes them like broiler hens will create the irresponsible society.' Possibly the most extreme paragraph quoted was: 'Legislation and state interference could be cut back and limited to a requirement that all should insure against ill-health, misfortune and old age; and that the minority whose resources are insufficient to pay the premiums because of mental or physical handicap, would be helped by some form of reverse income tax with the cash or vouchers necessary to pay their way on the free market.' I certainly still agreed with both of those paragraphs, but my new post was one in which I had to administer the existing system.

Two weeks later *Community Care* gave me a two-page profile under the title 'The Colossus of Rhodes' with a full cover-page colour cartoon. It described me as 'One of the most colourful and controversial of Mrs Thatcher's team'. It was a generous profile. It reported fairly my view of the welfare state:

I certainly believe that for those with a mental and physical defect society has a responsibility. It also has a responsibility in these days of unemployment for the unemployed of all ages to maintain them to ensure they don't lose their self-confidence, it is responsible for the pensioner. I don't say that they are feckless but where people are making a conscious choice not to work, then I don't believe that they have a claim on society.

I still like the definition I gave in this article of a minister's responsibilities and the principles to which he should be accountable: 'Every man has two masters – his philosophy and his daily responsibilities. If you take decisions without bearing in mind what you are moving towards you destroy your philosophy. If you get bogged down in administration and don't keep asking yourself questions, you destroy yourself.' I hope, as a minister, that I always remembered that.

New Commentary in its edition of 6 September, was probably the most interesting. Bill Davies wrote the profile:

At a time when we are being urged to take our values from the Victorian era it should come as no surprise to find the most vociferous exponent of that self-help philosophy on our doorstep at Social Security. With a stroke of the prime ministerial pen Dr Rhodes Boyson has been translated from the Department of Education to the DHSS. With his mutton-chop whiskers and gold watch chain he could be mistaken for a northern ironmaster or millowner of the type sent up so uproariously by Timothy West in the TV series *Brass*. However, the Lancashire manner disguises a keen intellect as many a political pundit has found to his cost.

My change of post affected at least one other Conservative Member of Parliament. The *Sunday Express* on 3 July had the following paragraphs in its 'Cross-bencher' column:

Next a tale which might have come straight out of a script for *Yes, Minister*. Shortly before the election, Tory MP Mr Trevor Skeet (Beds N.) sought out Dr Rhodes Boyson, then junior Minister at the Education Department.

Poor old Trevor was in no end of a state over two village schools in his constituency which had been earmarked for the chop. The good folk of Stevington and Little Staughton were in a mighty rage. Could Rhodes help?

Now Dr Boyson is by nature a helpful chap. Especially at election time. And his message to Mr Skeet added up to a 'Don't worry, I'll see you all right.'

Mr Skeet scurried home to spread the word. He was '75 per cent sure' the schools were safe. Sighs of relief all round. The issue never really surfaced during the election and Mr Skeet romped home with an increased majority.

Alas, alas.

Just a few days after the election, the helpful Dr Boyson was promoted to a new job at Social Security. Seizing their chance, the civil servants back at the Department of Education immediately slid the school closure papers in front of Secretary of State Sir Keith Joseph. Without the rough, tough Dr Boyson around to growl out any objection, Sir Keith signed. Leaving two Bedfordshire villages stunned and an angry Mr Skeet looking a bit of a Charlie.

On 27 July we had the yearly uprating of benefits debate. The Opposition Members had by then checked my writings. The most effective speech was that from Gordon Brown, who had joined the House after the 1983 general election and chose this opportunity to make his maiden speech. Gordon said: 'Does he [Dr Boyson] still believe what he wrote in *Centre Forward* in 1978? Does he still believe that there are plenty of jobs for the unemployed as window cleaners? He wrote, "I shall believe that there is a shortage of jobs when two window cleaners call for my custom within one week, one month or one year." Perhaps the Government's answer to mass unemployment is for Britain to become a nation of window cleaners. In the same book, *Centre Forward*, the Minister wrote that, "To become a window cleaner little equipment is needed – a bucket; a leather or two and a ladder." When the Prime Minister talked regularly during the election about ladders of opportunity, I had not realised that the next Conservative Government would have something so specific in mind. Perhaps the Minister is to do for ladders what the Secretary of State for Employment has done for bikes. Perhaps the exhortation "Up your ladder" will become as intellectually compelling as a solution to unemployment to Conservatives as "On your bike" was in the previous Parliament.'

My window-cleaner test has still not brought two such cleaners in a week, month or year!

In the Department I took responsibility for all the welfare benefits apart from those for the disabled, Tony Newton becoming the Minister for the Disabled. I thoroughly enjoyed my time with the Department. My private office was excellent and the subject, especially the ins and outs of the new housing benefits scheme, was stimulating in the extreme. I was under pressure all the time, with regular speeches and verbal battles in the chamber of the House of Commons and with various organs of the press. I found my new Department much more open-minded and easier to get on with than I did the schools department in education. My staff enjoyed the challenge of debate and of varied views and I was touched when eventually I left the Department that the senior staff insisted on treating me to lunch. I arrived at the time when housing benefits were being introduced to replace the 4 million on supplementary benefits help and the 3 million on rent rebates. This covered one-third of all the houses in the country.

The housing benefits introduction was a major change and up to one-third of local authorities were already behind in its introduction from April 1983. Some had started on computers and were back on hand calculators. The initial scheme had broken down completely in certain authorities. It had originally been advocated by Professor David Donaldson, the husband of my deputy chairman of governors at Highbury Grove, for some time. It was introduced, however, too quickly and without enough money to ensure that there were no losers. I have always believed in a specific Boyson's Law: everyone who gains from a change says thank you and forgets about it, while those who lose remember for years. Anomalies that arise when a new scheme is introduced always need money spent on them and in this case the money was not available.

The position was made worse by an attempt to cut the cost of housing benefit by 5 per cent – £230 million – at the end of 1983. Some of those affected by this cut were the most vulnerable, while others of the half-million who would on the changed scheme lose part or all their housing benefits were Tory voters with small pensions or savings. In politics one must always remember that one cannot take a bone away from a dog that is eating it without being bitten!

The death grant also began to haunt me. I was constantly questioned about it. It was £20 in 1949, raised to £30 in 1967. This was totally inadequate, since in 1983 funerals were costing between £350 and £600. Indeed, where families could not afford funerals, the state had to pay: in 1982 the Department paid out £2.6 million for the funerals of 13,000. The Department made three suggestions for changing the death grant: giving £250 or £200 or £150 grants to people on supplementary benefit, family income supplement and war pensioners, but none of these suggestions gained favour with even half of the people asked, so the Department did nothing.

The various benefits with their various allowances were highly technical – they could have been a test for entrance to Mensa. There were regular debates on them all, often late at night or on the consolidated fund, and the fifteen months I spent in the Department acted as a mental developer. During the consolidated fund debate in December 1983 I had to reply to six Labour and Liberal MPs, including my own pair, from 4.17 a.m. to 6.25 a.m. I then wished them all a happy Christmas break.

I was at the Department at the time of the miners' strike. I ensured that the miners' families were given their dues under the law, I answered questions in Parliament and I also met a delegation of Labour mining MPs. The law was clear: a miner's family could have help, but not the striker. We also presumed that the striker was receiving £15 strike pay from his union. This had been put in our 1979 manifesto and had been brought into law. The National Union of Mineworkers, despite reserves according to the *Financial Times* of £27 million at that time, paid nothing to a miner's family. While social security could help the family, any gifts to the family of more than £4 a week would bring a cut in social security. This was the law we inherited from the previous Labour Government, but to which the Labour Party now so strongly objected. By 26 April 1984 I had 800 social security officers working on miners' family benefits and £500,000 had been paid out. Indeed, when there was a strike at our Newcastle headquarters regarding roster changes, I worked very hard to ensure that all needing help, including the miners' families, received it.

On 12 March 1984 Michael Meacher waved in the Commons what he claimed was a secret document about the miners' strike. It was 'Guidelines Additional to that in the S Manual – Miners' Strike'. I immediately informed him that I had already put a copy in the Commons library and there was no change of policy in it.

Left-wingers, supported by the *Morning Star*, organized a march on my constituency surgery on 7 July 1984 in support of the miners, but all it achieved was to inconvenience my constituents with genuine problems.

With my political hat on I did speak out on the issues of the miners' strike after I left the Department. I reminded the public on 18 September 1984 that every miner was being subsidized by £130 a week through national taxes – this was two and a half times more than the single old age pensioner received. The average coal-face miner was also receiving a wage 26 per cent higher than the average earnings in manufacturing industry. I thus said: 'Every expensive ton of coal bought by the electricity industry will only increase the price of heat and light for old age pensioners and those on low incomes.' I added: 'The violence on the picket lines reminds many of us of riper age of Hitler's National Socialists in the 1930s when their mobs fought to destroy a democratic government and to replace it with a government which brought horror and agony and degradation in its wake.'

The level of the burden on the Exchequer of the state pension was already a major problem for the Government. There were some 650,000 more pensioners than there had been five years previously. The pensioners' organizations regularly asked for increases to keep up with the rising standard of living as against the level of inflation, while the Government hoped that over the coming years the increasing number of occupational pensions would help solve much of this problem.

I was soon involved in meetings on 'early leavers'. Originally I thought an early leaver was a schoolchild who left school at the first opportunity. However, to the Department, early leavers were those who left their occupation for other employment and needed to take their 'portable pensions' with them. This and the need for the disclosure of where the assets of pensions funds were invested were becoming major matters of concern.

I was the first minister to address the pensioners' annual

conference, which was held in 1984 at Blackpool, and I had a very reasonable reception despite the fact that I bluntly, but unaggressively, told the conference that there was no way that their pension demands could be accepted by the Government.

The pensioners were also concerned about the end of the earnings rule – the amount a pensioner could earn without its affecting the level of his pension. We did, however, raise this amount in 1983 by 4 per cent – well above the level of inflation.

Fortunately, all public opinion polls indicated that the pensioners were more concerned about defence, law and order and especially inflation, which destroyed their savings, rather than the level of the state pension itself. They well remembered that the 110 per cent inflation during the years of the 1974–9 Labour Government had taken away half the value of their savings.

We had one major debate on senior citizens' pensions on 25 November 1983, when Sir David Price brought forward a Private Member's Bill on the lines suggested by the Social Services Select Committee in 1981–2 which would have begun a move to the equalizing of the male-female pension age. But this Bill proceeded no further than its second reading, though I did learn that not only was the pension age for women reduced by Winston Churchill in 1940 to sixty because of their great war effort, but it was then presumed that men normally married women five years younger than themselves and the sixty/sixty-five rule would allow husband and wife to retire at the same time.

The only really unpleasant incident I had as Minister for Social Security was when, against my better judgement, I agreed to speak to 600 people at a London conference organized by Child Poverty Action and SHAC, the London housing and homeless centre. This was on 20 December 1983. I had a very tight diary that day and had previously informed the conference organizers that I could be there for only a quarter of an hour. I arrived and was delayed before being asked to speak, so there was no time for questions. I was heckled and booed in my speech and given a slow handicap at the end and advised to 'get on your bike'. I certainly felt sympathy with those on housing benefit if these were the social workers who claimed to speak on their behalf. I heard Michael Meacher say as I left this conference, 'It's a pity he can't stay. I have to tell you that he is kindly man who has fallen amongst Thatcherites.'

In pleasanter mood, while taking part in a debate on social security in the House on 14 February 1984, I interrupted my speech to announce that Torvill and Dean had won their Olympic gold medal. I then sent a copy of *Hansard* of that day to them.

By the summer of 1984 we were spending some 20 to 25 per cent more in real terms on social security than the Labour Government had spent in 1978–9. One quickly learnt in social security that, whatever one spent, there would be immediate demands for more. Early in 1984, Norman Fowler had set up a number of committees to look in detail at various areas of welfare spending. These were chaired, as suggested by the *Daily Express*, by 'Mr Fowler's Four Just Men'. Social welfare was then costing some one-fifth of public expenditure. Norman claimed that it would be 'the most substantial examination of the social security system since the Beveridge Report forty years ago'. We were to report by the end of the year.

I chaired the children and young persons review. There were great anomalies. A young person who left school in July and found a job and then became unemployed received £27.05 a week. One who left school but could not find a job received nothing until the end of the holiday following his leaving school. The ones who remained at school also received nothing. Those, however, who joined the Youth Training Scheme received £25 a week.

We also looked into child benefit, then worth £6.50 a week, Family Income Supplement and One Parent Benefit. Child benefit was the one that caused most controversy, especially as two-thirds of families receiving it also paid tax back to the state.

These reviews were open to the public and my committee, which included T.G. Parry Rogers, director of personnel at Plessey, and Dame Barbara Shenfield, chairwoman of the Women's Royal Voluntary Services, took evidence in public at Central Hall, Westminster. We saw the Low Pay Unit, the DHSS unions, Youth Aid, the Centre for Policy Studies, Gingerbread, Professor Peter Townsend, Ralph Howell, MP, Charles Kennedy, MP, health spokesman for the Social Democratic Party. . . . We also accepted written evidence and commissioned reviews, including a report by Professor Jewel of the City University on what recipients of welfare thought of the existing system. It was presumed that all these reviews would lead to a green or white paper and suggestions for government action.

I decided to visit a conference of European social security

ministers in April 1983 in France and at the same time to look at the social security system in that country. I was impressed by the French system, especially the fact that recipients knew the cost of their health treatment by the way their charges were repaid. I decided to return there in September 1984, to make further investigations into the French system and, as before, I made arrangements to stay with Sir John and Lady Fretwell at our beautiful Paris embassy.

Meanwhile Labour in Brent continued with its far-left-wing policies, and at the Brent Show in 1983, which cost the ratepayers £40,000, the armed services were not allowed to attend, while a special stand was allocated to the Greenham Common ladies. However, in early December 1983, the very courageous councillor Ambrozine Neil moved from the Labour to the Conservative benches. Labour thus lost control of Brent Council and the Conservatives took the chairmanships of the committees. On 7 December there were then rent-a-mob scenes in the Brent Council chamber, with three hours of organized barracking, two separate bouts of egg-throwing and an invasion of the council chamber by a mob wearing 'Vote Labour' badges organized by the Labour Party. The matter was raised in Prime Minister's questions in Parliament the following day by two Conservative MPs and Mrs Thatcher replied: 'I saw reports of the disgraceful scenes, which really amounted to mob rule by the Fascist Left. This is what happens when they take power. . . . One can only totally and utterly condemn it as being contrary to every tenet of democracy.'

A month later the Conservatives took a seat from Labour in a by-election in St Andrew's ward in my constituency, the first time since re-warding that this seat returned a Conservative councillor. This meant that only one Labour councillor – the other councillor for St Andrew's ward – remained in my constituency. The high rates in Brent had brought their just deserts.

Meanwhile in the constituency I had ensured that popular schools were not cut back in pupil numbers and I continued to visit all activities. Indeed, when I visited the new Michael Sobell Sinai School I was welcomed by Geoffrey Leader, the deputy headmaster, who had been one of my head boys at the Robert Montefiore School. I was also helped by the election of a Conservative mayor in May 1984 – the first time I had had a Conservative mayor since my election to Parliament.

On 28 June I made my last major speech as Minister for Social

Security. It was on a Labour motion on the rich and the poor. This was a subject that greatly interested me. I liked the wide sweep and I was surprised that I was not initially asked to wind up the debate. I heard that another minister had been invited to do so and I went to see Norman Fowler, since I thought I was being marginalized, and he said that he thought I did not want to do it. I certainly did.

I have always seen the question of the rich and the poor to be relative to one's time and country. I replied to Frank Field in oral questions on 15 November 1983: 'There is no general accepted income level below which people can be regarded as poor.' Frank Field replied: 'The Minister may not accept that there is a common definition for poverty, but does he accept that everybody else does?' I replied: 'In 1976, under the Labour Government, the right hon. Member for Salford East [Mr Orme], the then Minister for Social Security said, "Poverty is a relative matter and the Government do not accept that a single poverty line can be drawn."' Similarly, in 1978, the Labour Chief Secretary of the Treasury said: 'The Government do not accept that a single poverty line can be drawn.'

Roy Hattersley opened for the Opposition, attacking the Government's parsimony. The Chief Secretary to the Treasury replied, and when we came to the wind-ups the Labour Party put up Gwynneth Dunwoody. She claimed that we were making cuts in the welfare system.

In my speech I quoted Professor Townsend about the difference between absolute and relative poverty. Relative poverty was 'The state where people cannot purchase the goods or engage in the activities which the majority take for granted.' I added: ' . . . as long as society has people earning different amounts, there will always be some people at that level' and 'unless one has an egalitarian society . . . there will always be some form of relative poverty; what Christopher Jenks, the American sociologist, called the inability to fit into a social group'.

I then turned to list the great rise in living standards in Britain since the Second World War. I quoted what Lord Harris defined as poverty in the Lords on 29 April 1981: 'The world of flypapers, of gas coppers, of black-leaded grates, of mangles, meat safes, boiled meat in the summer and acres of lino.' I went on to list the material improvements between 1979 and 1982: 'The number of households with some form of central heating increased by

5 per cent to 60 per cent. . . . Those with a deep freezer increased by 11 per cent from 40 to 51 per cent. . . . The number of people with telephones increased by 9 per cent from 67 to 76 per cent.' I ended: 'Conservatives want a Britain in which, through the full development of the talents and motivation of our people, there is an increased standard of living and in which over the next ten or twenty years the luxuries of the rich become again the necessities of the less well off. Let the rising tide lift all our people. Let us have rising and fulfilled expectations and not the dull equality that is wanted by the Opposition.'

I liked the tribute paid to me earlier in the House of Commons by Charles Kennedy, MP: 'Hon. Members who correspond with the Minister on constituency issues will agree that the hon. Gentleman is always reasonable and open-minded and that he goes to great lengths to explore the problems we raise with him.' Mrs Margaret Beckett paid me a rather different compliment when she said on 2 May 1984: 'No one has seen anything as fast as the Minister for Social Security in closing loopholes and getting through the House regulations to ensure no loophole can be left through which someone might obtain a little more money. If loopholes appear during determinations and appeals . . . the Minister displays a turn of speed that would be the envy of a young lady whose name has been mentioned recently in the House – Zola Budd.'

On 1 August 1984, in the timed half-hour debates before the House rose for the recess until 22 October that year, I replied to a timed debate from the MP for Cunninghame North and waited until the House adjourned at 3 p.m. before returning home. I was looking forward to my second visit to France and the continuance of my enquiry into social security affecting children and young people, which was to continue taking evidence throughout the summer. I was enjoying my social security posting.

21

Northern Ireland

*

As I was leaving St John's Church, Wembley, after the Battle of Britain service on Sunday, 9 September, the vicar told me that he had heard on radio that there were rumours of a government reshuffle. I replied cheerfully and confidently that it certainly would not affect me since I was in the middle of a social security enquiry.

At mid-morning the following day I went into my Department. There was silence in the outer office and my principal private secretary asked immediately to see me. I called him into my room and he informed me that No. 10 had asked that I should remain in my Department until early afternoon, when I would be receiving a call from the Prime Minister. I was shattered: the following day Florette and I were due to go to France to stay with our ambassador and I was going to make a full study of how children and young people were treated under the French social security system.

It was a long and tense morning and my outer office was totally silent. I saw Norman Fowler at one stage and he obviously knew where I was going and said he would like to know in six months' time what I thought about it. By then I decided I was going to be transferred to the Department of the Environment as Minister of State in charge of the abolition of the Greater London Council and the metropolitan countries. I thought I would enjoy this.

In the afternoon we had a scheduled meeting for my review team, which involved taking evidence from Professor Minford and others, and this was due to be televised in public and I would have to be there whether No. 10 had rung or not, otherwise rumours would abound. No. 10 was informed of this. Meanwhile I rang Florette to tell her that something was afoot and it was unlikely that we would go to France as had been planned. I indicated that I thought the new post would be interesting, thinking of course of the abolition of the Greater London Council. Florette had a bath and wondered, what if I were asked to go to Northern Ireland?

Just before the deadline of 1.45 p.m. Mrs Thatcher rang and said that she would like me to go to Northern Ireland as Minister of State to Douglas Hurd, who was taking over as Secretary of State. Surprised and rather shell-shocked I immediately said 'Yes'. I rang Florette, who had already sensed where I might be going, and then rushed off to my enquiry. The ministerial changes were announced in early evening and I went to an Indian dinner in my constituency where I met Sir George Young, MP, who was responsible for room allocations in the Palace of Westminster, and I made sure that I retained my own favourite ministerial room there.

The following day I was offered my choice of portfolios by Douglas Hurd and chose the Department of Finance and Personnel and the Department of Economic Development. The other ministers already *in situ* were Nicholas Scott, Chris Patten and Lord Lyell.

There was some press surprise at my Northern Ireland appointment. The *Financial Times* reported: 'The appointment of Dr Boyson to the number two job at Northern Ireland is unexpected. . . . In his case, however, it is his right-wing views that have commended him to the Prime Minister.' The *Daily Mail*'s London column stated: 'At first sight there may appear a touch of mischief in appointing the abrasive Rhodes Boyson as the polished Hurd's number two: the rough with the smooth. But Boyson's Lancastrian loquacity may even perplex the roaring Paisleys of Ulster into unaccustomed silence. Certainly his rough views on law and order go down favourably with the Protestant majority.' The *Daily Mail* contrasted our two images: 'Mr Hurd, 54, is a smooth diplomat and a Tory "wet", a tall, cool protégé of Mr Heath, whom he once served as political secretary. Dr Boyson, 59, is straight out of the hard-line Thatcher mould, a fast-talking former comprehensive head who has a rough, tough reputation for knocking heads together to settle an argument.'

The next morning in the *Today* programme Mr Hurd was asked: 'There is a great deal of press comment this morning about what some people call "the odd couple", because you're looked upon as a wet, a former Heath man and as an ex-diplomat, and Dr Boyson is very much on the dry side with a reputation, one paper says, for settling arguments by banging heads together.' Mr Hurd replied: 'This is not my experience of him at all. . . . I am actually very pleased about it. He is someone of very great experience and great integrity and a great power of communication, and we'll need all those things in the team.'

After musing on this change, what did I think of it? I was confused. I had entered Parliament not to be the equivalent of a colonial governor but to influence national policy. My time in Northern Ireland could marginalize me from this. In a way it was like returning to the Royal Navy at flag rank – high security, top meetings – but one's responsibilities were akin to the administration of a province as against influencing educational and economic priorities in the overall British scene. I had, however, always accepted challenges as they came and this was yet another. It was a most responsible job affecting the future of large numbers of people and I was determined to do my best for the province. At the same time I also resolved to keep my parliamentary and political contacts intact so that I was not marginalized away from the Westminster scene.

One odd compensation for the change of post was my rooms. I had a large room with three huge windows overlooking Horse Guards Parade in London, where I could entertain splendidly for the fortnight of rehearsals leading up to Trooping the Colour; I had a pleasant bedroom/study in Stormont House, two large rooms in Stormont Castle, one with a remarkable view over the area, and another large room at the Department of Development. Never would I have private access to such real estate again!

During the two years I spent in this post I flew more than 170 times forwards and backwards to Northern Ireland. I would have been worth something for my air miles. I kept separate sets of clothes in Northern Ireland and London and averaged two days a week in Ulster, with additional weekends and holiday duties. Whenever I was in the province for more than one night, Florette came with me. When we were on weekend duties, we stayed at Hillsborough Castle in Co. Down, where the grounds are magnificent, and we generally attended service at the Church of Ireland church there and sat in what was once the governor's few where I was too short to look over and see what was happening. On such weekends we journeyed around the province and gave dinners for leaders of the Ulster community.

I had always visited all the churches in my constituency at least once a year and I hoped to be able to visit various church denominations in Northern Ireland, but it was not to be. On security grounds this was considered out of the question in the Catholic churches. Only when there was the rare joint service across denominations was such a visit allowed. We thus usually worshipped in the Church of Ireland or a Presbyterian church. Once we worshipped in the church of the Revd Martin Smyth, MP, and heard him preach and then lunched with him and his family afterwards at his home.

In July 1985 we were on duty in Northern Ireland when we were visited by Eunice Shriver, sister of John F. Kennedy, and two of her sons, and we discussed the Northern Ireland situation for more than an hour.

Belfast is a northern city, where there is a strong working-class culture in both communities. Having grown up in a working-class village with the same values and religious division – Irish Catholic and English Protestant – I felt quite at home in Northern Ireland.

Within a month of my taking on my new responsibilities we had the Brighton Conference bomb. The day before I had been in Brighton with Florette, but decided to return to London that evening to clear correspondence. So did James Pawsey, my PPS, who was also there with his wife. Indeed, James had originally decided to book a room at the Grand and stay the night, but he had then changed his mind and driven back to Rugby.

In the middle of the night my home telephone rang. It was a friend who had heard of the bombing and wondered if I was safe. I immediately returned to Brighton, arriving there before breakfast, to see if there was anything I could do to help. The bombing made my move to Northern Ireland even more traumatic.

On the following Sunday I attended a service at a Catholic church in my constituency. The priest, shocked by the bombing, asked Florette and me to bring up the elements at mass that morning, which we considered a great honour.

There was one irony regarding the Conservative Party Conference that year. For the first time I had been put down to reply to a debate from the platform. I had looked forward to this but my change from Social Security minister to Northern Ireland minister meant that I lost the opportunity, something I greatly regretted.

I concentrated on my portfolios of finance and industry, to me critical for the future of the province. I believed that if we could cut down unemployment, fewer men would be standing on the street corners to be recruited by the paramilitary groups. A man needs to be important to his wife and family and, if he has not a wage to bring home, a rifle may seem a good substitute. Unemployment was then 22 per cent in Northern Ireland, reaching as high as 50 per cent in Strabane, where many men had never had any work. The problem of the province was it was far too dependent on the public sector. Some 70 per cent of employment was dependent directly or indirectly on the public purse. A thousand pounds a person was transferred to Northern Ireland from London to keep the economy and the province afloat.

There were two major agencies that reported to me: the Industrial Development Board, which dealt with large firms; and the Local Enterprise Development Unit, which dealt with smaller firms. We had just seen the end of the De Lorean car project with a huge loss of public money and I wound up the Lear Fan plane project in 1985, which had cost over £57 million of public money. I resolved then that any firm coming to the province must put in a goodly sum of its own money, while we helped with buildings, advice, grants and so forth. Much of my time was spent in meeting businessmen from the province, the mainland and abroad. In 1985 I also spent thirteen days in the United States visiting actual and potential investors, and I was due to go there again just before I again changed my government post. One in eight of the work-force were employed by twenty-seven American firms, and we had begun to attract European and even Far East interest and investment. It was in 1985 that Du Pont, from America, agreed to build a 300-job fibre plant in the province. Indeed, three-quarters of the new jobs created in 1984 came from firms whose headquarters were outside the province.

Soon after I came to Northern Ireland there came a threat to the level of the existing employment. Molins, the cigarette-machine makers, decided to close their Maydown plant, the last engineering works west of the Bann. They called the shop stewards together at Aldergrove, Belfast's airport, and gave them the news. I immediately rang John Hume, the Social Democratic MP, and told him I was going to ring the firm and tell them that if they closed they must give the plant to the men. At the same time I was determined that we would raise money from the Department of Development, from the men's own redundancy money and from charities and the churches to ensure the future of this plant. I had joint meetings with John Hume, the Anglican Bishop of Londonderry and the Catholic Bishop of Derry. It was then that I met Frank Hanna, the brother of Vincent Hanna, from the well-known legal family.

The plant was saved and I reopened it several months later. Molins gave it pledged orders and the plant has since further widened its range of products. It was a proud moment for Florette and me to open the plant under the new management and see the plaque with its tribute to me – especially since I was the son of a trade-union official who had known the ravages caused by unemployment in my childhood. I hailed it as 'the flagship of the north-west of the province'. John Hume said on this occasion: 'I want to place on record my appreciation of the Minister's commitment to the work-force from the very beginning. He expressed his determination to do all in his power to maintain an engineering base in the north-west. In all our meetings with him and with the workers' representatives he showed that same commitment and his attendance here today on the first day of Maydown Precision Engineering is further proof of that confidence.'

One of the problems of Northern Ireland is the lack of an indigenous energy fuel. There is no natural gas, no oil and no coal. Thus energy is expensive domestically and in the factories. I began the phasing-out of town gas, which was hugely subsidized up to £12,000 per man employed, encouraged the import of coal from Scotland to our mutual advantage and did all I could to move to the exploitation of lignite (brown coal), of which there are huge reserves in Northern Ireland. I visited Germany to see the use of lignite in their power stations and in 1986 we fired 200 tons of lignite at the Belfast Power Station. I also tried to revive the traditional linen industry of Northern Ireland, linked with its own flax growing. The linen industry had then an annual turnover of £110 million a year, 95 per cent of the linen being exported to Italy, Japan and the United States.

Northern Ireland has a great deal going for it to attract outside investments. It is a beautiful area with clear roads, marvellous golf-courses, fishing in rivers where the top half is water and the

bottom half fish, good food, a welcoming populace, the best schooling standards in the United Kingdom and the lowest ordinary
crime rate. American firms had difficulty persuading executives
in the first place to come to Northern Ireland, but then found
that they had even greater difficulty getting them to leave at the
end of their term of duty. Florette and I thoroughly enjoyed the
hospitality of both communities, certainly until the difficulties
caused by the signing of the Anglo-Irish Agreement.

Tourism is another important industry which could expand enor-
mously but for the troubles. Even so, nearly a million people,
many of them Americans, visited the province in the first year I
was there.

The two large, world-renowned firms are Shorts, aeroplane and
specialist engineers, and the shipbuilders Harland and Wolff. These
are the Belfast flagships of the province, employing large numbers of workers, and all ministers work hard to try to keep their
order-books full. I had regular debates in the Commons on orders, bringing into effect legislation that had already been passed
for England, Wales and Scotland, often late at night or in the
early hours of the morning. These debates were resented by the
Ulster Unionists, since they wished for full integration with other
parts of the United Kingdom and Enoch Powell was very effective in his speeches on such occasions.

The fact that I was always willing to meet Ulster delegations
and Members of Parliament and concentrated on my portfolios
was appreciated by the Ulster MPs. On 17 December 1984 the
Revd William McCrea, a Democratic Unionist MP, said in the House
of Commons: '. . . I appreciate the Minister of State's efforts on
our behalf. He has shown clearly his interest in these matters
since coming to Northern Ireland a short time ago, and I appreciated
his grasp of the many problems which he displayed clearly a few
days ago when he addressed the Northern Ireland Assembly.'

Catholic unemployment was far higher than Protestant unemployment. The Fair Employment Agency was established to ensure that the two communities had equal access to the jobs available.
This was easier said than done. One has only to think of the geographical separation of the two communities, their different work
traditions and even the differences of the historic school curricula,
with the Protestant schools giving more emphasis to science subjects, to appreciate the problem. Yet the fact that we had established the Fair Employment Agency was itself helpful. It monitored

the employment statistics. It concluded that 32.7 per cent of the non-industrial civil servants were Catholic, 58.4 per cent Protestant and 8.9 per cent had no known religion. The Catholic percentage had risen 5 per cent in the last five years.

I increased the staff of the agency so as to give it more teeth, without putting at risk any existing jobs. As we approached the Anglo-Irish Agreement, the matter became even more important. One of the big problems was Shorts, which was well over 90 per cent Protestant. I came under pressure from the United States for reverse discrimination under the McBride Principles, which to my mind would have led to unacceptable laying-off of existing workers.

Possibly I concentrated too much on the economic problems of the province. Aiden Hannigan, who once lived in my constituency and comments on Irish affairs, wrote: 'This week I called at the Westminster office of Dr Rhodes Boyson, Minister of State for Northern Ireland, who more or less leaves the politics and security to Tom King and Nick Scott and pursues a singularly dedicated course in obtaining the maximum economic benefits for the north.' That was both my job and my concern.

I supported the bringing in of the Anglo-Irish Agreement because I considered it essential if we were to keep, never mind increase, American investment in the province. My personal conversations with men like Harrison Golden, Controller of New York State and a full supporter of the McBride Principles, was decisive for me. I also hoped that the United States could be encouraged to give American firms tax relief if they invested in Northern Ireland.

Patrick Murphy wrote in *Hibernia* in August 1985:

Chris Patten and Rhodes Boyson would hardly be considered card sharks by their colleagues in the Northern Ireland Office. Patten is a mild-mannered monetarist, exceedingly loyal to Mrs Thatcher, while Boyson is a boisterous ex-headmaster, Dickensian in both face and values. But it is these two men who have been given the job of testing the early worth of the green card. The Two have been selected by Douglas Hurd because, like all cards, the green one has two heads. The first, which Patten has been dealing secretly in his negotiations with the SDLP, is the cultural and political head. The other, which Boyson has now played, openly for two months and which apparently genuinely disturbed him when he saw it face up for the first time, is the social and economic head. Of the two Boyson has the more difficult task. . . .

Improving the lot of Catholics will prove particularly difficult for the unfortunate Dr Boyson. Already he has set up an internal Civil Service team to go over the head of the Fair Employment Agency in an effort to establish some sort of socio-economic power-sharing.

In September Mr Hurd was recalled to become Home Secretary. In the light of the importance of the projected Anglo-Irish Agreement I considered this an odd decision of the Prime Minister. It treated Northern Ireland as a backwater.

In 1985 relations between the two communities in Northern Ireland were improving. The number of troops required to keep order had declined to roughly garrison strength of 9,000 regulars and 6,500 in the Ulster Defence Regiment, 10 per cent of the police then being drawn from the Catholic community, with current recruitment reaching 12 per cent of recruits. When things are improving it is generally wise to leave them alone and simply encourage what is happening.

In October the *Newsletter* reported in Northern Ireland that I was concerned about the political upheaval associated with any projected Anglo-Irish Agreement, but on the grounds that I have already stated I continued to support, rather reluctantly, the Agreement. I was then telephoned by the Prime Minister and asked to wind up on the first day of the two-day debate on the Agreement, presumably to help to keep the right wing of the party in line. Rereading my speech I realize it was far from my best utterance in the House. My heart wasn't really in it. I stated that political instability was the biggest obstacle to more investment in the province. I continued: 'This Agreement represents the first occasion when in a binding international agreement the Republic of Ireland has affirmed that there will be no change in the status of Northern Ireland without the consent of the majority and that the present wish of the majority is for no change. The sense of the Agreement is an attempt to distance ourselves from a past in Northern Ireland which has recently had severe difficulties both politically and economically. On one side it gives a firm commitment from the British Government and from the Government of the Republic of Ireland that Northern Ireland will remain part of the United Kingdom as long as the majority wishes. On the other side, it accepts the legitimate identity of the nationalist community and recognises that the two parts of the island of Ireland have interests in common. The Agreement thus gives to the people of Northern Ireland the promise of a more settled, confident, co-operative and more prosperous future. Such a future is possible if both communities in Northern Ireland are prepared to work for it and I commend the Agreement to the House.'

The Treaty was passed overwhelmingly by 473 to 47 votes, the Ulster Unionists and right-wing Conservatives voting against it, and I remember particularly the speeches of Ian Gow and Ian Paisley, which held the House.

Whatever the rights and wrongs of the Agreement, the Ulster Unionists to my mind made a major mistake in then withdrawing from the Commons and fighting by-elections in their own constituencies. I warned them in my Commons speech against such action. I believe that they should have immediately said that, while they would continue to oppose the Agreement, they would certainly ensure that the Nationalist community and the Irish Government delivered their part of the bargain on security. Instead, the House considered this withdrawal a very silly move – rather like that of the boy who takes his bat home when he is bowled out – and by the time they returned, life had moved on. It is never wise to disappear from the main battlefield and in this case it was the House of Commons. The Ulster Unionists were certainly badly advised. The 'Ulster Says No' campaign had little or no impact in the Commons or the mainland; rather, it spoilt the atmosphere in the province during the rest of my stay.

The Anglo-Irish Agreement came into operation on 29 November and the first meeting took place in Belfast on 11 December, when the relationship of the Catholic community with the security forces was discussed, along with security co-operation and a reference to economic development. The Ulster Unionists were not present at the next Northern Ireland questions on 12 December when Mr Nellist, a left-wing Labour MP, asked what in retrospect was the best question: 'What is the point of the Anglo-Irish Agreement if it provokes sectarian murders and increases the risk of civil war?'

For the rest of my time in Northern Ireland many individuals continued to be very friendly, but security had to be stepped up and one had to be careful not to be annoyed by tactics which irritated rather than wounded. That New Year's Eve (of 1985/6) we were warned not to join a party to which we had been invited and accepted. Instead we had a cold supper at Hillsborough Castle.

Florette and I were also met by Democratic Unionist protesters whenever they knew our movements, and Florette was not enamoured by those who shouted at her 'English go home', since she is of Scottish/Welsh descent.

On 5 January 1986 I warned those concerned that the protests against the Agreement were affecting future business plans for more investment in the province. Outsiders saw the protesters as far more dangerous than they were.

In May 1986 Florette and I went to Rathlin Island to see the amazing bird cliffs at the time of nesting. Word got out of our visit and the ferry at Ballycastle was invaded by a dozen noisy Democratic Unionist protesters, until the police cleared them before we sailed. While we were on the island more protesters gathered at Ballycastle to await our return, so we came back by army helicopter. When the protesters saw what was happening, they tried to follow the helicopter by road in their cars. It was like a mad Keystone Cops scene and one could not help seeing the funny side of it.

I made sure that I did not lose the close contacts with my constituency during my time in Northern Ireland. I still did my weekly door-knockings, with some six to fifteen volunteers on each occasion, and attended most local events. My constituents were happy that under Conservative control there was no increase in the Brent rates in 1984 and 1985. Alas, in 1986 Labour regained its majority on Brent Council. In my constituency nineteen of the twenty-one councillors elected were Conservative and we polled 53.84 per cent of the votes as against 28.78 per cent for Labour and 17.38 per cent for the Social Democrats.

On 10 April 1986 I had an interesting *Question Time* in the famous television programme. The Government had put a three-line whip on the deregulating of Sunday trading and I thus had no choice as a minister but to vote for it. I made it clear, however, in *Question Time* that my vote was being given under duress. On the same programme I also opposed any government plans to bring in the single GCSE examination at sixteen. I said: 'I am sure some of the whips will not be very pleased with what I have been saying.' Peter Riddell, who was then political editor of the *Financial Times*, commented on the programme: 'We are seeing the lid being taken off what is being said in Whitehall.' The Government, however, narrowly lost its vote on Sunday trading, despite my voting for it!

Two years after the 1983 general election Praful Patel, a leading figure in the Indian community in Britain as well as in India, was selected to be my Labour opponent at the next general election. At the Labour Annual Conference that year Praful was reported to have drawn cheers from delegates when he stated his intention of sending Dr Rhodes Boyson 'on his bike' at the general election.

I realized all the time I was in Northern Ireland that if I was not careful I would be half forgotten in Parliament, since I would be spending half of the four Monday-to-Thursday important Commons days in Ulster. I thus continued to take weekend speaking engagements for my colleagues, to address area conferences and to give my views on important political issues. Indeed, I had a full page in the *Daily Express* on law and order in the summer of 1985. I also regularly spoke for the Freedom Association. I warned against Labour's threat to pension funds if a future Labour Government were to take over a proportion of these funds in a government-controlled national investment bank, and I also supported publicly our involvement with our American allies in the air attack on Libya.

In 1985 Francis Pym, ex-minister, formed a group called Centre Forward, without realizing that this was the title of my very Thatcherite 1979 book. I suspect his views were very different from mine! Mrs Thatcher took advantage of my book title in Prime Minister's question time on 16 May. She was asked by a Labour member: 'In view of the formation of the Centre Forward group and the statement by Ian Picton, Chairman of the Tory Reform Group, will the Prime Minister now state whether the Lady is for turning and if not, why not?' The Prime Minister replied: '... The name Centre Forward was, of course, first coined by my hon. Friend the Minister of State, Northern Ireland Office, who wrote a book called *Centre Forward: a Radical Conservative Programme*. Honourable Members can see the book which I have here. It was written in 1978, and I am delighted to find that my hon. Friend has so many new supporters.'

This helped to torpedo the new group, about which Francis Pym made a statement to the 1922 Committee. He was alleged to have told the Committee that he was not challenging Mrs Thatcher's leadership and was not interested in setting up a party within the party. I took advantage of the publicity to address the Ludlow Conservatives the following evening on the book and the achievements of the Thatcher government.

Early in 1986 there came rumours that Sir Keith Joseph wished to retire from his education post. Two names were regularly mentioned for the succession – those of Chris Patten from the left of the party and mine from the right. Chris was already *in situ* as Minister of State in that department. For three months the newspapers were full of our rival strengths, along with those of other ministers, particularly John Moore and Peter Morrison. I thought *The Times* first leader of 29 April was significant:

> The choice should fall on someone who approaches the problem unambiguously from the position that the more schools are obliged to respond to parental choice the more effective they will be. On that basis Mrs Thatcher would be right not to give the department to its present Minister of State, Mr Chris Patten, the candidate the department itself would most like. He is an enthusiastic minister who minds about the subject, but his own approach seems insufficiently differentiated from the educational orthodoxies which have got education where it now is.
>
> At the other end of the opinion scale is Dr Rhodes Boyson, the candidate of a significant number of Conservative MPs. Dr Boyson knows about education as a remarkably successful and popular headmaster of a London comprehensive school who fought against many of the educational fashions which led to a loss of standards in the Sixties.
>
> However, although Mrs Thatcher seems to share his opinions, he was promoted not within the DES but sideways to Social Security and then to Northern Ireland. Mrs Thatcher, while recognising his opinions as diamond-sharp, may think him somewhat too rough a diamond in style for her taste. If that is so, the odds are against his succeeding Sir Keith.

The same day Robin Oakley in the *Daily Mail* forecasted that neither of us would get the job. He wrote: 'Senior Tories say Mrs Thatcher has accepted that to promote either would set off a bitter Left-Right battle within the Party.'

The following day, never behind in coming forward, I addressed the Conservative graduates on education, advocating more parental choice of school and more power to the family. I said: 'Just as the Government of the country is subject to electors' choice at elections so should the individual school's continuance, expansion or contraction be subject to parental choices.'

On 15 May the *Daily Mail* and *Today* came out in support of me, the *Daily Telegraph* against me. The following day I warned publicly against suggested moves towards a policy of closer curriculum control of schools and said: 'It would be tragic if Britain ever considered going down the continental road of centralizing educational control by turning its back on education's origins and history in this country which were based on individual, group and local control. Teachers should be given scope to deploy all their talents to teach children in the way that will give the fullest satisfaction to pupil and parents and, therefore, to future employers and the community at large.' I still believed in simple pen-and-paper tests in basic subjects, with enhanced parental choice of school ensuring that schools delivered a good all-round education. The *Gloucestershire Echo*, in the locality where I delivered the speech, wrote: 'Nothing if not outspoken, Dr Rhodes Boyson, heir to the thorny crown of Secretary of State for Education, chooses Gloucestershire as a platform from which to launch a damning indictment of the Government's latest educational foray. He may have done his own cause no good by attacking so vigorously deeper Whitehall involvement in the running of state schools, but truth and commonsense have been given good service.'

I was right then, but it was probably unwise of me to have put my views on record at that specific time. The over-repressive national curriculum, as against simple tests of achievement, has damaged education in this country and the balance of power between national and local government and professional teachers, upon which freedom and responsibility depend, has been seriously undermined. I certainly did not lose the education number one job by silence or kotowing to 'enlightened' or even government opinion.

So Kenneth Baker was appointed Secretary of State for Education. I was in London when I was informed of this and I got into my government car to be driven to the airport and return to Northern Ireland, sad at heart as if going into exile. I was greeted in Belfast by a senior civil servant who said, 'Never mind, Minister, it will make sure you will soon return to London.' He was right but I was also right. I would never get Cabinet office and as a natural number one I would never have my own department to show what I could do.

The following Sunday I was on duty in Northern Ireland when I opened the *Sunday Express* and read in 'Crossbencher' under the subhead 'Hairy Hopeful':

> On then to the fellow who failed to get the job. I give you the rumbustious Dr Rhodes Boyson, still languishing as Minister of State for Northern Ireland. As a former headmaster, Dr Boyson knows more about education than most. He desperately wanted the job. He is an able communicator. . . .
>
> What then is holding Rhodes back? Could it be that the back-stabbing campaign mounted against him by the Conservative Wets has finally blighted his career? That he is paying the price for being one of the few Government Ministers who still believes heart and soul in the principles of Thatcherism? Or could it just be that with his enormous Victorian sideboards no one any longer takes him seriously?

Certainly the reading of this press comment did not improve my Sunday.

22

Local Government Minister

*

In early September 1986 newspapers were again speculating about a government reshuffle. *The Times* of 8 September considered that Chris Patten and I were once more vying for a Cabinet post, this time the Secretary of State for Health and Social Security. The *Daily Telegraph* on the same day considered 'There could be a sideways move or even a party post' for me, and the *Irish Times* also considered that I might be offered the Secretary of State for Health and Social Security.

On 10 September I was visiting factories in Northern Ireland, a day when everyone expected there to be ministerial changes. Thus I returned to Stormont House for lunch. The following week I was due to go again with Florette to the United States to beat the drum for American investment in Northern Ireland following the Anglo-Irish Agreement. I considered, however, that my two years were up. Then the telephone rang and it was the Prime Minister ringing two years exactly to the day from the time she had moved me to Northern Ireland. I was to go to the Department of the Environment in charge of local government. I immediately agreed, and with all my kit I was on the 6 p.m. plane to London. In one way it was like returning from India after the Second World War. I had enjoyed my time in Ulster, but it was an interregnum in my life as against part of a life plan.

I was pleased with my new post. Some 12 per cent of the country, including Brent, was under 'far left-wing local government occupation' and needed help and direction to return to saner ways. I had for years advocated a poll-tax to bring responsibility back to local government, and the party had agreed to move to this with the community charge. Local government interested me and I had spent ten years as a councillor in Lancashire and London. I had also chaired the London Boroughs Management Services Unit.

The *Daily Telegraph* welcomed me back to the mainland as 'The indefatigable workhorse'. *The Star* saw me as 'another tough campaigner'. The *Daily Mail* called me 'the darling of the Tory Right' and 'the scourge of the Left'. Robert Hedley in the *Local Government Chronicle* later welcomed me 'not only as an authority on London's Labour Left', but as 'an old guard local government traditionalist'. I certainly believed in local government as long as it was local and government. My antagonism against the loony Labour left arose from the fact that it was their total confrontational attitudes, their propaganda on the rates and the networking of Labour councillors and paid local officials between various boroughs which were destroying responsible local government, which was once – and in many areas still is – an honourable, responsible job.

The day after my appointment I met Nicholas Ridley, the Secretary of State, with William Waldegrave, from whom I took over local government, William moving to the planning and environmental part of the Department. Nicholas informed us that he had had nothing to do with our appointments, which were made by the Prime Minister. With his usual consistency, when I went back to the back-benches after the general election he similarly informed me that it had had nothing to do with him and was purely a decision of the Prime Minister.

The Parliamentary Under-Secretary in my part of the Department was Christopher Chope, who had made his name as leader of Wandsworth Council in privatizing services and reducing rates. He had not expected to be appointed to government and was abroad. It took several days before he was found. I thought at one stage I would have to go and look for him myself, like Stanley in search of Dr Livingstone.

The party was keen to introduce the community charge. Rates had been unpopular for years and the huge expenditure of the loony left had made them even more unpopular as a way of financing local government. The Prime Minister promised in the October 1974 election, when she was Environment spokesman, that rates would be ended. Now was the time and I was delighted to be part of the exercise.

The vast majority of Conservatives were weary of non-ratepayers voting in spendthrift Labour councils whose high rates were bankrupting industries and businesses as well as individuals. I said in the Commons on 4 March 1987: 'The great advantage of the community charge is that everybody who is voting is paying something towards the cost, whereas in Lambeth and Liverpool, where there are nonsense Councils, only one voter in five pays.' In Manchester only two voters in nine paid rates. I consider it is immoral to vote to spend somebody else's money without contributing any of one's own. The community charge would be paid by all, apart from people like the mentally ill and those in old people's homes who paid nothing, and students and others who paid 20 per cent of the full charge. To me this seemed an equitable system.

We were also committed to change the business rate. This was then levied separately by each council and it was argued that businesses were being established not where they really should be based according to resources and communications, but where the business rates were lowest. The anti-business prejudice of some of the left-wing councils was also likely to cause them to increase the business rate and drive firms elsewhere, creating areas of high unemployment. Thus the Conservative Party became committed to a universal business rate, the same all over the country fixed and collected by government and then redistributed to the councils.

I now think that the universal business rate was a mistake. It separated businesses from their areas and diminished the calibre of councillors because local businessmen no longer stand for election to be financial watchdogs on local councils.

In the 1986 London elections four Conservative councils fell to Labour. The first was Waltham Forest, which in 1987 put up rates by 67 per cent, the second was Ealing, which in 1987 put up its rates by 72 per cent, and the third council was Hammersmith and Fulham, which raised the rates in the same year by an horrific 127 per cent. Only Brent, the fourth council, was spared such increases. This was because Brent was rate-capped already following high spending when under Labour control in previous years. Some 6 million people were living under what I called, 'the bullying rule of socialist Soviets'. Others were 'living in fear of an Orwellian or a McCarthyite challenge to their integrity against which there seems little or no defence'.

The loony left were organizing race meetings, women's meetings

and gay meetings. Labour Haringey decided to 'promote posi-
tive images' on homosexuals and lesbians in their seventy-eight
schools, setting up a lesbian and gay unit with eight officers costing
£120,000 a year. Labour Lambeth banned the word 'families' and
ran twenty homosexual courses. Labour Ealing resolved to let gays
and lesbians adopt children. Labour Brighton had a women's
committee, a police committee, a nuclear-free zone committee and
spent £66,000 on a campaign to persuade their electorate that they
were short of money. Labour Manchester spent £500,000 on a
'nuclear-free Europe' and had five full-time officers employed in
this unit.

There was also the use of creative accountancy whereby councils mortgaged their future, selling buildings and even equipment
to be bought back from Japanese, Swiss and other European banks
over many years. Up to £5 billion of additional local government
debt was created by this method. Camden even sold its parking-
meters to a French institution at £125 a time and lamp-posts at
£200 a time. Some authorities went so far as to mortgage library
books and bathroom fittings. The Secretary of State and I warned
the banks involved in such 'creative accountancy' that these loans
were not backed by the Treasury and there would be no government help if such councils refused to redeem their debts. We also
legislated against this process.

Two other serious matters were the putting of political restrictions on the giving of local authority contracts and the appointment of Labour councillors in one borough to be paid full-time
political advisers to Labour councillors in other boroughs. Leicester
City Council asked contractors if they had any links with nuclear
missile projects. Newham asked if any of a firm's directors were
Freemasons. St Helens asked for gifts to South Vietnam Hospital
funds. Some forty councils refused to accept tenders from firms
with any South African link. Labour councils were also using *Labour
Weekly* to advertise their vacancies, and the wordage often was
such that it implied that sympathy with the aims of the council
was at least as important as were professional qualifications.

In November this matter was raised in oral questions. Jack Straw
compared Labour councils advertising in *Labour Weekly* with Conservative councils advertising in *The Times*. I replied: 'Anyone who
cannot see the difference between *Labour Weekly* and *The Times* is
very short-sighted. I note that, like myself, the hon. Gentleman
wears glasses, but I suggest he consults my oculist.'

Brent, of course, joined in this dangerous nonsense. Plans were prepared to appoint thirteen full-time political advisers – one for each committee chairman – at a cost of £178,000 a year. Their tasks would include liaising with Labour Party headquarters nationally.

An attempt was made in Brent to use Home Office money to appoint 180 'race spies' to cover all of Brent's schools. This was stopped by David Waddington, the Home Secretary, who took back £2 million of a grant and insisted that the remaining money had to be used in teaching English as a second language, not for race spies sniffing out offenders like latter-day Gagools. I said at the time, 'Somebody can be destroyed by being accused of racism without any substance at all and it's getting to the point where nobody can speak out for fear of the witch-hunt.'

The persecuting of Maureen McGoldrick by Brent Council became a national issue. She was the able headmistress of Sudbury Infants School who was suspended for alleged racism. The matter went to the High Court and she was defended by the National Union of Teachers until her suspension was revoked. *New Society* referred to 'the Salem witch trial of Maureen McGoldrick' and one teacher referred to a 'a climate of fear in Brent schools'. I said: 'There is a cloud of fear over the whole borough and it has got to the point where parents and teachers dare not speak out for fear of having their careers destroyed. It is real intimidation. People are truly frightened.' I was quoted in *The Sunday Times* on 26 October 1986 as saying, 'McCarthyism is alive and well in Brent today, and as in Nazi Germany and Soviet Russia, we are moving towards a society where children are encouraged to inform against their parents and their teachers.'

Four 'women' advisers were appointed at a cost of £60,000 a year, and the Brent town hall and other civic buildings were sold in creative accountancy for between £200 and £300 million. A Brent Gay and Lesbian Unit was established at a cost of £120,000 a year. There was an 'Out in Brent' campaign with homosexual and lesbian exhibitions in the local libraries, including the children's libraries, to which parents and local ministers of religion strongly objected. I called such exhibitions 'obnoxious'. It was no wonder that one in four Brent children were attending schools outside the borough. The attack on the family was no accident. It followed the teachings of Trotsky where family, locality and religion were to be destroyed so that 'human dust' was created which could then be totally remodelled in a revolutionary fashion.

Of course Brent was named a nuclear-free zone with a 'nuclear-free zone co-ordinator'. *The Times* leader of 21 October 1986 quoted my description of his duties: '... presumably to daily point the nuclear-free sign outside the Town Hall away from the direction in which the wind is blowing'.

One other issue was decisive in marginalizing the local Labour Party. This was the tolerance, if not the direct encouragement, by the Labour Party of huge gipsy encampments in the north of the borough to harass the local population. Indeed, it was alleged that the gipsy occupation was to teach the north of the borough, which voted Conservative, a lesson! On the beautiful Fryent Country Park – metropolitan open land – 130 caravans, many with all modern conveniences, with some 500 gipsies stayed for two years and did tremendous damage. Ten thousand of my constituents petitioned the town hall for their removal and thousands joined with me in a march on the town hall.

There was also the gipsy threat to the Vale Farm sports ground, again in Brent North Conservative territory. The Labour council at a government enquiry failed in an attempt to take part of the centre for a gipsy site, but the local residents feared that the site would be taken over, as at Fryent Way, illegally. Thus they guarded the entrance to Vale Farm as vigilantes each night, with the telephone numbers of hundreds of locals who would turn out, given a gipsy warning. Whenever I came back late at night or early morning from the Commons I visited them for ten minutes or so and sat by their camp-fire. These vigilantes continued until the threat had passed. Brent was then really under siege with an identified enemy: the Brent Labour Party. John Banham, controller of the Independent Audit Commission, said in 1987 that Brent was one of eight Labour-controlled boroughs where mismanagement was such that they were spending £80 a household more to give the same service as other London boroughs.

I was also fully committed to competitive tendering of almost all services, since they brought the town hall a saving of between 20 and 30 per cent in each case.

A most worrying problem was that the relationship between the Conservative Government and many Labour local authorities was breaking down, and this was neither good for the Government nor for the local authorities. I said in Parliament on 3 March 1987: 'We have been forced to take action because of the breakdown, from a small minority of the local authority side, of consensus. There used to be an acknowledgement by local government that central Government governs in the national interest, but that has been challenged by a handful of reckless authorities. This handful of authorities is tarnishing the reputation and honourable tradition of the majority.'

I suspect it was the Conservative local government reorganization of 1964 and 1974 into huge units that had made this matter worse. Such large units created a need for more full-time local politicians and they became ever more party politicized. In local government, as in most spheres, small is not only more beautiful but more efficient. One needs only look at the percentage voting to realize that small local government units have much more commitment from their citizenry than have large units. Certainly in London the fact that there are not yearly elections for at least a quarter of the councillors means that councils can ignore their electorate for four years, once elected. This also means there are great swings at election time. Jack Straw offered in the 1986 Local Government Bill that he would support a clause bringing yearly elections of a third each year in London boroughs as they had before reorganization, but to my regret the Government was not interested.

I always tried to keep a good relationship with Opposition members. To me they were and are opponents not enemies. Jack Straw was my opposite number two at the Department of Environment and I had known him from the time he was the President of the National Union of Students. When on 5 May 1987 I introduced the fourth rate support grant debate in six weeks, I said: 'It was the writer of Ecclesiastes who wrote, "of making of many books there is no end" and "much study is a weariness to the flesh". Misquoting him a little, I might say that "of the making of many rate support grant reports there is no end".' Two months earlier, on 11 March 1987, just before midnight, while moving a guillotine motion in the House, I said: 'I am surprised that it is I, rather than an opposition Member, who am moving the motion. I had assumed that opposition Members would have been so fed up with seeing me at the Dispatch Bos describing local government finance that they would have queued to support the motion.'

My good friend Colin Welch, then writing in the *Daily Mail*, noted in his column: 'The Gods have relented. The rehabilitation of Dr Boyson, now Minister of Local Government, proceeds apace ... Dr Boyson's affable grin has returned.'

In April I went to Brigham Young University in Utah to address their commencement ceremony and to receive an honorary doctorate in humanities. The audience was made up of 2,834 students receiving degrees and 14,400 others. This was the largest live audience I have ever addressed.

Soon the general election was announced and in the Government's dying days I spoke on two Bills and in one debate. During one of these debates – on local government – I made up a limerick, since it was Edward Lear's birthday:

> 'There was once a doctor of Brent
> Who said, some councils have spent
> Far too much.
> If alas this amendment should pass
> We would all have great cause to lament.'

Jack Straw in his reply also had a limerick:

> 'There was once a doctor of Brent
> Writing verse was not quite his bent.
> He claimed inspiration from Lear –
> T'was a terrible smear
> On a poet whose ideas were heaven-sent.'

On 12 May at 9.26 p.m. I wound up a debate on the green belt: 'Conservative ministers stand by the green belt, they will flock to the polls to support them. We look forward to that day in four weeks' time when we will see the Conservative green benches in the House populated even more than the Opposition green benches.' Those were my last words from the front bench – not the most distinguished, but in good humour.

23

A Free Man Again

*

I always like elections and in the 1987 election I again spoke all over the country. I like best canvassing in my own constituency and meeting my people. With Brent Council upsetting so many ratepayers, I hardly needed to mention national issues on the doorstep in the 1987 election. In addition to Praful Patel, the Labour candidate, I had an Alliance opponent, Chris Mularczyk. The result was:

Dr R. Boyson	(Conservative)	26,823
Mr P. Patel	(Labour)	11,101
Mr C. Mularczyk	(SDP/Alliance)	6,868
Conservative majority		15,722

This was my highest majority and there was a swing of 3.6 per cent in my favour. The *Wembley Observer* wrote: 'He [Dr Boyson] had the air of a seasoned headmaster presiding over the end of term examination where the results are academic – and the only question is whether the class will be allowed home early if they behave.'

Two days later I was made a member of the Queen's Privy Council in the Queen's Birthday Honours list and I presumed I would continue as Minister for Local Government. But this was not to be.

On the following Monday morning I was rung early from No.

10 and asked to come in to see the Prime Minister. I knew immediately this was the 'black spot', that I would be out of the Government. Florette drove me to Harrow, where the station was crowded. At a time when I just wanted to be unrecognized, people came over to me to congratulate me on my election and my privy councillorship. With a strange irony of fate a cheerful, voluble Irish constituent, who had already partaken of the glass of cheer, then attached himself to me on the station platform to begin a wide-ranging conversation which lasted until the train came in. Suddenly the whole irony of the situation began to amuse me. It was as if I were watching myself in a play in a situation where everybody knew what was happening apart from me. At last a fast train came, which did not stop in my constituency so I left my cheerful constituent swearing eternal friendship.

I walked to No. 10 from Westminster station and within a few minutes saw the Prime Minister. She came to the point immediately and I accepted the situation. Over a cup of tea we discussed a matter affecting the Indian vote in our country which I wished to tell her about and which I later followed up by a letter. She informed me that she had recommended the Queen to make me a knight, which pleased me. Few people within three days become both a privy councillor and a knight.

I returned to my Department to arrange for my possessions to be sent home and went over to the Commons to empty my ministerial room. Then my government driver drove me home for the last time. That evening I did a number of cheerful radio and television interviews and I later received a letter from the Prime Minister which said: 'You enhanced every department in which you served with your wit, down-to-earth approach and knowledge of how ordinary persons think. I want to thank you for the notable contributions which you have made in explaining and defending Government policies on radio and television.'

A couple of weeks later I was sworn in as a member of the Privy Council; the following day I was knighted at the Palace and the third day I attended a royal garden party.

It took me a few weeks to adjust to back-bench life after three years as an Opposition spokesman and eight years as a minister. One part of me missed the ministerial routine, another part was delighted to be free again. I had come into politics to influence policy and not for office and I was now free to take up wide-ranging issues again. *The Times* of 16 July referred to me as 'one of the Conservative Party's more eccentric and colourful figures'.

I spoke in the debate on the address in the new Parliament. I began by saying that this was like a second maiden speech and closed by quoting Matthew Arnold: 'Hath man no second life? – Pitch this one high!', followed by my last sentence: 'Tonight I have begun/ My second political life.' I defined clearly in my speech the areas I intended to concentrate on: education, local government and the cutting back of government and taxes within the philosophy of Classical Liberalism. On education I welcomed the extension of parental choice and the direct funding of schools. I asked, however, that groups of parents – Christian fundamentalist schools and Muslim schools, for instance – should be allowed to opt in to grant-maintained status from private status. I welcomed the national curriculum as long as it was basic only in subjects and in matter, while I reiterated my support for tests – simple pen-and-pencil and paper tests – at seven, eleven and fourteen in the basic subjects of English and mathematics and possibly science. I said: 'By all means let us have a minimum curriculum, but let us also have maximum freedom for teachers who go beyond it and teach from the textbooks and syllabuses that they choose as long as they cover the minimum curriculum.' I also advocated a great variety of secondary schools, all with specialities which were taught in depth at least two hours a day, if necessary by extending the hours of instruction. I warned the Government that the educational reforms would go wrong if we insisted on too tight a curriculum and if we packed the organizing committees with so-called educational experts as against practising heads and teachers.

I said in the House on 26 October 1987: 'I am concerned by the fact that 80 per cent of the curriculum is laid down – I think this is too much, especially when it leaves out classics, home economics, business studies, art, music, drama and religious studies.' I wrote in *The Sunday Times* on 29 November that year: 'A common curriculum being offered for 70 per cent or more of the week is an egalitarian concept.'

In January 1988 I warned against the extension to a ten-subject curriculum going up to the age of sixteen, which would be a total nonsense for non-academic pupils who should by then be on specialist courses which had meaning for them. I said unless such specialist courses were provided from the age of twelve, thirteen or fourteen, 'teachers would need the tongues of angels and the amazing qualities of the Magic Circle to interest their classes. I was also concerned about the downgrading of religious education which, with physical education, were up to then the only two compulsory subjects!

I saw the 7-plus, 11-plus and 14-plus tests as minimum competence tests. These could be set nationally by a teachers' panel, should take up to no more than three hours in total, should be sent away to be computer marked and the results returned to the schools and the local education authorities. I opposed teacher assessments, since these are totally subjective and in most cases a waste of time. Alas, the education establishment moved in and built up a great empire. I said in April 1988 that to put 'the tests under the control of an educational establishment which has lowered our educational standards compared with other advanced countries over the last 25 years would simply be a formula for educational non-achievement, and a government which has been so successful in privatising industry should also begin to apply a similar philosophy in educational and social fields.'

Two and a half years later, on 18 October 1990, I told the House of Commons: 'I have considerable sympathy with teachers who feel that if one called a meeting of six infant classroom teachers and six infant school heads, chosen at random from a list of teachers, and brought them together for a day, they could solve all these difficulties by drawing up the tests themselves, instead of leaving it to the educational establishment which did so much to destroy standards.'

I was also concerned about the centralization of the GCSE examination under the control of the Department and not of the universities. I asked time and time again for at least one 'O' level university-controlled 16-plus examination to be retained to ensure that there was no drop in standards. I wrote in the *Daily Mail* on 9 October 1989 that government control of both the national curriculum and the new examination system was 'a centralisation of power alien to the free society which the Conservative Party would have fought had it been introduced by the Labour Party'.

As early as 1988 I also advocated very simple tests when children joined their schools at the age of five. I did this because schools could then be tested on the value-added education they

221

gave between the years of five and seven. Without such a 5-plus simple test the teachers in downtown, inner city areas would always be at a grave disadvantage compared with those in affluent areas, where children could often read before they went to school. What matters is the improvement between the ages of five and seven as well as the standard achieved at seven.

I thus moved on to draw up a list for parents as to the standard their children should achieve before they joined school at five. This list could be given to all parents when they registered their child soon after birth. It began with the ability to dress oneself, to go alone to the toilet, and to use a knife and fork. It then moved on to the knowledge of their names, addresses and ages, the primary colours, numbers up to ten, the ability to put five or six objects in order of size and to put together a ten-piece jigsaw. I recommended that from at least the age of six months if not from birth parents should read regularly every day to their children stories from books which became so well known that the children would eventually be able to read them themselves.

I also advocated that pupils who failed the minimum 7-plus competence test should have to return to school throughout the summer and sit the test again in September. There is no point in moving children up automatically just because of their age when they cannot cope with the work. This only makes them bloody-minded.

I warmly supported the grant-maintained schools as a further extension of parental choice and of parental control of the educational system. Indeed, one of the schools in my constituency – Claremont High School – had a 'yes' vote to become grant-maintained as early as March 1989, and by now all but two secondary schools in my constituency are grant-maintained.

As for the high rates of truancy, which are still with us, especially in the later secondary school, I said in November 1989 that it had been a fearful mistake to rename school attendance officers as educational welfare officers. Once the name was changed, they saw themselves as social workers on the side of the children instead of enforcers of school attendance on the side of the local education authority. I thus recommended that they should be renamed school attendance officers and paid according to the average attendance at the schools for which they were responsible. Such a change of title and purpose would transform school attendance figures in the country overnight.

One earlier educational decision concerned me greatly. This was the introduction of the 1,265 hours per year teachers' contract. When I was at the Education Department I argued against this and stopped its introduction. The 1,265-hour yearly contract treats teachers as hourly workers and gives a weapon against the school and the education authority to trade-union orientated teachers and the clock-watchers. Teaching is a profession and I expected my staff and myself to finish whatever job was in hand in the school when it was needed, instead of counting the hours spent. I also opposed the introduction of the so-called Baker days for professional improvement, since teachers should attend such courses in their own time. I wrote a letter in *The Times*: 'History will make clear that this "contract" has sadly turned teaching from an honourable profession to, in many cases, a clock-watching exercise. At the same time as industry was "buying out" the rule book the Department of Education and Science insisted on introducing such a rule book into teaching.'

Jack Straw, when he was an education spokesman, gave me two compliments which I appreciated. On 2 July 1989 he wrote in *The Sunday Times*: 'Cox and Boyson were editors of the *Black Papers* – probably the single most successful exercise in pamphleteering this side of the War', and a year earlier on 23 March, at the report stage of the Education Reform Bill he said: 'I also pay tribute to the right hon. Member for Brent North [Sir R. Boyson] who always presents himself as some sort of latter-day Gradgrind. However, I represented Islington on ILEA when he was Headmaster of Highbury Grove School, and I can tell the House that the image that he presents is wholly confounded by his reputation as a progressive headmaster who sought high standards for every child in the true spirit of the comprehensive school that he ran.'

After speaking in favour of the community charge in the 1987 general election I had a period of silence on this subject when I returned to the back benches. It was now Michael Howard's brief and I had great respect for him.

One day, however, all this changed. In the early summer of 1989 Tony Favell, the able Conservative Member for Stockport with a majority of 2,853, asked if he and some other northern, largely Lancashire, MPs could talk to me. We decided to dine that evening in the Members' dining room at one of the larger tables. The discussion outlived the meal. Tony brought figures indicating the effect of the community charge in his constituency, where very many of his Conservative voters in small terraced houses would be massive losers because of the greatly increased level of the community charge that they would have to pay in comparison with the previous rating system. The following day I checked the figures with Dr Tony Travers at the London School of Economics and I gave them to *The Times*. This opened the battle of the poll-tax, which would indirectly bring down the Prime Minister.

Much of the north of England had low-rated terrace houses dating back to before the First World War. If there were, for argument's sake, one large house which paid £1,000 in rates alongside four small houses which paid only £100 each in rates, then under the community charge £280 would have to be raised from each house to keep up the town's income, which would mean a near-200 per cent increase on the smaller houses. Indeed, in areas like Hyndburn, Pendle and Stockport up to 70–80 per cent of families would prove to be losers as a consequence of the community charge. This was political dynamite and had not been foreseen and the position could be improved only by putting more money in the government grants to such areas. It was also coming to light that on the changed business rates some 928,000 businesses would lose, some 590,000 would pay less and some 108,000 would pay the same. The whole change in the rating system was becoming a suicide pill and it was a lesson of how not to run a country. Detailed figures should have been prepared before the scheme was put through the Commons.

The Times of 7 July 1989 also stated that I wanted another £1 billion of public money to be put in to cover the cost of the safety net which would otherwise penalize careful Conservative boroughs by forcing them to switch money – up to £75 per head – to wasteful Labour boroughs. I was reported as saying: 'With an act of demonic genius we are undermining all the political good it will do. The main advantage of the community charge as far as ratepayers are concerned is that they will be paying for their own authority's spending. In this case, there is a subsidy to left-wing authorities with their absurd Third World policies.'

To add to the increasing madness Brent, the second highest spender in London, had to transfer £41 per head via the safety net to other London boroughs through a formula which was beyond understanding. *The Observer* the same month quoted me as saying: 'The community charge as it stands is a Labour Party benevolent fund.'

Meanwhile Chris Patten, who had taken over as Secretary of State for the Environment, was receiving more money from the Treasury and I took a delegation of Conservative MPs to see him. By now Ralph Howell, Conservative MP for Norfolk North, was advocating the abolition of the community charge and the putting of the whole cost of local government on a 6 per cent increase in VAT. Other MPs wanted the end of the safety net and the capping of all council community charge levies at £300 per head.

With the London local elections due in 1990, I also took a delegation of London Conservative MPs to see Kenneth Baker, the party chairman. Meanwhile the Conservative Party Conference in October 1989 heard that even more money was going to be put in. This continued drip-feed was inadequate to make the community charge acceptable, but the fact that more money kept becoming available meant that pressure for further government subventions continued. If the Government had in the beginning put in the extra money necessary in the right way the community charge could have been saved, but the continued delay in getting it right proved a death sentence to it.

On 18 January 1990 I voted against the Local Government Finance Bill, along with other Conservative MPs, and our majority dropped from a hundred to thirty-six. I said in the debate that 60–80 per cent of the lower-rated properties in the north would still lose and the safety net, whereby careful boroughs transferred money to spendthrift boroughs, was totally flawed, as was the statement that the maximum increase was £3 per person, since this would apply only where local authorities spent at the norm expected. This Labour councils certainly would not do, and thus their residents would face huge increases. In the same debate I said: 'The Government started out with good intentions. Ministers have passed through and civil servants passed through, so no one guides the legislation from beginning to end. Eventually, as the old saying goes, a camel is a horse invented by a committee.' This is why the legislation was so flawed. Whichever minister sets out the beginning, as Mr Baker did in his green paper, of the new policy, then this minister and the civil servants working with him should take the proposal through from green to white paper to legislation and to its implementation. The continued change of ministers means that each one makes alterations and then passes them on to the next holders of their office without anybody being finally responsible.

Meanwhile I had, at the request of other Conservative MPs, warned Margaret Thatcher privately that the community charge was now fatally flawed and it would damage her position. She did not take kindly to this information and spoke about my loyalty. I replied that loyalty means telling people the truth.

The Times of February 1990 quoted me as saying: 'I am worried that we shall create a new poor. Twice as many people will require help, yet we came in as the Government who wanted to end or lessen dependency.' In early March 1990 I suggested that all education expenditure should be financed by the Government by making every school a grant-maintained school and I said: 'We will have to make concessions sooner or later on the community charge. Surely it is better to make them now than later, when the Government will be portrayed as walking from one elephant trap into another.'

In the debate in the House of 26 March 1990 I not only attacked again the now £70 switch of the safety net from careful to spendthrift boroughs, but the injustice meted out to the wife who did not work but looked after her children: she would be the only person without income who had to pay the community charge. I called this a tax on marriage and it was certainly another blow against the family. I also spoke against a system whereby aged relatives who were kept at home had to pay the community charge, though if they were put into an old people's home there was no charge. This was a further penalty clause against the family.

The community charge was by now unsaleable. Already more than £3 billion more had been put in by the Government and yet more money still was required.

We then had the fall of Margaret Thatcher and Michael Heseltine's appointment as Secretary of State for the Environment, when more money was again put in. I said to the Secretary of State on this occasion, with what one newspaper called my 'mastery of the metaphor', that before the replacement of 'the poll tax is set in concrete there has to be a head-banging session.... It must not be brought down like the tablets from Mount Sinai. We cannot afford more mishaps'.

The March 1991 Ribble Valley by-election, when a 19,528 Conservative majority was transformed into a Liberal Democrat majority of 4,601, made the decease of the community charge certain. We simply waited for the funeral. Norman Lamont's budget, in which he took £140 away from the average community charge and put it on VAT, was decisive. Ironically, however, this was sufficient money to make the community charge saleable, but it was too late. There was nothing wrong with the principle of the community charge; what was wrong was its level, which arose from wrong government calculations which would not have achieved a GCSE Grade 9 in mathematics. A universal tax must be kept low for the mass of the people or it will be indefensible for the lower earning groups.

I said in March 1991: 'If we go back to a property tax we will be going not from the frying pan into the fire, but the flaming cauldron.' We went back, however, to the council tax – a mixed system which benefited the north and generally disadvantaged the south, where the Tory seats are. I then asked for a 50 per cent discount for single householders and a separate set of bands for London and the south-east or for the valuation of the houses to be done purely on house rebuilding costs, ignoring the heavy cost of the land which inflates London property prices.

Because the average price of houses varies in different parts of the country, Wales and Scotland each have their own set of bands, yet London and the south-east, where there is the greatest difference of house prices compared with the rest of the country, were not allowed a separate set of bands despite the request of London MPs and the London Boroughs Association.

The same size of house in the north-east can cost only 40 per cent of the cost of a London house of the same size. Forty-seven per cent of houses in Barnet are in the top two bands as against 1 per cent in the north-west. London and the south-east have 45 per cent of their houses above the average price, while the cost of houses in the north is 25 per cent below average. Since the amount of money put in by the Government is in reverse ratio to what is assumed can be raised locally, the over-valuation of London houses compared with the rest of the country moved £200 million out of London in 1992 and another £175 million out of the rest of the south-east. This money was switched largely to the north and the Labour seats there. This affected the 1992 local government results in the south of England. With the cost of transport as well as housing being so much higher in London, it is estimated that a person needs to earn £6,000 per year more in the metropolis before he can live at the same standard as someone in the north.

It is interesting that the Department of Health accepts the difference of housing prices in London from the rest of the country and has four sets of bands to reimburse doctors for their surgery housing costs. It is presumed that a doctor in London will have to pay one-third more for his housing surgery than a Cliveden doctor. I thus suggested that an environment minister should collect a copy of these health allowances from which to calculate a new set of bands for the council tax in London.

Sadly, real local government has almost been destroyed in Britain. I do not think Mrs Thatcher ever liked local government except in Westminster and Wandsworth. The Conservative Government has centralized both power and finance and now the local council tax raises only 15 per cent towards local government costs. The rest comes from central government. I said in the debate on the address in November 1991: 'We do not want all power to be vested in central government – or anywhere else for that matter. The tension that has existed between national and local government under the present Government has been bad for the country.'

I always opposed the local government reorganizations of 1964 and 1972 – both by a Conservative Government. This was part of the destruction of Edmund Burke's 'little platoons' where people feel at home, valued and involved. These reorganizations were also highly expensive and created a semi-professional class of local councillors as against the involvement on two or so nights a week of local councillors.

Compared with France, with its 37,000 communes, we have almost regional government in Britain. Everywhere on the Continent the average size of local government units is far smaller than it is in Britain, and it is really *local government*. The time is surely right in Britain to allow local communities that wish to opt for smaller council areas to do so. This is now easier, since education through the grant-maintained schools is leaving local government, housing has almost left local government, and police and regional planning can be controlled elsewhere. We should thus aim for smaller units set up by the areas themselves with their council tax covering a far higher share of local expenditure than under the present system. The nineteenth century was keen on 'enabling' legislation. This allowed areas that wished to change their local arrangements to do so, while leaving other areas as they were. This may make a country untidy but is surely part of freedom and democracy and we badly need our 'local platoons' back.

On the national and international scene I have become more and more suspicious of the European Community. I voted for our continuing membership in 1975 in the referendum. Since then, however, other European countries have made clear that they intend to drive on to a federal Europe, which I certainly do not want. I am also becoming more and more suspicious of the economic future of the European Community which, I fear, through over-regulation, could become a bureaucratic morass unable to compete with the rest of the world. On 15 May 1989 I voiced these fears in a speech when I said: 'Britain faced the danger of a post-1992 high tariff protectionist Europe' while 'our future lay in open markets, open seas and open skies'. I said in the debate on the address that year: 'I do not like the social market and I do not want any form of political links. I am not a Federalist.'

At the time of the resignation of Nicholas Ridley in July 1990, after his aspersive comments on Germany, I called for a referendum before we made any closer links with Europe.

Before Mr Major went to Maastricht I met him with a number of other Euro-sceptical MPs. I said that if he kept us out of the social charter, out of a single currency, out of a single European bank and out of a federal Europe, I would carefully consider my position in any subsequent vote in the House, but otherwise I would have to oppose such legislation. At Maastricht he achieved these opt-outs and on Boxing Day I praised his achievement as a negotiator. I wonder what Margaret Thatcher would have done. I fear she might finally have settled for such a compromise when the chips were down!

I thus voted reluctantly with the Government at the second reading of the European Communities (Amendment) Bill, which passed by 336 to 92 votes. In my speech in this debate I did spell out my reservation: 'I am still concerned about over-regulation . . . it could make economies in Europe uncompetitive with those in the rest of the world. . . . I am still concerned about the exchange rate mechanism.'

By the time of the paving resolution on 4 November 1992 I had become even more sceptical. I lost sleep over what I should do so soon after a general election which was won, to my mind, by the Prime Minister. A Member of Parliament must follow his conscience, yet he must make sure it is not a personal ego-trip. He must also weigh up what effect his vote will have in the long run on his constituents and the country.

The day before the vote I was still undecided. I then met with four other members of the 92 Group, all of us elected members of the 1922 Executive, and we decided to see the Prime Minister. We telephoned him and he gave us a time and George Gardiner, Bob Dunn, James Pawsey, John Townend and I went to the Prime Minister's room to talk for almost half an hour. We gave our views – frankly and clearly – as to how much we disliked the Maastricht Treaty. We asked for no concessions and when we came away we decided to support the Prime Minister. We feared that if he lost the vote he might resign and we would have a much more pro-European replacement, or if, at very long odds, a government defeat meant a general election, there was a risk that the Conservative Party would lose it and this would not be only a disaster on defence and economic and educational policies, but we would have a government much more pro-Maastricht than the Conservative one.

Once we had made our decision we wrote to the Prime Minister, sending a copy of the letter to the *Daily Telegraph* in which, the next day – the day of the vote – it appeared on the front page. It must have also influenced others to support the Government. The votes on that night were 319 to 313 and 319 to 316. It was a close shave!

Having made up my mind, I had two good nights' sleep, particularly as the Labour Party made the situation easier by playing politics with the issue and voting against the Government, while they were more pro-Maastricht than the Conservative Party!

I initially intended to play a part in the committee stage of the Bill being taken on the floor of the House as a constitutional Bill. On the first day I prepared a speech and sat in the chamber. There were continuous points of order, which I always find tedious, and after some four hours I noticed one of my daughters was in the gallery. Obviously she wanted me and I came out, threw away my speech and gave her a meal. Charity begins at home.

I had by then decided that I would vote against the third reading and in favour of the referendum, but I had no intention of getting involved in the minutiae of the Bill at committee stage. I voted against the Government twelve times, abstained thirty-eight times and voted with the Government eleven times on the various substantive and procedural motions. When I look back, what I regret is that the whole Bill – now an Act – seems to be a confidence trick of the three parties against the people of our islands. When the three parties agree and their agreement is blessed by the Archbishop of Canterbury, one must be very suspicious – unless it is a declaration of war. I firmly believe that the passage of power from the Commons to Europe should have been a people's decision and not a government or whipped party decision. The vote, to my mind, thus has no credibility and the British people can revoke it at any time. We joined the European Community originally for trade purposes, and the preservation of GATT is in my view more important than the European Community, and this could allow us to leave it if we so decide.

Alas, the British people seem bored by the whole proceedings, as is seen by the low vote of anti-Maastricht candidates in recent by-elections. Maybe the British public, with their instinctive sense of history, have made up their minds that Europe is going to break up in any case, so that the Maastricht Treaty is not worth bothering about.

Another matter affecting foreign policy was our relationship with China and Hong Kong. I voted against the motion to offer 50,000 passports to some 225,000 ethnic Chinese. I saw no sense in this at all, since China does not allow dual nationality and consequently such passports would not help to keep people in Hong Kong but condemn them to exile. I said in the House on 19 April 1990: 'The British Empire is as dead as the Roman Empire. This is a Chinese problem while we have to make our own destiny.' I would simply have offered passports to those who had served in Her Majesty's forces and their families. If anyone else should have been offered passports, it should have been the ethnic minorities there, such as the Indians. I also think that after 150 years of British rule in Hong Kong the attempt by Chris Patten and the British Government in the dying days of our rule to attempt to introduce democracy there is wrong and the Chinese Government is right to oppose it. It seems to me to smack of the worst of Western hypocrisy.

After the invasion of Kuwait in 1990 I was very concerned that Parliament was being ignored and I wrote a letter to *The Times* on 18 August, asking for its recall. I wrote: 'Our legitimate pride in our Parliamentary government is weakened if the elected government can virtually declare war at the behest of the United Nations or any other group of nations without this having been currently debated and agreed in Parliament.'

Needless to say, I spoke in the two-day debate, giving the Government full support and making a parallel between Saddam Hussein's aggression and the failure to check Hitler and Mussolini in the late 1930s.

With regard to defence, I have made clear in Parliament and in letters to *The Times* that there should not be any further cuts in our defence capacity in a world which in many ways has become much more dangerous since the end of the Nato/Russian Communist balance of power.

Over the last few years law and order has continued to decline in Britain, notably from 1983, and the Government continues to deal with symptoms not causes. A classic example of this is on the question of identity cards. On 10 February 1989 Ralph Howell moved the second reading of the Bill to bring in identity cards for all. Only three countries in Europe have no identity cards and it is obvious to me and to the man in the public bar that the existence of such cards would help cut down undetected crime. I said outside the House: 'Anybody not prepared to carry such an identity card is up to no good or is suffering from advanced libertarianism.' Such cards would also cut back social security and credit card fraud. I favoured a card carrying the name, date of birth, address, photograph and fingerprints of the owner, along with the blood group in case of accident and whether he or she wished to be an organ donor. With no government help, the Bill passed by forty-eight to thirty-seven votes one Friday, but since fewer than a hundred had voted, this Private Member's Bill fell.

Four months later, however, the Government introduced its Football Spectators Bill whereby all spectators of professional football leagues had to carry cards issued by their home team. Football hooliganism is but a symptom of widespread juvenile revolt arising from massive school truancy, the lessening of community ties which once held people together and the virtual disappearance of the three-dimensional family of grandparents, parents and young adolescents. The Football Spectators Bill was unworkable, biased against what was seen by many as a working-class sport and would have caused huge problems if it had become law. Together with thirteen other Conservative Members, I voted against it. Fortunately it was dropped the following year, when football hooliganism was already past its peak.

I have little sympathy with the continued reorganization of the Health Service, ostensibly to save money and to become more efficient. In the Commons and in the press I have opposed the destruction of the London specialist hospitals, as I had earlier opposed the destruction of the old grammar schools. Both the old grammar schools and the old London hospitals were built on loyalty and *esprit de corps*, not on accountants' reports. Nor do I believe that we have too many hospital beds in London, when I have to battle every week to get constituents of mine into hospital.

We could easily spend 105 per cent of the gross national product on health, yet people would still demand more. With increased affluence, people expect to buy their cars, their household goods and their overseas holidays without long waits and they automatically now demand the same in health. The continued attempt by the Government to reorganize the Health Service is then blamed – in my view with considerable credibility – as the reason for the long hospital queues! I think a period of no change in the Health Service, during which everybody would be expected to be responsible for the job they are doing, would be much more helpful.

I also believe that some form of personal insurance will have to be introduced to bring in sufficient money to satisfy the continued demands for better health services, and patients must certainly be told the cost of their treatment and operations, as is the case in other European countries. Personally, if we were making a change, I would have much preferred the hospitals being put back into the control of charities, churches, local authorities, trade unions and other bodies as against the *ad hoc* trusts which have no territorial base in their areas and are totally artificial. They seem a typical uninspiring product of a semi-quango age.

I used to tease people at meetings when I spoke of the great increase of people working in the National Health Service, the biggest employer in Europe. On 19 January 1988 I said in the

House of Commons: 'On one set of figures . . . 510,000 more people are employed in the Health Service now than were employed in 1970. Since 1970, the population of this country has grown by 500,000. So we are employing 510,000 more staff for a population that has grown by 500,000. Thus on a straight line graph projection there will come a time when more people are employed in the Health Service than live in this country.'

On the economy I expressed my serious reservations about joining the European Monetary System, considering the pound to be overvalued by between 10 and 15 per cent, and I regularly pressed for a reduction in interest rates whose size was crippling the British economy. I compared the EMS to a twelve-legged race in which twelve people had their legs tied together and were then made to run. Of course they all fell down. The value of a currency is simply the observers' assessment of what it will buy in the near future.

I thus welcomed our withdrawal from the EMS on 16 September 1992, but regret that we then wasted months before we cut our interest rates to encourage the growth of our economy.

As for taxes, I not only wanted the bottom rate reduced to 20 per cent, but the top rate cut to 30 per cent. The drastic cuts in taxation under the Thatcher government fired the enterprise of our people and even helped to win the 1992 general election. I warned in the debate on the address on 8 May 1992 that the Government had again begun to increase its share of the national cake. I said: 'We can have low taxes only if we keep Government expenditure under control. In this century, the more Parliament meets and the more Ministers there are the more Bills costing money in the long run are passed. I was delighted that the gracious speech said that the Government will reduce the share of national income taken by the public sector. Up to 1987 we achieved that – we brought it below 40 per cent – but in the last four years it has crept up again, as it always does, to about 43 per cent. We must get it back to below 40 per cent as in Switzerland and Japan. The 40 per cent level is very important. The various taxes that are taken from people in this country currently represent £10,000 per person at work. Nobody can say that we are a low tax country at the present time. The more that people make decisions about their own money the better society is – rather than such decisions being made by Government committees, however elevated.'

Much has been written about the replacement of Margaret Thatcher as Prime Minister by John Major. There was first the 1989 kite-flying by Sir Anthony Meyer and then in 1990 the real challenge by Michael Heseltine, an exciting figure, a favourite of the Conservative Party Conference, an interventionist and a keen European. The pro-Thatcher campaign did not exist. On numerous radio and television programmes I spoke in favour of the retention of Mrs Thatcher as Prime Minister, but no contact was made with me by the official team that was supposed to be running her campaign. On the other hand, I was regularly approached by the Heseltine campaign team, despite the fact that they knew that I was committed to Mrs Thatcher.

I was speaking on an extended Radio 4 *PM* programme when the news came through that Margaret Thatcher had gained a majority on the first ballot but was four votes short of the number needed to win outright. William Powell, MP, was with me, representing the Heseltine supporters. I do not know what I said on radio but I do know what I said to William: 'Tell your man to withdraw now in the name of party unity and say his services will always be at the party's disposal and he will be the Prime Minister in a year's time.' I wonder whether William was able to pass the message on to Michael Heseltine.

The following day there were continuous meetings and speculation and I went home late, believing that Margaret Thatcher would stand in the second ballot. I rose early and worked in my study at my desk and suddenly I had a call from Robert Kilroy-Silk to go on his programme, with the information that Margaret Thatcher had withdrawn. I was shattered, but I went and it was not until the end of the programme that I suddenly realized that no right-wing candidate had been nominated. The nominations had closed at noon.

On the previous ballot I informed my constituency chairman what I was doing – indeed everyone knew – but on the second ballot I asked my constituency chairman to poll my ward chairmen. I was at first tempted to vote for Michael Heseltine, since if we were to have a change we might as well have a complete one. Over the weekend I received my constituency opinions –

overwhelmingly for John Major. On the Sunday morning I went up to the Midlands to address the National Young Conservative Conference and they – largely right-wing – were also very much for John. I was also informed that Margaret Thatcher preferred John Major. Thus on the Sunday evening I rang Michael Heseltine, as I had promised, and informed him that I was voting for John Major. I then rang John Major and the rest, as people say, is history.

I do think that John Major won us the 1992 election. I said in the debate on the address on 8 May: 'The Election was clearly won by the Prime Minister's firm stand on constitutional issues. In the last resort constitutional matters are even more important than economic ones. Those constitutional issues were proportional representation, devolution and the unity of the United Kingdom.'

I am privileged in Wembley to represent John Betjeman's Metroland. Most of my constituency was built in the late 1920s and 1930s, with a few earlier streets and some post-Second World War estates. People moved to the suburbs for gardens and fresh air and I am becoming more and more concerned that this fresh air is being threatened by the planning laws which, with other MPs, I have tried to have changed. The law is far too much on the side of the developers in back-garden development. Houses can be knocked down without planning consent to force the hand of the local council and the minister to give planning consent for unpopular replacements. Developers are also allowed to appeal against a council rejection of their development plans yet the householder, whose life-style will be changed or even destroyed if a development goes ahead, has no right of appeal to the minister when the local council agrees a planning application. It is also an astonishing situation when somebody, without owning one square foot of the land, can put in for planning permission affecting thousands of houses. Such applications frighten existing householders, so that they often sell cheaply to the developers.

On 28 November 1988, and on 12 November 1990, I, along with other MPs representing suburban seats around London, Birmingham and Manchester, tried in vain to have the planning laws changed to protect the suburban environment. With no government help – indeed probably with government hindrance – we failed.

People in my constituency are rightly more concerned about

the green belt of their own and their neighbours' gardens and the adjacent school and university playing fields, which they see every day, than they are about the rolling green acres of the green belt which are a long drive away. During my time as Member of Parliament for Brent North, playing field after playing field in my constituency has been built over, to the serious detriment of the area, but no one in the Government seems to care. Tiny flats have replaced the green gardens and playing fields and we are becoming a 'window box' rather than 'garden' society. Indeed, I said in the 12 November debate that some of this development 'was worse than the back-to-back developments of the nineteenth century. An exaggeration, perhaps, but still a justifiable comparison.

Brent continued to be a problem area. In 1987 Sir David Lane was appointed to report on the use of Section 11 money – English as a foreign language – in Brent. The gipsies were eventually removed after almost two years, in June 1988. Brent also achieved a shortage of teachers, the sale of council house flat keys in Africa, the largest percentage of rates and rent arrears in Britain and a rates increase in one year (1989) of 32 per cent.

The Conservatives polled well in council by-elections in Brent and in the 1990 local elections, despite Labour being 20 per cent ahead in the public opinion polls nationally, we gained 9 seats from Labour. Brent Council then consisted of 31 Conservatives, 29 Labour and 6 Liberals. A mayor and a deputy major were then elected, but there were no committee chairmen. Every committee meeting began with the election of a chairperson. This problem ended only when a number of Labour councillors left the Labour Party to form the Democratic Labour Party in order to support the Conservatives and to take chairs and official nominations as Conservative allies. This created other problems, but allowed the Conservative group to improve services while reducing the council tax. Instead of being the fourth highest in London, Brent became in 1994 the fourth lowest.

The state of London Transport has long been a matter of great concern to my constituents. On 9 December 1989 I asked the Secretary of State for Transport: '. . . is he aware that it is generally felt in London that massive capital expenditure on the London Underground is required if London is not to come to a stop? Is he aware that people of all political opinions are weary of delays, breakdowns, inaudible announcements, the greatest concentration of broken-down escalators in discovered space, beggars, tramps and children selling lavender, all of which are a disgrace in a national capital?' I opposed the cuts in staff on the London Underground, believing that people will not travel from unmanned or skeleton-manned tube stations in late evenings or even on winter afternoons.

I also think that London is disadvantaged in not having a central body to speak on its behalf. On 5 June 1991 I suggested a directly elected lord mayor for the people of London to join with the City lord mayor to sell London to the world. We still need such a voice, just as we need massive up-rating of the Underground and the building of two or three new underground lines.

All Conservative MPs were concerned about the future of the Government when the general election was announced in 1992. I had continued, as always, on my regular walkabouts and contact with constituents and this was the first general election since 1974 in which I could concentrate my energies on my own constituency. I found it difficult to assess the mood of the public. People were very pleasant on their doorsteps but they were obviously concerned about the state of the economy in London. One in eight of my male electorate was unemployed, with the figures for the eighteen- to twenty-four year-old males reaching as high as one in five unemployed. Many people did not tell me or my canvassers that they were unemployed, and it was only after fairly long conversations that this fact came to light. There were real human tragedies in every avenue, with people wondering how long they could hold on to their houses, having lost their jobs and their earning prospects.

My Labour opponent was local and fought a hard campaign. The result was a drop in my majority of 5,589 and a swing to Labour, but I still had 56.4 per cent of the total votes. My Labour opponent referred to me as a 'doughty fighter'.

Sir Rhodes Boyson	(Conservative)	23,445
Mr J.G. Moher	(Labour)	13,314
Mr P. Lorber	(Liberal Democrat)	4,149
Conservative majority		10,131

Nationally it was a narrow victory, but the British people with their political genius probably achieved the result they desired – a narrow Conservative victory. They still distrusted the Labour Party and they had no enthusiasm for the Liberal Democrats, yet though they were disappointed with the Conservatives, they felt safer with them than with any other political party.

One personal sadness for me has been the decline of Highbury Grove School after Laurie Norcross retired as headmaster in 1987 because of political interference. The headmaster who replaced him was not in the Boyson or Norcross mould, to say the least. By 1991 the school was in trouble and an HMI report on it in 1992 was one of the worst I have ever seen.

There have been other education shadows. Ramsbottom Secondary Modern School is no more; Lea Bank was closed because of its buildings and smallness despite its great achievements; and Robert Montefiore Secondary School was closed because of its problems, despite its success from 1961 to 1966.

My father often repeated that he had outlived his friends. I seem to have outlived my schools, apart from Stonefold St John's Church of England Primary School, to which I went as a boy and which I helped to save when it was under threat. The wheel of life has indeed come full circle.

24

The Future

*

I have travelled from childhood to maturity and I have seen great changes in our society and in our place in the world. What of the future? Let us ignore Sam Goldwyn's remark that we should never forecast, especially about the future. There is one constant factor, however, that we ignore at our peril: the unchangeability of human nature. I do not believe that it has changed since God breathed actually or figuratively on man in the Garden of Eden and gave him a soul and the opportunities of choosing between good and evil. Ross McWhirter used to say that if we stroke a cat one way it purrs, but if we stroke it the other way it growls. The secret of good government is to understand human nature and stroke people the right way. The study of human nature in the classical cultures, in history and in great literature is the best preparation for the understanding of man and politics. Modern media studies are no substitute. Such modern studies have much breadth but no depth.

We have seen the decline of the power of Britain. This was possibly inevitable from 1880 and it has continued in my lifetime. We were not aware, however, of this decline when as a schoolboy I walked in the coronation procession in Haslingden in 1938, nor when I returned from the Royal Navy after the Second World War in which, with our allies, we had won a righteous war and saved European civilization from barbarism. In 1947 I had hoped that we would build a socialist paradise in Britain. It was not to be. I slowly recognized and accepted the doctrine of original sin and that man was not perfectible in this life, and that if we could make life even tolerable, this was a great achievement. Then we had Thatcherism – partially the age and partially the lady – and it seemed that we would have an economic miracle to be admired by the rest of the world. The last four years seem to have put paid to that dream.

What is the future for Britain? Historically we were a nation of merchant adventurers buying in the cheapest and selling in the dearest markets. Is this still possible, now we have chosen closer and closer links with what seems a restrictive, bureaucratic yet large European market? Certainly Hong Kong, Taiwan and the other rising economies of the Pacific basin have shown that, if a country makes goods of the right quality and at the right price, the world will still beat a path to its door. If the world does divide itself into three or four huge rigid trading blocs, there is a strong argument that we have to be in the European bloc. I do not think, however, that this will happen and I am glad that at last we achieved a GATT Agreement in 1993. I suspect that if the European Community becomes, as it may, even more bureaucratic and restrictive, we shall have to consider at some stage withdrawal from it, painful as this may be. One should never ally oneself with a declining power. The 1996 Intergovernment Conference is the crunch date. If the Conference comes out for a Federal Europe, really a Euro superstate, we shall have to withdraw. The Labour and Liberal Parties are totally married to Europe, but the Conservative Party is split and it should offer our people a referendum on whether we withdraw or remain in Europe. This would also change the face of British politics to Conservative advantage.

Internally, I believe that the best government for Britain will be one believing on the one hand in the free market, low government expenditure, low taxes and preferably debt free, while in social policy it promotes national unity and creates a climate of concern for the welfare of the young, the handicapped and the old.

The Thatcher government cut back the share of gross national product going to government from 49 per cent in 1979 to 39.25 per cent. This rose to 45.5 per cent in 1993. Forty per cent going to government is to me the absolute maximum before the psychology of the country becomes corrupted by the populace being concerned more to obtain their share of the government gravy train than to increase productivity and their direct incomes.

When Gladstone was in charge of our finances over a hundred years ago only 9 per cent of gross national product went to government. By 1914 the figure had risen to 15 per cent, to 25 per cent in the 1930s and to almost half the national income today. In Japan only 30 per cent of national income goes to government, and in Hong Kong the figure is only 18 per cent. I suspect that these lower figures have had a great deal to do with the rapid growth of their respective economies.

I believe that the difficulty of cutting government expenditure and bureaucracy in Britain is linked with the great increase this century in the number of ministers and aspirant ministers and the over-activity of the House of Commons with full-time Members of Parliament. All ministers are backed by large numbers of civil servants believing, like most of their ministers, that the government in which they serve has a wisdom far beyond that of the ordinary populace. Both ministers and civil servants thus become wedded to big government.

Cutting government should start at the top. In 1900, when Great Britain was still the greatest power in the world and we governed a huge empire upon which it was said the sun never set, Lord Salisbury was both Prime Minister and Foreign Secretary and was supported at the Foreign Office by just one under-secretary in the Commons. Now with our empire gone and our responsibilities drastically reduced, we have six Foreign Office ministers. In 1900 there were only seventeen ministers outside the Cabinet in both Houses. There are now over sixty. Until 1939 only ministers were full-time politicians. Now most MPs are full-time whatever their outside interests. The burden of constituency ombudsman work is very demanding, although it does keep Members of Parliament in touch with reality. A reply to a recent survey indicated that 40 per cent of Members of Parliament worked over a seventy-hour week, which leaves little time for detached thought or reading.

There is also a tendency for Members of Parliament to join at an earlier age, before they have full independence of profession, calling or property. The independent Tory squires have almost disappeared, as have the chairmen of big companies and national trade-union officers. We now have a Parliament where most are ministers, ex-ministers or aspirant ministers. There is thus a risk that the Commons could become a kind of closed shop of a narrow political interest group totally dedicated from university age or even earlier to a lifetime's political career, although there seems to be a new fashion of ex-Cabinet ministers not remaining on the back-benches but going to the Lords at the first opportunity.

Our Parliament also meets far longer than that of practically any other country. The amount of legislation increases yearly, and Lord Rippon said in 1990 that Parliament had become 'a sort of legislative sweatshop'. The more legislation is passed, the less it can be checked carefully and the more amending legislation has to be carried in subsequent years to clear up faults and anomalies. Objections are made, quite rightly, to over-regulation from Europe while we in Parliament over-regulate British industry. As one American judge is alleged to have said: 'No man's liberty or property is secure while the legislature is in session.'

I would suggest one way to tackle this problem. Let there be a sabbatical year when Parliament debates the great issues of our time but no Bills are allowed. At the same time we should learn from the success of the education league tables and construct a departmental league table published every three months to show how much each department has cut its expenditure and the number of its employees. The future honours to the departmental permanent secretaries and the senior civil servants should be linked with these tables. This would be a very interesting experiment as to how far government was then cut back.

The wonder is that despite the number of ministers and shadow ministers and the number of aspirants to ministerial office so many, particularly Conservative, Members of Parliament revolted on Maastricht irrespective of the effect on their parliamentary career prospects. It still gives one faith in the basic independence of the British character.

One department which should be protected from any more cuts is defence. The world is now a much more dangerous place than when there was a balance of power between the Soviet Empire and Nato. Peace in international relations is akin to that in marriage – there has to be a dominant power or a balance of power. In the nineteenth century Britain was the dominant power and the Royal Navy was the world policeman. From the Treaty of Vienna in 1815 to the outbreak of the First World War in 1914 there was relative peace. From the breaking of the Berlin blockade in 1948 to the collapse of the Soviet Empire in 1990 there was a balance of power between the Soviets and Nato, and again we had relative peace. This balance of power has now gone and we have minor wars and threats of such wars all over the world, many of which could escalate into major conflicts threatening world trade and security.

I believe it was a mistake that the Gulf conflict was not continued until Baghdad was taken and Saddam Hussein replaced. That would have been a lesson to the world that the United States and her Nato allies, along with local alliances, would keep the world's peace. As it is, Saddam Hussein is still there cocking a snook at the rest of the world. I suspect that the United States might not have gone into the Gulf War without the iron will of Margaret Thatcher and her close relationship with President Bush. I also suspect that if Mrs Thatcher had remained as Prime Minister, her influence on the American President would have been forcibly exercised in favour of taking Baghdad and the downfall of Saddam Hussein. In war, as in school discipline and in all conflicts, the first battle should effectively be fought so that it is also the last.

Bosnia has indicated that Europe cannot even look after its own backyard properly and this could influence the United States to pull out of Europe, which would be a sad day for our continent, since, with a question mark remaining as to Russia with her huge nuclear arsenal, the future has many danger signs. The return of all United States military personnel from Europe would certainly create a dangerous power vacuum.

We must retain our Trident submarine nuclear deterrent or we shall be at the mercy of any rogue state that threatens us with a nuclear attack. We also need a strong Royal Navy and Royal Air Force to deter any future threat to our country. We do not need a large standing army, but we should have considerable numbers of army reservists on the Israeli model, who after three to five years full-time service are regularly retrained over the following thirty years ready for any conflict. Our forces should be adequate not only for our own defence but to help our allies, especially the United States, in any joint conflicts.

Good defence forces are not only necessary for our own protection, they are in many ways the best training schools in discipline, responsibility and leadership in our society. They are, with the local company and regimental army system, one of the best of Burke's 'little platoons' to hold society together.

Locally recruited, they are a social cement. Arrangements should also be made for automatic transfer at the same rank, after further training, from the armed services to the police, the fire services, the ambulance services, the railways and London Transport.

One other suggestion regarding the armed services. Having a high proportion of my electorate from India, East Africa and other parts of the world, I have always advocated that there should be not only a brigade of Scots, Welsh and Irish Guards, but that there should be an Indian Guards brigade and a West Indian Guards brigade officered from the same communities. Such brigades would do more for race relations than twenty Equal Opportunities commissions. The collapse of law and order in our society has arisen from the breakdown of the 'little platoons' on one side and a total misreading of human nature on the other side, whereby governments of all colours have listened to do-gooders or rather well-meaners. Men and women are not naturally good. They need firm enforcement of law and order.

Edmund Burke started from the smallest unit. He held: 'To love the little platoon we belong to is the first principle of public affections.' Alas, the breakdown of the smallest 'platoon' – the three-dimensional family of grandparents, parents and children – has been the most disastrous change of my generation. Respect for others and oneself, good behaviour and a sense of continued responsibility and purpose come naturally from the extended family, with the young males modelling themselves on mature fathers, grandfathers and uncles. This is now often totally absent in the one-parent family with father absent.

We have also added to our problems by withdrawing corporal punishment from schools, whereby the male teachers cannot now act *in loco parentis* to the male young. Social workers are no substitute and may even increase the problem. Vigorous team games are also in decline in schools so that the young create their own more brutal games to fill the vacuum. Boys also create their own little gang platoons at war with society as substitutes for the family and school games.

Taxes, benefits and social services should be totally reorganized to support and advance the nuclear family without being balanced against the one-parent family. Someone is always responsible for a youthful misdemeanour – the child or the parent. If the Government decides that children up to the age of seven or ten are not responsible for their actions, then the parents or guardians should be put in the dock. Cautions are rarely any use in controlling the behaviour of children. When children misbehave intentionally, immediate retributive action is necessary. The police are a law-enforcing body, not a social service, and they must be seen as persons of authority.

We need a return of the residential approved schools as well as day misbehaviour and truant schools, which children have to attend for elongated days of eight or more hours, where they receive education in the basic subjects and two hours minimum of physical training daily. Ex-service non-commissioned officers would be ideal for this task.

The view that the British are a kind, automatically law-abiding people is a dangerous myth. Our sports and pastimes have always included many which were and are amongst the most brutal and our infantry bayonets have been feared all over the world. We had a hundred years of relative law and order from the introduction of the police in Victorian times until the early 1960s when the well-meaners took control, totally undermining the peace and security of our society. Punishments themselves, however, are not enough. We must rebuild our 'little platoons'. We need in addition to the family the local village, town and county loyalties, the churches, the schools, voluntary societies and all other intricate patterns of social life. Conservative governments in the name of efficiency and economy destroyed hundreds if not thousands of 'little platoons' in their local government reorganizations of 1964 and 1972. Local government should be both 'local' and 'government', and local people should be allowed to decide their own local boundaries by referendum and not by central government diktat. Every country in Europe has far smaller local government units than we now have in Britain and there is far greater local pride in Europe. Local government boundary tidiness is no virtue in a free society.

One course of action to help law and order and local pride would be to insist that all young males between the ages of twelve and eighteen had to belong to a local uniformed organization which meets together at least one evening a week, one weekend a month and one week a year. These could be the Scouts, the Church Lads' Brigade, St John's Ambulance juniors or the existing pre-service units. In addition, there should be established in each local area a twelve- to eighteen-year-old uniformed general service unit run by ex-servicemen on the lines of a cross between the Outward Bound schools and Dad's Army. Each unit drawn from a specific local area would compete against other local units on a regular basis. I would restrict these units to being male only because the problem of adolescent misbehaviour is basically male, since boys, unlike girls, are pack animals and because I do not worship at the shrine of political correctness.

It would help our youth both in learning and behaviour if there was a return to the apprenticeship system. Germany has 700,000 apprentices in 430 different occupations. One-third of German apprentices have already attained *Abitur* standard for university entry and they complete an apprenticeship before taking up their higher education place. This means that they can then work with hands and brain. Holland allows apprenticeships to be started up to the age of twenty-seven. It would be even more helpful if each apprentice was articled to a mature, trained journeyman who was responsible for his progress. Each journeyman would then be a male parent substitute for the youth from a one-female-parent family. The apprentice would have a pattern of mature behaviour to follow. The journeyman would by his responsibilities also become more concerned and mature.

In higher education it is vital that we keep up the standards of our best universities, which are world renowned. I do not understand why the Conservative Government has made all higher education institutions universities. I wonder whether this could be challenged under the Trade Descriptions Act! Eight to twelve universities should be funded to keep them equal to any in the world. Some twenty to forty other universities should be reasonably funded, and the rest of the higher education institutions should become specialized according to the likely requirements of administration, commerce, industry and the professions.

We must also reassess how we fund higher education students. With the great increase in numbers yet only limited national finance, we risk creating a politically motivated poor by inadequate funding. I would suggest that the top 20 per cent of higher education students should be given on their 'A' level results full maintenance grants. This would mean that the academically most gifted students would be encouraged to go to university for their own sake and for the sake of our country. They would keep learning alive. A second group of 40 per cent could on their 'A' levels have half their maintenance paid, the rest being offered by way of loans. The last 40 per cent should he offered full-cost loans, which would test their motivation and also encourage them to take courses that would lead to paid work in adult life.

A word about the monarchy, which has served us well over hundreds of years. The election of a president divides a nation, while the crowning of a king unites a people. All people like a little mystery in their lives, but our age of full-frontal news nudity risks putting all people at risk. A little more self-censoring would produce more mature news media, concerned for the preservation of our unique constitution. The monarch continues to have a vital part in our national life.

I believe the Conservatives won the 1992 election because John Major appealed to the country in his opposition to devolution, proportional representation and the break-up of the United Kingdom. This brought him fully in line with the national mood. The old verities are the strength of the Conservative Party. The Conservative Party succeeds when by instinct it represents the feelings of the people. British people do not want unnecessary change. Lord Falkland said in the Root and Branch debate concerning the abolition of Episcopacy in 1641: 'When it is not necessary to change, it is necessary not to change.' The Conservative Party represents continuity. Cicero held that not to understand what happened before we were born is to be children all our lives. Edmund Burke declared: 'People will not look forward to posterity, who never look backward to their ancestors'; and he saw society as a partnership between 'the living, those who are dead and those who are to be born'. Conservatism favours the natural evolution of society in which millions of people make their own decisions and change them when they are obviously wrong and develop them when they are successful.

I always say that man sits on a three-legged stool: one leg is moral and religious, one's view of why we are here on earth; a second leg is tribal – men in particular like to belong to groups of kindred spirits; a third is economic – we all like an improvement in our economic lot. The future of the Conservative Party and the future of our country are linked together. If the policies of the party are responsive to the views and aspirations of the British people, it will continue to win elections. If the party ceases to represent these views and aspirations, it will cease to be the governing party.

Brent deserves a postscript. In the 1994 local elections Brent, via the casting vote of the mayor, retained a Conservative council, one of only five in London. Some 56 per cent of voters in Brent North voted Conservative. This was due to a £112 reduction in the council tax, better privatized local services, like street cleaning, and continued close contact with the voters. There is a lesson here for the Conservative Government nationally.

I have enjoyed my life and continue to do so. Life is a privilege for which we must thank our Maker. We are not asked when we want to be born or how long we wish to live. Yet within our physical and mental make-up we have amazing free will in how we react to events and how individually we order our lives. Fortunately mine continues to be a very interesting one.

Index

*

251

Taking it easy in the Dead Sea, Israel 1983